PRACTICAL DIGITAL
IMAGE PROCESSING

ELLIS HORWOOD SERIES IN DIGITAL AND SIGNAL PROCESSING
Series Editor: D. R. SLOGGETT, Principal Scientist, Software Sciences Ltd, Farnborough, Hants

G.D. Bergman	ELECTRONIC ARCHITECTURES FOR DIGITAL PROCESSING: Software/Hardware Balance in Real-time Systems
R. Lewis	PRACTICAL DIGITAL IMAGE PROCESSING
S. Lawson & A. Mirzai	WAVE DIGITAL FILTERS
J.D. McCafferty	HUMAN AND MACHINE VISION: Computing Perceptual Organisation

PRACTICAL DIGITAL IMAGE PROCESSING

RHYS LEWIS B.Sc., Ph.D.
IBM, UK Scientific Centre, Winchester, Hants

ELLIS HORWOOD
NEW YORK   LONDON   TORONTO   SYDNEY   TOKYO   SINGAPORE

First published in 1990 by
ELLIS HORWOOD LIMITED
Market Cross House, Cooper Street,
Chichester, West Sussex, PO19 1EB, England

A division of
Simon & Schuster International Group
A Paramount Communications Company

Printed and bound in Great Britain
by Hartnolls, Bodmin, Cornwall

British Library Cataloguing in Publication Data

Lewis, Rhys
Practical digital image processing.
CIP catalogue record for this book is available from the British Library
ISBN 0–13–683525–2

Library of Congress Cataloging-in-Publication Data available

Table of Contents

List of Figures

To Angela, Peter and especially Andrew

And to Joan and Alvin, for making everything possible

Preface

A large number of books have been written about digital image processing in the 30 or so years since the subject's inception. There are a number of classic works, written by eminent people in the field and containing vast amounts of detailed information. You might well be forgiven, therefore, for questioning the need for yet another title covering the basic subject material.

Image processing is, by its very nature, intensely mathematical. The major works on the subject are written by mathematically literate authors for a mathematically literate readership. They tend to take an academic approach to the subject, concentrating on the derivation and proof of important results. There is nothing wrong with that, particularly as mathematics provides a very precise way of defining the detailed concepts involved. However, the presence of a large amount of formalism means that many works on image processing are inaccessible to readers without the necessary mathematical skills.

This book is an attempt to describe image processing without the reader being required to understand complex mathematical formalism. It does contain formulae, but in the main these are used to augment explanations rather than being fundamental to them. It is, I suppose, the book I would like to have read when I started working in image processing some years ago. A background in the biological sciences meant that my mathematics were never of the strongest. A period of several years, spent writing commercial computer software, dulled still further my recollection of university maths courses. My subsequent tussle with the image processing literature was enough to convince me of the need for a book dealing with the subject by description and by example rather than by definition and derivation — a book describing the subject in easily assimilable form — a book aimed at people who use image processing systems, rather than those who implement them. This is my attempt to produce such a book. It is for others to decide how successful I have been.

The book came about as a result of more than six years spent working at IBM's United Kingdom Scientific Centre (UKSC), located in Winchester, England. During my time there, I took part in a number of medical research projects involving digital image processing. More importantly, from the point of view of the book, I became heavily involved in the development of two interactive image processing systems, one of which (IBM IAX Image Processing) is now marketed by IBM.

A number of people have helped me directly, during preparation of the book, through discussion and by providing material. I would like to thank Gavin Brelstaff, David Prendergast, Mike Ibison, Peter Elliot, John Ibbotson, and especially Ricky Turner, for the principal components analysis code. I would also like to thank Terry Harris, John Knapman, Colin Bird and Eric Janke who reviewed the manuscript in its various stages.

The IBM UK Scientific Centre has given me considerable support by making equipment available for creation of the numerous figures, which the book contains, and for preparation of the camera ready copy. I would like to thank John Knapman, Rodger Hake and Dave Steventon for making these facilities available.

I would like to thank Dave Slogett, my editor, for his invaluable suggestions, and Sue Horwood and her team, at Ellis Horwood Ltd., for their advice and assistance.

Many people have offered me help, guidance and education whilst I have been working in image processing. It would be quite impossible to mention them all. However a few names do stand out. My thanks go to Paul Jackson, Mike Cowlishaw, Steve Davies, Mike Cocklin, Myron Flickner, Mark Lavin, Peter Muller, Wayne Niblack, Rick Simpson and Virginia Hetrick. To all my friends and colleagues involved in image processing, both inside IBM and elsewhere, thank you. You have all contributed in some way to this book.

Finally, and feeling a little like someone giving the acceptance speech for a media award and trying, breathlessly, to ensure that everyone in the production company gets a mention, I must thank my sons Andrew and Peter for putting up with a father who hid himself away and typed at every opportunity and my wife Angela for keeping everything running smoothly at home throughout the preparation of the manuscript.

1

Pictures

A picture is a representation of some form of visual scene. We are all familiar with colour or black and white photographs. A black and white, or **monochrome**, photograph records the brightness of each point in the scene. A colour photograph records each point's colour as well as its brightness. In conventional photography, the mechanism by which the record is made is chemical. It depends on interactions between the light falling on the film and chemicals in the film itself. The subsequent chemistry, in the process known as development, amplifies the changes caused by the light and makes them permanent.

To a computer, however, a picture is a large array of numbers. Such an array is termed a **digital image**. The whole subject of digital image processing is little more than the application of various forms of arithmetic to the arrays of numbers which are the computer's representation of pictures. Before we can begin to examine the kinds of arithmetic used in image processing applications, we need to look at the digital representation of various kinds of pictures, their properties, and the techniques by which the data can be acquired and displayed. These are the topics for the current chapter.

1.1 THE DIGITAL IMAGE

Digital images occur in a wide variety of forms. In the following sections we will look at the most commonly encountered types of image.

1.1.1 Monochrome Images

Figure 1.1(a) is a representation of a monochrome photograph. The information in the photograph is solely a variation of brightness with position. To capture the pictorial information in digital form, we must find a means of encoding the brightness at each point in the picture in a way which can be represented numerically.

1.1.1.1 Image Coordinates

Before we deal with encoding the brightness, we must provide a way to specify the position and size of the point whose brightness we are measuring. By convention, digital images have their starting position or **origin** at the top left corner. Position is specified by an x coordinate, which increases from 0 as we travel from left to right, and a y coordinate which increases from 0 as we travel from top to bottom. It is unfortunate that this choice of coordinate system is in conflict with those used in computer graphics systems. These commonly have their origin at the bottom left corner. Each convention is widely used within its own user community and there seems little opportunity for reconciliation.

1.1.1.2 Sampling

To produce the digital version of a photograph, we take samples of its brightness at regular intervals. The process involves laying a sampling grid over the data and then measuring the average brightness in each square of the grid. We will see how this sampling is carried out in practice in section 1.3. In Figure 1.1(b) the original photograph is shown sampled 256 times. There are 16 rows of samples and each row contains 16 samples. The sampling process itself takes the average brightness of the picture underneath each square in the sampling grid and assigns it a value. That value is placed in an array of numbers at the location corresponding to the position of the square in the grid. Figure 1.1(c) shows the grid of numbers corresponding to the top left corner of the sampled image. The values used correspond to the brightness. In this case, 0 represents black and 255 represents the brightest area which the sampling system can record. This range is called the **grey scale** for the image. 255 may seem like a strange choice for the maximum brightness. It is, in fact, the largest value which can be represented in a single **byte** of computer storage. A byte consists of 8 **bits**. Each bit can take the value 0 or 1. Using standard binary number representation the values 0 to 255 can be encoded in a single byte. A byte is normally the smallest unit on which a general-purpose computer can conveniently perform standard arithmetic operations. Brightness values between the extremes of 0 and 255

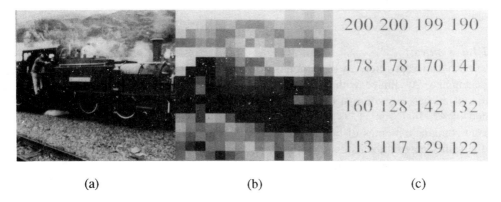

(a)   (b)   (c)

Figure 1.1. Monochrome images. (a) Original image sampled 262 144 times, (b) image
sampled 256 times, (c) numeric values of top left corner of the data in (b)

are represented on a linear scale. A sample with value 42 is twice as bright as one
with value 21. As we shall see, this is by no means the only way to encode image
brightness. Monochrome images can be encoded in a variety of ways with different
brightness ranges or grey scales. It is quite common to refer to monochrome images
as grey scale images. The terms can be considered interchangeable.

1.1.1.3 Picture Elements

The samples which make up a digital image are commonly known as **pixels** or **pels**.
These are contractions of the term **picture elements**. A pixel is the smallest part of a
digital image which can be assigned a value. The physical size of the piece of photograph represented by each pixel is determined by how precisely we wish to record
the data.   In Figure 1.1(a) the photograph is actually represented by 262 144
samples. Essentially, all of the detail of the original photograph is retained in the
digital version. However, this is clearly not the case in Figure 1.1(b). Each sample
covers such a large area that much of the detail has been lost. Figure 1.1(c) shows
the values of the pixels in the top left hand corner of this image. The term **resolution** is used to describe the level of spatial detail captured by the digital image.
The digital image in Figure 1.1(b) is termed **low resolution**.

   The technique of collecting samples and assigning values to numbers in particular
positions in an array does not explicitly capture the real dimensions of the photograph being digitised. Also, any measure of resolution is specified only in terms of
numbers of pixels. In order to relate the size of the image to some physical measure
of distance, scaling information must be collected in addition to the brightness data.
Typically, the scaling information records the number of pixels which represent some
standard distance, for example 1 pixel per millimetre. The scaling information allows

distances measured on the image to be related to the actual dimensions of the photograph.

1.1.1.4 Contrast
The term **contrast** refers to the amount of variation in brightness which occurs in a
given image. An image with a maximum pixel value of 100 and a minimum pixel
value of 50 has less contrast than one with a maximum value of 200 and a minimum
value of 42. In Figure 1.2(a) is a monochrome image showing high contrast. The
image contains extremes of brightness from full black to full white. In Figure 1.2(b)
is the same image after its contrast has been very much reduced. We will see how to
achieve modifications in contrast in section 3.6.

1.1.1.5 Scenes
Throughout this section we have considered the digital image as a numeric representation of a physical photograph. This is very convenient when discussing pixels,
sampling and so on. However, not all digital images are created from photographs.
In many applications the digital data is collected directly from the real scene without
a photograph being involved. The principles are, however, exactly the same. The
variation of brightness over the scene is captured in exactly the same way as if a
photograph were being sampled. The only difference is that the light is coming to
the detector directly from the scene rather than being reflected from a photograph or
being transmitted through a photographic negative or transparency. It is also worth
pointing out at this stage that images can be created by detectors which do not use
visible light at all. For example, detectors exist for infrared, ultraviolet, microwave
and X-ray radiation, to name but a few. We will meet these sources again in section
1.3.2.

1.1.1.6 Monochrome Image Representation
In Figure 1.1, we saw examples of images in which each pixel can be represented in
1 byte of computer storage. The values which can be represented range from 0 to
255. Fractional values cannot be recorded. The available values are **integers**. Many
types of image data can be recorded in this kind of representation. Each pixel is an
8-bit unsigned integer. The term **unsigned** refers to the fact that only positive
values can be represented this way. This is no problem for conventional, visible light
images as brightness is a positive quantity. The 8-bit unsigned integer is perhaps the
commonest representation for image data. When used for monochrome pictures, the
number of brightness levels available is sufficient for reasonably high quality display
whilst being the most compact of the commonly encountered forms. We will look at
more compact representations which are suitable for other purposes in section 1.1.4.

We can calculate the amount of storage required for 8-bit unsigned images very
simply. Since each pixel occupies 1 byte, the amount of storage required is the same

(a)   (b)

Figure   1.2. High and low contrast images.   (a) Image with high contrast, (b) the same image
          with reduced contrast

as the total number of pixels. As an example, the image from Figure 1.1(a), which
has 512 rows with 512 pixels per row, requires 262 144 bytes of storage. This image
has approximately the same spatial resolution as a standard television picture but has
rather better reproduction of shades of grey. Computer storage is commonly referred
to in terms of units of 1024 bytes. Known as a **kilobyte**, this is written 1k. The
image requires 256 such units, or 256k. A larger unit, the **megabyte**, is also in
common usage. It is 1024 kilobytes and is written 1M. Our image can be described
as requiring a quarter of a megabyte of storage. Regardless of which notation we
choose, it is clear that even a modest image, like that in Figure 1.1(a), requires a
considerable amount of storage. For comparison, a standard 3.5 inch diskette used on
the IBM Personal System/2† holds 1.4 megabytes of data (1.4M). This type of
diskette can hold five complete 8-bit unsigned integer images which are 512 pixels
square.

   Some sources of image data, particularly those in the medical field, routinely
produce data which cannot be represented as 8-bit unsigned integer data. Often, this
data is stored as **16-bit signed integers**. This representation can hold values between
−32 768 and +32 767. This signed representation is also useful for storing intermediate results during computations without the overflow and underflow which can be
associated with 8-bit data. Of course, for special applications it might be desirable to
have a 16-bit unsigned integer image. Such applications are uncommon.

---

† IBM and Personal System/2 are trade marks of the International Business Machines Corporation.

A 16-bit image requires precisely twice as much storage as an 8-bit image of the same size. Each pixel requires two bytes of storage. To store our 512 by 512 pixel image in this form requires 524 288 bytes or 512k. We are now down to two complete images per diskette.

A still wider range of values can be represented with 32-bit signed integers. This representation can hold values between approximately -2×10^9 and 2×10^9. The usefulness of this representation is again in its ability to hold intermediate results without overflow. In addition, it can be used for **fixed point** arithmetic. In fixed point arithmetic a proportion of the bits of the number representation are used for the integer part of the number. The rest are used for the fractional part. For example, with 32-bit integers, 16 bits could be used for the integer part, giving the same resolution as a 16-bit integer value. The remaining 16 bits can be used to represent the fractional part to a precision of about 1 part in 65 000. All arithmetic operations are carried out using normal 32-bit integer arithmetic. However, results are interpreted by splitting the data into the integer and fractional parts and considering each separately. Fixed point arithmetic allows fractional values to be computed without requiring that **floating point** number representations be used. We will look at floating point data in the following section. On many small computers there is a very significant difference in computational performance between integer data and floating point data. Floating point computations can easily be an order of magnitude slower than equivalent integer operations even when special hardware is installed. Without the hardware assistance, the operations are slower still as they must be emulated in software. On mainframe computers and on high performance workstations, such as the the IBM RISC System/6000[†] , floating point performance is more nearly comparable with integer performance. Consequently less performance benefit is achieved by using fixed point arithmetic.

A 32-bit image requires four times as much storage as an 8-bit image of the same size. To store our 512 by 512 pixel image in this form requires 1 048 576 bytes or 1 megabyte. Only one such image can be stored on our 3.25 inch diskette.

1.1.2 Floating Point Images

1.1.2.1 Real Images
Real numbers are used to represent values with an integer and fractional part. We have already discussed fixed point representations of such data. However, real images are more commonly expressed as **floating point** numbers. Floating point numbers can represent a very wide range of values with a limited though useful precision. For

---

† IBM and RISC System/6000 are trade marks of the International Business Machines Corporation.

example, the standard precision floating point representation used on the IBM Personal System/2 can hold values between about 1.18×10^{-38} and 3.4×10^{38} with a precision of about 1 part in 10^6. This representation takes the same amount of storage as the 32-bit integer image, namely 4 bytes per pixel. Again our 512 by 512 pixel image requires a megabyte of storage when represented in floating point numbers. However, the floating point form can hold a much wider range of values than the integer form, albeit with less precision. As with the 16 and 32-bit integer representations, the floating point image is very useful as an intermediate form allowing fractional information to be preserved during a computation as well as being able to handle a very wide range of values. Also, seemingly mundane operations may require floating point results if precision is to be maintained. A trivial example is the multiplication of an integer image by a decimal fraction.

For applications where very high precision and a very wide range of values is required, double precision floating point numbers are also available on most computers. Again, using the IBM Personal System/2 as an example, this representation can hold values between about 2.2×10^{-308} and 1.8×10^{308} with a precision of about 1 part in 10^{15}. Double precision floating point numbers require 8 bytes per pixel. Our 512 by 512 pixel image now takes up 2 megabytes and cannot be stored on a single diskette.

1.1.2.2 Complex Images

Complex numbers are used in many branches of mathematics and science. They have specific set of uses in digital image processing. In the main they are required when image data is transformed into alternative domains, for example by the Fourier transform. The functions involved are discussed in chapter 7. A complex number consists of 2 parts. There is a **real** component and an **imaginary** component. For example, the value $4 + 2j$ is a complex number with real part 4 and imaginary part $2j$. Similarly, $4 - 2j$ is a complex number with real part 4 and imaginary part $-2j$. Here, j represents the square root of -1, a troublesome concept for traditional arithmetic. It is not necessary to understand in detail the mathematics of complex numbers in order to appreciate their use in image processing. However, if more details are required there are many standard mathematics texts which deal extensively with the properties of complex numbers (for example Kreyszig (1972).)

The real part of a complex number is represented by a real number. The imaginary part is represented by a second real number. The fact that this real number represents an imaginary value is implicit in the way the data is stored. No attempt is made to store i explicitly. A single precision complex number requires twice as much storage as a single precision real number, namely 8 bytes per pixel. A 512 by 512 pixel single precision complex image occupies 2 megabytes. A double precision complex number requires twice as much storage as a double precision real number, or 16 bytes per pixel. Consequently, a 512 by 512 pixel double precision complex image needs 4 megabytes of storage.

1.1.3 Colour Images

So far, we have looked at image representations in which only one intrinsic value has varied with position. When dealing with colour, however, we have to encode not only the brightness of a particular point but also its colour. Whereas brightness is an immediately understandable quantity, the same is not true for colour. How can colour be represented in a form which can be sampled and stored easily?

The study of colour has a long history. Newton, in 1666, discovered that white light, when refracted by a glass prism, is split into a spectrum containing a wide variety of colours. He inferred that white light is composed of light of all these colours, and confirmed it with the famous Newton's disk experiment. In this, a circular disc is divided into 7 sectors. Each sector is coloured with one of the so-called colours of the rainbow. When the disc is rotated, it is perceived to be white, as the individual colours merge together.

It is the wavelength of light which determines its colour. The wavelength of a particular colour of light is usually expressed in units of nanometres (nm). A nanometre is 10^{-9} metres. Light with a wavelength around 430 nm is blue, that with wavelength around 550 nm is green and that with wavelength around 700 nm is red. It is an empirical observation that mixing red, green and blue light together in various proportions allows a wide variety of other colours to be obtained. There are colours which cannot be re-created this way. However the technique is sufficiently powerful for colour television to be based on it. Red, green and blue are said to be the **primary** colours for the **additive** colour system. The term additive refers to the fact that the system used in television is based on projecting the primary colours. As the screen emits light, the primaries can only be added and not subtracted. There are international standards governing the precise details of the primary colours used in television transmission. However, for our purposes it is only necessary to take note of the fact that colours can be represented as combinations of primary colours.

Sampling a colour image is just like sampling a monochrome image. A grid is effectively laid over the image in the same way, but now instead of just recording the total brightness of each sample, the brightness of the red, green and blue components is measured individually. As we will see, in section 1.3, this can be carried out either with a colour camera or with a monochrome camera and a set of special filters. The result, in either case, is 3 images, each of which represents the brightness of one of the primary colours at every pixel sampled. Clearly, in this form, a colour picture requires three times as much storage as a monochrome image of the same data type and size. In practice, colour images are almost invariably digitised as three 8-bit integer images. A 512 by 512 pixel colour image requires 768k of storage in this format. This kind of data is sometimes referred to as a 24-bit per pixel colour image, reflecting the total number of bits of information recorded for each pixel. Also, as each primary colour is represented to a precision of 1 part in 256, an individual colour can be specified to about 1 part in 1.6×10^7 (1 part in 256×256×256.) Colour display systems are usually described as being able to display 16 million colours if they are capable of handling this type of 24-bit colour data.

Colour is a major subject in its own right. The specification of a particular colour in terms of its primary components is a convenient representation but it is by no means the only one. Systems which require accurate representation of specific colours must pay great attention to the definition of the primary colours used. Corrections must also be applied when devices used to capture or display colour images have less than ideal colour characteristics.

The perception of displayed colour images is a large and complex field of study. Much research has been done, with colour television transmission providing much of the motivation. A detailed study of colour images is beyond the scope of this book, though we will encounter them again in section 7.4.3. Further information on colour can be found in Gonzalez and Wintz (1977), Niblack (1986) and Netravali and Haskell (1989), amongst others.

1.1.4 Binary Images

Binary images encode the least imaginable amount of information in each pixel. Whereas a grey scale image records the brightness of each pixel and a colour image records both the brightness and colour of each pixel, a binary image simply records the presence or absence of some property at each pixel. In a sense, it is a logical representation with each pixel being TRUE or FALSE. It is common to represent binary images using just 1 bit of information per pixel and to store 8 pixels of the image in each byte of storage. By convention the pixels are grouped along the rows of the image. The first byte holds the first 8 pixels on the first image row. The second byte holds the second 8 pixels on the first image row, and so on. For practical reasons, if the number of pixels per image row is not a multiple of 8, the remaining spare bits in the last byte are not used to start the next row. Each new image row starts with a new byte. The image rows are said to be **aligned** on a byte boundary. Some systems may require this alignment to be on the boundary of a larger grouping, for example a 16-bit or 32-bit integer. This is done to allow the data to be read in groups of 16 or 32 bits which may be advantageous for performance on certain systems.

Binary images have two main uses. First, they can store monochrome image data when only a very restricted grey scale is required. In fact a binary image can only encode two levels, namely bright and dark. However, there are applications where this is sufficient. For example, when printing image data, a representation is required which matches the printer capability. Printers usually make black marks on white paper. The encoding for output is binary. Either there is a mark at a particular position or there isn't. It is possible to simulate a monochrome image, with a wide range of brightness, using a binary image. The binary approximation can be printed directly. We will see how to do this in section 7.4.1. Figure 1.3(a) shows an approximation to Figure 1.1(a), using a binary image. Figure 1.3(b) shows the

(a)   (b)   (c)

Figure   1.3. Grey scale image and binary approximation. (a). A binary image which approximates the grey scale image of the train, (b) the central portion of the train image
zoomed up, (c) the central portion of (a) zoomed up.

central portion of the grey scale image in more detail. Figure 1.3(c) shows the
central portion of the binary image in greater detail. The pattern of black and white
pixels used to form the grey scale approximation can be seen.

Some image applications never use more than 2 levels. Document image processing applications use binary images to hold digitised versions of written, typed or
printed documents. These can easily be encoded as binary images with sufficient
resolution to allow them to be read when displayed on computer screens. The image
merely needs to record the presence or absence of marks on the paper. This information can be encoded by just a single bit per pixel. Binary images offer significant
space saving over other kinds of monochrome image. For example, our 512 by 512
pixel image requires only 32 768 bytes of storage, assuming we pack 8 pixels to the
byte. For applications where a large number of images need to be stored, this low
data requirement is important. It can further be reduced by the application of compression techniques particularly suited to binary image data. We will look at image
compression in section 7.3.

The second main use for binary images is in building masks which can be used to
control other image processing operations. In particular they can be used to determine whether or not an operation is applied to an image on a pixel by pixel basis.
We will look at the construction and use of masks in section 3.4.4.

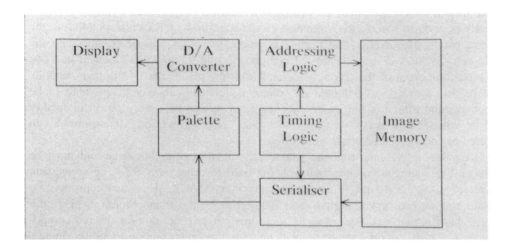

Figure   1.4. Simple monochrome display

1.2 DISPLAYING IMAGES

The cathode ray tube (CRT) is, almost without exception, the device used for the display of image data. The technology involved is essentially the same as that used in domestic television receivers. The main difference between a television and a monitor designed for image display is one of quality. Image display monitors have higher resolution and better geometric accuracy and are consequently much more expensive than television sets. A monitor on its own is insufficient for displaying an image. There must be additional electronics to store the image data and to convert the digital data into a signal which the monitor can use. This electronics is contained in the **display controller**. The process carried out by the display controller is very like the reverse of the sampling process by which a digital image is created from a photograph or a scene. Figure 1.4 illustrates the operation of a simple monochrome display controller. Each pixel of the image is retrieved from the storage area in turn. Retrieval starts with the pixel at the image origin and proceeds along each row of the image in turn. This process is known as **serialisation** and the hardware which performs it is called a **serialiser**. The timing and address logic ensures that pixels are retrieved in the right order and at a rate suitable for the display monitor. As each pixel is retrieved, it is presented to a **palette**, also known as a **look-up table** (LUT.) The palette is a high-speed table look-up device. It contains one table entry for each of the possible pixel values which can be in the display's storage. For example, if the display holds 8-bit unsigned integer values, the palette will have 256 entries. If a pixel value of, say, 42 is retrieved by the serialiser, the palette will return table entry 42. The contents of this table entry are used to determine how to drive the display.

If the display is monochrome, the palette will return a single value which will subsequently be used to specify the brightness of the spot on the CRT corresponding to the current pixel. However, if the display is colour, 3 values will be contained in the table entry. One will specify the red component, one the green component and one the blue component of the colour associated with the pixel value, 42 in this example. The palette allows the brightness or colour associated with any pixel value to be varied without affecting the image data itself. This can be a very powerful facility and we will see how it is used for monochrome images in section 3.8 and how it can be used to encode colour images in section 7.4.3.

The value, or values, from the palette are still digital at this stage and must be converted to analogue voltages before being used to drive the CRT. The conversion is carried out by a **digital to analogue converter** (DAC). This device produces a voltage proportional to the digital value applied to it. In a monochrome display only one of these is required. For colour, 3 such units are needed, one for the red component, one for the green component and one for the blue component of the image. The resulting voltage, or voltages, can be applied to the CRT.

As well as specifying brightness levels, the display controller also needs to provide timing information to the CRT. This keeps the position of the beam, which scans across the CRT to produce the image, in step with the serialiser. It ensures that each pixel's brightness or colour appears at the appropriate position on the screen. Display controllers often provide additional hardware support for other operations not strictly associated with image display. Very often, graphics operations such as line drawing or area filling are provided. In part, this reflects the fact that most display controllers are designed to support both graphics and image display. The graphics functions can be very useful for image processing applications which frequently need to plot graphical data or to indicate parts of an image by drawing or colouring.

1.3 ACQUIRING IMAGES

There are essentially two ways of acquiring image data for processing. First, there is a wide variety of recording devices specifically designed to produce digital image data from scenes or from various kinds of photographs. Using this kind of equipment, digital images can be formed of any subject which can be photographed conventionally. Second, some kinds of device produce digital image data directly. This is either because they have digitisation equipment attached to an image sensor, or because they form images indirectly from computations on other kinds of measurements.

In this section, we look at examples from both these broad categories of image acquisition.

1.3.1 Analogue Sources

We have already seen in, general terms, how sampling the brightness or colour of a photograph or scene can lead to a digital image. Fundamentally, we divide up the area to be digitised into pixels and measure the colour or brightness of each pixel in turn. In this section we will look at how, in practice, these steps can be achieved and at the sort of hardware which is involved. Although the various devices used for image acquisition vary greatly in precision, speed and cost, many of the principles on which they operate are common to them all. We will examine these principles before looking at some of the devices themselves.

Figure 1.5 illustrates the general arrangement of a digitisation system. At the heart of any image recording device is an optical system which brings an image, of the scene or photograph to be digitised, into sharp focus on a sensor. The sensor converts the light falling on it into a small voltage or current. The sensor output is buffered and amplified and, if necessary, converted into a voltage suitable for sampling. This voltage is converted into a numeric value by an **analogue to digital converter** (ADC). This kind of converter compares the incoming voltage with a set of standard voltages. The result of each comparison is a single bit value indicating whether the incoming voltage is higher or lower than the reference. By suitable choice of reference voltages, the bit pattern resulting from the comparisons can be made to be a binary number of arbitrary precision. The timing and address logic ensures that the incoming signal is sampled at the appropriate time and that the resulting binary value is stored at the correct position in the array which represents the image. Naturally, if the system is digitising colour information, 3 values are returned from the sensor for each pixel. These are the red, the green and the blue components of the colour at that pixel.

It is an unfortunate fact that certain kinds of image acquisition equipment naturally lead to pixels which are not square. The actual physical distance represented by the horizontal sides of the pixel is different from that represented by its vertical sides. Even though a particular application may not need to know what these distances are, the fact that they are not the same may adversely affect the image processing algorithms which it uses. Image algorithms almost invariable assume square pixels. It is possible to correct for pixels which are not square and we will see how to do this in section 5.2.6.

The common components of equipment for image acquisition are

- the optical system
- the sensor
- the analogue to digital converter
- the data store

We will now examine some real devices to see how these components vary in practice.

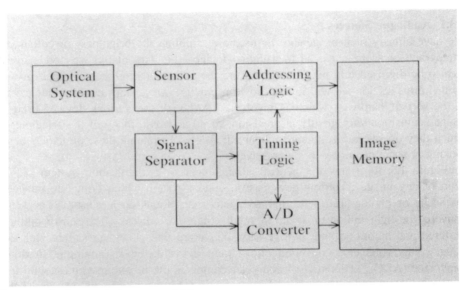

Figure   1.5. Schematic image acquisition system

1.3.1.1 Television Cameras

The most striking feature of image acquisition systems based on television cameras is
their speed.   In Europe, the television standard requires a complete picture, also
known as a **frame**, to be transmitted 25 times per second. We have already noted
that a single television frame contains approximately 256k of data. Simple multiplication shows that a television camera generates the equivalent of over 6 megabytes of
data per second.   There are very few systems which are capable of digitising and
storing this quantity of data continuously. It is much more common to digitise a
single frame at a time. Of course, digitising a single frame does not decrease the rate
at which the incoming data must be sampled. It does, however, reduce the total
amount of data to be recorded to about 256k, an amount which can readily be accommodated on a single adaptor card in a typical personal computer.

The optical system on a television camera is usually a compound lens. A very
wide choice of lenses is readily available and indicates the huge variety of applications for which television cameras are used. The sensor in these cameras is usually
either a **vidicon** tube or a solid state, **charge coupled device** (CCD). In either case,
light falling on the sensor causes a local variation of electrical charge which is then
read out of the sensor in a predefined sequence.

A vidicon is basically similar to the tube in a television set. It consists of an
evacuated glass envelope with a source of electrons at one end (the cathode) and a
special coating at the other.   In contrast to a television, where the coating is a
phosphor which emits light when struck by electrons, in the vidicon the coating is

light sensitive. It is known as a **photoconductor**. The electron beam sweeps across the coating causing a build up of charge. Light falling on the coating allows the charge to leak away. The brighter the light, the more leakage occurs. The leakage causes a variation of charge across the coating depending on the brightness of the light falling on it. When the next sweep occurs, the charge variation affects the current flowing in the electron beam. The variation in the current is a measure of the brightness of the light falling on each point of the coating. In practice, of course, the vidicon is more complex than this. Various other electrodes are needed within the tube to direct the electrons and to accelerate them towards the photoconductor. Also, coils are required to generate the magnetic fields needed to sweep the beam across the photoconductor. These coils require considerable current and, together with the high voltage circuitry needed to accelerate the electrons account for the bulk and weight of this kind of camera.

CCD based cameras, on the other hand, are usually small and very light, being based on semiconductor technology. The detector chip consists mainly of a large number of small cells, one for each pixel. Unlike the photoconductor used in the vidicon tube, charge builds up rather than leaking away when these cells are illuminated. The brighter the light, the more charge accumulates. After an appropriate sampling period, the charge must be read out from the cells and converted into a voltage. This process uses the charge coupling inherent in this form of semiconductor. By the application of appropriate signals, the cells are made to pass their charge to a neighbouring cell. In this way, the charges are moved to the edge of the chip in the appropriate sequence for construction of the television picture. Amplifiers convert the charges into an appropriate voltage. Whilst the timing electronics associated with CCD devices is quite complex, there is no need for any heavy coils or high voltage circuitry and the whole system can be miniaturised into a small number of high density chips. It is the advance in CCD technology which has made possible relatively inexpensive domestic colour video camera/recorders and the light weight broadcast cameras used increasingly in television.

Both vidicon and CCD cameras produce an output signal related to the brightness of the incident light. Circuitry in the cameras converts the output of the detector and provides amplification so that the signal is sufficiently large to be transmitted in a coaxial cable over a distance of several metres. The resulting signal conforms to one of the several video signal standards. In addition to the brightness information, the video signal carries **synchronisation pulses**. As we shall see these are used to allow the digitisation system to associate a position with each part of the brightness signal. Incidentally, in broadcast television systems, the synchronisation pulses are used to keep the receiver in step with the camera and to ensure that the correct part of the picture appears at the right place on the screen.

If the camera directly records colour information, the sensor and the electronics will be arranged to detect the amounts of the red, green, and blue primary colour components rather than the total amount of illumination.

In addition to their lower weight, CCD based cameras have a significant advantage over tube based types. Their imaging geometry is much more precise and does not drift with time. The sensor is solid state and the positions of the cells which detect the incident light are very accurately determined during manufacture. In a tube camera, the positional accuracy depends on how precisely the electron beam sweeps across the tube. This in turn depends on how well controlled are the magnetic fields used to deflect the beam. The components are prone to drift with time affecting the precision of the image. Tube cameras must be carefully and regularly maintained to achieve consistent results.

The other components of a television camera based digitisation system are normally not part of the camera itself. Often they will be mounted on an adaptor card which can be used in a personal computer or workstation. Such an adaptor is commonly known as a **frame grabber**. A coaxial socket brings the video signal to the analogue to digital converter. This must be a very high speed device to cope with the large data rate of the signal. The converter produces the digital values of the signal. Additional logic ensures that the values are placed in the correct entries in the image array. The positional information is present in the video signal as synchronisation pulses produced by the camera. These pulses occur, for example, at the start of each row of the frame. Along any given row, the position is determined by an accurate timer. The time taken to transmit one row of the image is precisely defined by the video standard. A typical frame grabber will digitise each row of the incoming signal into 512 samples. It digitises the incoming signal at 512 points in time equally spaced throughout the duration of the row.

The digitisation of a single frame, using the European television standard, takes about 1/25th of a second. This is fairly rapid and images of moving objects can be captured, provided they are not travelling too fast. For comparison, hand held still frame film cameras are commonly provided with shutters capable of exposure times of 1/1000th of a second or less, allowing them to deal with rapidly moving objects. A further speed limitation, when acquiring data from television cameras, is the time taken to move the data from the frame grabber to some other form of storage to allow another frame to be acquired. Typically this will require many times longer than the time taken to acquire a frame. It could be many seconds, if the data is being written to a slow medium, such as diskette. This does not affect the time taken to acquire a single frame, but it does limit the repetition rate at which frames can be captured. It implies, for example, that to be able to capture a short lived event, it is vital that the acquisition of the frame be synchronised to that event.

Systems based on television signals have a high **bandwidth**. The very high data rates involved necessarily mean that high frequency information occurs in the video signal. High bandwidth systems are inherently susceptible to **noise**. Noise is composed of random fluctuations of the signal. It comes from a variety of sources, including the electronics of the camera. It is also caused by the quantum nature of light itself. As noise is random, it tends to mask the signal which the system is trying to detect. A common way to express the amount of noise in a given system is by its **signal to noise ratio**. As its name implies, it is the ratio of the size of the signal to the size of the noise in a particular system. Television systems have high bandwidth and tend to suffer from poorer signal to noise ratios than do other, slower detection systems. However, they are relatively inexpensive, are easy to use, and are robust. They can be used in many digitising applications.

1.3.1.2 Scanning Cameras

A scanning camera differs from a conventional camera by using a sensor which acquires only one row of image data at a time. To capture an entire image the sensor must be swept mechanically across the field of view. Scanning cameras are often mounted in an arrangement rather like a photographic enlarger. Conventional lenses can be used and the camera can be racked up and down a long column to place it at an appropriate distance from the photographs to be digitised.

Because scanning cameras are not constrained to adhere to any television standard, most digitising cameras based on this technology offer a wide variety of capture speeds. Even the fastest scanning camera will take very much longer than a television camera to digitise the same scene or photograph. It will, however, produce a much higher quality result. Most of this improvement is due to the scanning camera's superior noise performance, which comes from the lower bandwidth employed. The relatively slow operation of scanning cameras makes them best suited to digitising photographs.

Scanning cameras almost invariably use solid state sensors. The CCD technology already described is commonly employed. The reduction in speed, when compared with a television camera, is achieved simply by allowing light to fall on the sensor for a longer period of time before reading out the accumulated charge. The longer the period during which charge accumulates, the slower is the recording process and the higher is the signal to noise ratio of the final image. The increased signal to noise ratio comes from the extra averaging of the noise which occurs during the longer exposure.

Each time data is read from the sensor, one row of the image is acquired. A stepping motor is then used to move the sensor across the field of view by a precise distance ready to capture the next row of the image. The time taken to acquire a complete image, using this kind of camera, varies from a few seconds to several minutes, depending on the number of pixels to be captured and the signal to noise ratio desired.

Scanning cameras suffer one major operational drawback when compared with television cameras. A television camera produces a complete image many times per second. While the digitisation system is being set up, the camera's output can be viewed directly on a television monitor. This makes it very easy to focus the camera, to select the area to be digitised, and to ensure that the illumination levels are appropriate. In a line scan sensor based system, there is no equivalent facility.

The image is available for viewing only after a complete scan has been carried out. Optical viewers are normally provided to allow the camera to be focused and to allow selection of the area to be digitised. However, the images they provide are often too small for accurate focusing. In addition, the field of view offered by the optical viewer is not always exactly the same as that of the camera itself. There are also interactions between the various settings possible on the camera. For example, slowing the camera down to improve the signal to noise ratio naturally increases the voltage produced by the sensor and may mean that the camera lens must be set at a smaller aperture to avoid **saturation**. Saturation occurs when the output of one or more cells of the sensor is at its maximum. This limit is imposed by the electrical characteristics of the sensor, not by the illumination level. Consequently, the cell's output does not correspond to the amount of light falling on it and gross errors are caused in the digitised image.

In general, scanning camera systems are more difficult to use than television based systems. However, some applications depend on the better quality and the higher spatial resolution of these systems. Scanning systems are available which can digitise at resolutions up to 4096×4096 pixels and at up to 16 bits per pixel. In practice, less than 16 bits of grey scale resolution is achieved, due to the effects of noise. However, high quality monochrome and colour digitisation is possible with these devices.

1.3.1.3 Line Scan Cameras

Line scan cameras are closely related to scanning cameras and use the same kind of sensors. However, in a scanning camera the sensor is fixed in position with respect to the optics. Any scanning which occurs is due to the motion of the object past the field of view of the camera. These very specialised cameras are used in applications, such as manufacturing, where the objects being monitored are in motion. For example, this kind of camera can be used to observe and even measure objects passing below it on a conveyor belt. As the objects being observed are often moving, speed of data acquisition in this kind of application is vital. Line scan cameras tend to have their sensors operated at high speed and consequently they loose the high signal to noise ratio associated with the same sensors used in scanning cameras. Their advantage when compared with conventional cameras is that it may not be necessary to acquire a complete image in order to recover sufficient information from the scene for the purposes of a particular application. There is a consequent increase in speed and reduction in the cost and complexity of the hardware associated with the application.

1.3.1.4 Document Scanners

With the trend towards the reduction in the usage of paper in the office environment, there is an increasing need to digitise documents so that they can be stored in and retrieved from computer based filing systems. The document scanner is another application of the line scan sensor. A transport mechanism moves the page past a strong light source and an optical system. Light reflected from the paper is carried by way of mirrors and lenses to fall on a line scan sensor. Successive rows of the image are digitised as the document passes over the light source.

Using a typical CCD line scan sensor with 1024 cells, a scanner can digitise A4 sized documents at about 120 pixels per inch, along each image row. A stepper motor is used to advance the paper by an appropriate amount between scans. Document scanners often digitise at just 1 bit per pixel, which is adequate when the resulting binary image has only to be displayed or printed. The image has only to record the presence or absence of marks on the paper, so 1 bit is sufficient. Even so, an A4 page at 120 pixels per inch requires some 1.4 million pixels or 175k of storage. It is indeed fortunate that compression techniques exist which are capable of reducing the space required by binary image data by about a factor of 10.

1.3.1.5 Densitometers
A densitometer is a device which measures the amount of light transmitted by a given piece of film. The basic components are a narrow aperture light source and a photodetector. Light is shone through the film. The amount reaching the photodetector is a measure of the density of the film and hence of the brightness of the original object. Because only a single photodetector is used, each sample of the film must be taken individually. As with the scanning camera, the time over which an individual sample is accumulated can be varied to alter the signal to noise ratio. However, the densitometer is an inherently slow device as it samples only a single pixel at a time. Scan times can run into hours. Although capable of producing high quality results, these devices are being superseded by scanning cameras which can achieve similar quality while operating much more quickly.

1.3.1.6 Digitising Colour Images Using Filters
So far we have only really considered the acquisition of monochrome images. There are devices available which can directly record colour images. Indeed, they are commonly available in portable video camera equipment. However, to achieve high quality, colour digital images, it is usually necessary to use monochrome recording techniques and special filters. This approach is usually only viable when digitising material which is already in photographic form , though it might prove possible to use it for recording stationary objects.

We have already seen that the majority of the colours encountered when viewing the world can be represented in terms of the primary colours red, green and blue. It is possible to measure the components directly. The photograph is illuminated with white light and three images are recorded, one through a red filter, one through a green filter and one through a blue filter. Images can be recorded in transmitted or reflected light using this technique. This makes it equally applicable to recording transparencies or prints.

The coloured filters introduce an additional problem when digitising. Anything placed between the photograph and the camera reduces the total amount of illumination at the detector. The standard colour filters will almost certainly affect the total illumination in different ways. To achieve satisfactory brightness with good colour balance and without overloading the camera sensor may take some experimentation. For example, a camera setting which gives good brightness and contrast with the red filter in place may overload the sensor when the green filter is in use. It is often desirable not to have to alter the camera settings between the different filters as this may upset the colour balance of the final image and it complicates the digitisation procedure. Actually, the final colour balance depends on how well matched the filters are and on how the sensitivity of the camera varies with wavelength. Most photodetectors respond better to longer visible wavelengths than to shorter ones. Often, the highest camera output will be found with the green filter in use. Though the detector may be more sensitive to red light, red filters are often denser than green ones. The filter which produces the greatest output can be used to set the camera aperture so that the full sensitivity of the sensor is being used without saturating it. Images taken with the other filters will then not overload the camera. This approach is suitable for most, typical colour images. However, difficulties can occur. For example, suppose that green is indeed the filter to which the overall system is most sensitive. We set the camera using the green filter. However, the image which we are digitising has very little green content. We set the camera aperture to get a large output from the detector. The detector then saturates when we use the other filters because the red and blue components of the image are much larger than the green component. Clearly, digitisation of colour images requires some experience. The approach described above can be useful but may need to be modified for difficult images.

Because of the various factors which can affect the colour balance of the final picture, it is almost always necessary to adjust the relative amounts of each of the three bands. In most cases, this can be done simply by viewing the resulting colour image. Some applications, however, require that the displayed image be a faithful reproduction of the original scene. These so-called true colour applications are very demanding and account must be taken of the particular colour display on which the final images are to be viewed as well as of the camera, filters and light sources. Applications in which precise colour rendition is important are often connected with archives of paintings or rare artifacts. In one case, an archive of images of paintings will be used by scholars and also by designers of art exhibitions. In both cases, the digital images must convey an accurate representation of each painting to people who do not have direct access to the original.

Probably the most important single factor to bear in mind when digitising colour images is to ensure that each band has sufficient strength of signal. Then, regardless of the subsequent operations required to balance the final image, at least the source data is of sufficiently high quality.

1.3.2 Digital Sources

As the technology for the acquisition of digital images improves, it is becoming more common for digital data to be available directly to image processing applications. Two areas have led the drive towards digital acquisition. We will look at each briefly.

1.3.2.1 Remote Sensing

Remote sensing has come to be synonymous with aerial or satellite based observation of the earth. Whilst film based techniques can be employed in reconnaissance involving aircraft, they are not really suitable for use on board satellites because of the cost and difficulty of retrieving the film! Consequently, the commonly known satellites used for earth observation and meteorology employ sensors which produce digital data. The sensors themselves are often related to the line scan cameras which we have already discussed. One row of the image is digitised at a time. The motion of the satellite relative to the earth's surface provides the scanning motion. Of course, this kind of scanning cannot be used if the satellite is **geostationary**. In this case, the satellite remains fixed above a specific point on the earth's surface, orbiting at exactly the same rate as the earth turns.

Images acquired by the satellite's sensors are transmitted via a radio frequency signal which is picked up at a ground station and relayed to the control station for the satellite. Signals sent from the control station via the ground station to the satellite can be used to alter its position or the position of its sensors to allow the desired images to be acquired.

One interesting aspect of remote sensing is that satellites often carry several sensors. Each of these detects radiation in a different part of the spectrum, for example infrared, visible or ultraviolet. Each detector is said to record a specific **band** of the electromagnetic spectrum. The reason for recording data from multiple bands is to increase the amount of data available for each point on the earth's surface. This aids the task of discriminating between the various kinds of ground cover which can occur, making it possible to distinguish between, for example forests, urban areas, deserts and arable farm land. Once distinguished, various areas can be monitored to see how they are changing with time.

There is, unfortunately, little standardisation in the way in which remote sensed data is made available by the various agencies which collect it. There is a wide variety of formats for the files of computer data which are distributed. This is made worse by the fact that each file usually contains not only the image but also a great deal of data related to the image. For example, the date and time when the image was acquired, the location of the satellite and the direction in which the sensor was pointing are vital pieces of information which will allow the image to be analysed later. Perhaps, eventually, some standard method of making this information available will appear. For the time being, it is often necessary to write special programs to allow these different data formats to be imported into various image processing systems.

1.3.2.2 Medical Imaging

It has become increasingly common for medical images to be recorded in digital form. This trend started with the so-called **body scanner** which uses X-rays to construct cross-sectional views of the tissue inside the human body. The technique used to generate the cross-sections was originally known as **Computer Aided Tomography** and as a consequence the machines are sometimes termed CAT scanners. More recently, another type of scanner has been introduced. Instead of X-rays, this scanner uses the absorption of radio waves by atomic nuclei aligned in a strong magnetic field. The technique is known as **Magnetic Resonance Imaging**. In both kinds of scanner, there is no directly measured image data. Instead, the output of the scanner's detectors is used to compute the required image which is then naturally in digital form. Figure 1.6 shows three cross-sections at different positions through the head of a particular patient. Various tissues are clearly distinguishable by eye in this kind of image and though expensive to acquire, they can be of great diagnostic value. In two of the images shown, a tumour is clearly visible. It is the area delineated with a light boundary behind and a little above the eye. To show the boundary of the tumour more clearly, the patient has been injected with gadolinium. This accumulates in the surface tissue of the tumour and provides extra contrast in the images. This particular tumour is known as an astrocytoma.

Other kinds of medical image are available in digital form. However, it is not yet common for conventional X-rays, still by far the commonest form of medical image, to be digital. However, the ever increasing cost of silver and the continuing reduction in the cost of mass digital storage devices, such as optical discs, mean that the switch to the digital acquisition, archival and display of all medical images is not too far in the future. Indeed, research organisations such as the National Institutes for Health in the United States, are already beginning to plan systems which will enable them to distribute digital medical images around their hospital sites and even via telephone links to remote medical centres.

As with remote sensed data, there is as yet no widely accepted standardisation in the forms in which medical image data is made available. Again, data related to the image, such as the patient's details, are often stored in the same file as the image itself. The situation has actually been a little worse than in the remote sensing field. Some manufacturers have regarded the format of the data from their equipment as proprietary and have not been prepared to publish the relevant details. This has made it difficult to use the data for image processing on any but the manufacturer's own equipment. In these days of the move towards open systems, a more enlightened

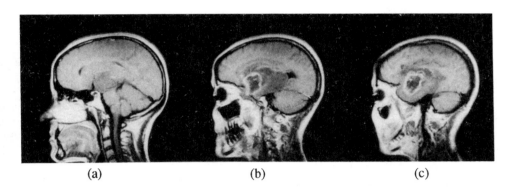

(a)   (b)   (c)

Figure   1.6. Images obtained using magnetic resonance techniques.. Three longitudinal
              sections through the head at varying positions. Data from Magnetic Resonance
              Imaging (MRI). (Images courtesy of Professor F. Galvez, Hospital General
              Gregorio Maranon, Madrid)

attitude is beginning to emerge and a standard known as the Picture Archival and
Communication System is becoming increasingly popular. Eventually this may form
the basis for the interchange of medical image data between a wide range of systems.

1.4 SUMMARY

In this chapter, we have looked at the nature of the digital image. We have seen the
data types which can occur. We have seen how monochrome and colour images can
be acquired and digitised. We have also briefly examined some standard sources of
digital image data and seen that a lack of standardisation is an inhibitor to the free
exchange of images between different systems.

    In the chapters which follow we will examine how digital image data can be
manipulated and processed to correct it and to extract the information which it contains. First, however, we look at the characteristics of typical image processing
applications.

2

Image Applications

Digital image processing has found application in wide variety of fields of human endeavour. Despite this, many image processing applications share broadly the same goals and achieve them using broadly the same strategies. Fundamentally, the objective of most image processing applications is to extract meaningful information from one or more pictures. The objective of many remote sensing applications, for example, is to extract information from images of the earth. This information might be about geology, land use, sea state or weather. The important common feature is that the information has to be deduced from the images. Similarly, the objective of many medical image applications is to derive information about a patient's state of health from X-ray, ultrasound, magnetic resonance or other relevant images.

In some applications, it is enough just to present the information to a human user. For example, in document image systems the objective is to replace paper documents by suitable, electronic images. Cost savings can be made by removing the need to store large amounts of paper. Also, access to the documents in electronic form is easier with less chance of their loss. This is an attractive proposition to businesses, such as insurance companies, which otherwise have to store huge numbers of hand written application forms. In document image systems, papers are digitised, stored and made available for viewing and printing. No analysis of the images is made, other than by the system's users. Though document systems are likely to be the most important type of image application in the near future, in economic terms, they represent only a tiny fraction of the problems to which image processing has been applied.

In the large majority of cases, image applications provide direct help in analysing the pictures and in extracting quantitative information.

There are a number of well defined processes which go to make up a typical image application. Some or all of these steps are needed by just about every application which involves image processing. The steps are:

Acquisition
> The capture of the image in digital form

Enhancement
> A rather non-specific improvement of the perceived quality of the image

Restoration
> Quantitative correction of the image to compensate for degradations introduced during acquisition. Restoration is used in preference to enhancement when there is sufficient information available about the degradations.

Segmentation
> Breaking up the image into areas which correspond to physically meaningful objects

Analysis
> Identification and measurement of the various objects apparent in the image

Each step in a typical application might involve use of a number of image processing functions. These functions, which we will look at in detail in the chapters that follow, are the basic building blocks from which image applications are constructed. In the following sections, we will look briefly at each of the steps in a typical image application. Each topic is revisited later in the book when the image processing functions involved are described in detail. The intent here is merely to put each of the processes into the context of the whole image application.

2.1 IMAGE ACQUISITION

We saw, in section 1.3, some of the ways in which image data can be acquired. The acquisition process introduces a certain level of noise into the images. In addition, the optical system in use introduces some geometric distortions and may also cause blur. Any motion of the objects being imaged relative to the optical system will cause additional blur. Whether the degradations which the acquisition process introduces are considered significant depends on the particular application. In many cases no action need be taken. If, however, corrections are required then either **image enhancement** or **image restoration** techniques will be applied. These two approaches to the improvement of image quality are mutually exclusive. The approach chosen depends on how much additional information is available on the exact form of the degradation. If little or nothing is known about the precise causes of the fault, image enhancement techniques can be used. If, however, the cause of the degradation is well understood, image restoration can be applied to correct for it specifically.

2.2 IMAGE ENHANCEMENT

In the absence of good, quantitative information about the form of any image degradation which is present, enhancement techniques may be employed in an attempt to improve the image in a subjective way. Image enhancement techniques are rather non-specific operations known to improve the visual appearance of images. Some techniques, for example, tend to reduce blur which may be present in the image. The techniques are non-specific in the sense that the blur will be reduced whatever its source. Blur due to motion is physically different from blur due to a poorly focused optical system, yet the same enhancement technique may improve the perceived quality of images suffering from either of these faults. Since enhancements are so non-specific and are not directly related to the degradation, it is difficult to predict which particular technique will be the best for a given application. The only way to select a suitable method is by trial and error.

Enhancements are often used to try to improve the detectability of certain features in an image, so that a human observer will be able to see them more easily. A reduction of blur may make it easier to see the features of interest, for example. Sometimes, it may be necessary for the enhancement to change the overall appearance of the image dramatically to allow the important features to be seen. The term enhancement may seem a strange one to apply in this case, since the result is quite different from the original. In this case we can think of the technique as enhancing the detectability of the features of interest, rather than enhancing their perceived quality.

There are many image processing functions which can be used for image enhancement. They appear throughout chapters 3 to 6.

2.3 IMAGE RESTORATION

When information is available about the forms of the various degradations present in an image, restoration techniques can be employed for correction. It is important that a good model of each degradation is available. For example, a great deal is known about the physics involved in a mis-focused optical system. In addition, direct measurement of the particular optical system used for acquiring the images may be possible. The degradation model and specific data together describe the

actual degradation in the image. Restoration techniques aim to correct the image
based on the model and the data. The objective is to remove all the effects of the
degradation, giving an image which is the equivalent of one captured by a perfect
acquisition system. Of course, restoration can never actually be perfect. However,
the results are in general superior to those obtained by image enhancement techniques, where no account is taken of the particular form of the degradation.

Image restoration techniques are discussed in chapter 8.

2.4 IMAGE SEGMENTATION

Images normally contain representations of multiple objects. For example, a
medical image will show a variety of organs and tissues, some normal, others
perhaps diseased. To achieve the goal of an image processing application, it is
almost always necessary to divide the image into regions each of which represents
one of the physical objects which have been imaged. A physician may be interested
in only one of the organs visible, for example, and may wish to analyse it in iso-
lation. The process of dividing the image up is known as **segmentation**.

Automatic segmentation of an image represents the single most difficult task in
modern digital image processing. At first, it is hard to see why this should be so.
After all, the human visual system allows us to separate and identify individual
objects even when we are viewing very complex scenes. Not only does it do that,
but it can cope with images which change many times per second with consummate
ease. If it is so easy for the eyes and brain to perform this task, surely it must be
simple for a computer. Unfortunately it most certainly is not. It is a very difficult
problem to solve. It is so difficult that many image applications do not even attempt
to perform segmentation automatically, preferring instead to rely on a human user to
provide the necessary information. Segmentation appears easy to us simply because
our visual system is extraordinarily good at doing it. It is only by trying to perform
segmentations on real images that we begin to appreciate just how difficult it can be.
Realisation of the fundamental problems associated with segmentation is one of the
most important steps in making a realistic assessment of the practicality of any particular application.

It is worth taking a little time to demonstrate just how subtle human sight is and
what a superb system we take for granted. Figure 2.1 shows some simple optical
illusions which illustrate a few of the subtleties of the human visual system.
Figure 2.1(a) shows the famous simultaneous contrast illusion. The lower row of
small grey squares are clearly all the same. In the upper row, however, the small
squares appear to get lighter towards the right of the image as the background gets
darker. In fact, the grey squares in the upper row are identical to those in the lower
row. The small grey squares are being viewed in relation to their surroundings. The
human visual system compensates for the background brightness change. Actually,

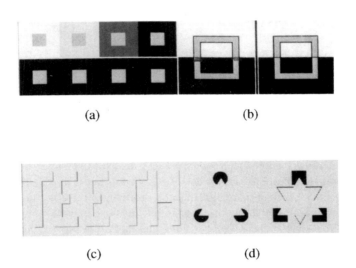

Figure 2.1. Optical illusions. (a) Simultaneous contrast, (b) Benussi's Ring, (c) Marks assumed to be letters making the word TEETH, (d) Kanizsa Figure.

this phenomenon of compensation is present in colour vision too. It helps to counteract the effect of the changing colour of sunlight throughout the day. To us, a London Transport bus appears the same shade of red whatever the time of day at which we see it. Yet in the morning and evening, when the sun is low in the sky, its light is relatively richer in red than it is at midday. Photographs of the same bus taken at various times of day will appear very different. The camera is quite unable to correct for the changing colour of the illumination. The human visual system does so continuously. Incidentally, the variation in the colour of sunlight throughout the day is due to the changing way in which it is refracted by the atmosphere as the sun's elevation changes.

Figure 2.1(b) shows another well known illusion based on simultaneous contrast. Benussi's ring is a grey ring on a split background. When the ring is whole, it appears to be of a constant brightness. The addition of two thin dividing lines cause the top half to appear darker than the bottom. The explanation for this effect begins to reveal some of the complexity of human vision. When the ring is whole, it is perceived as a single object. It is therefore reasonable for it to have a single colour, in this case a particular shade shade of grey. However, when the lines are added, the ring is perceived as two objects. The upper one is seen against a light background and is consequently darkened by the simultaneous contrast effect. Similarly the lower half of the ring is lightened. The only real difference between the two images is the addition of the lines. Note how subtle this effect is and how much additional knowledge, over and above the data contained in the image, is needed in order to generate it. Benussi's ring illustrates how in some situations, complex derived properties, such as whether particular regions of the image belong to one or two objects, can influence our most basic perceptions, in this case how bright something is.

Figure 2.1(c) clearly shows the word **TEETH**. Closer inspection, however, reveals that many of the lines which should make up the outlines of the letters are, in fact, missing. In this case, our visual system is basing its interpretation of the lines not simply on the image itself, but also on a vast store of previously acquired information. The visual system in some sense hypothesises that the marks are due to letters, in an effort to account for the phenomenon. It finds a good match, presumably better than for any other competing hypothesis and the resulting percept is a set of letters. Notice how sophisticated this process is. Not only must the visual system segment the image, admittedly rather easy in this case, but it must group the resulting lines appropriately and then recognise that the groupings constitute incomplete letters. It probably took you less than a second to do all of those operations.

Figure 2.1(d) shows the Kanizsa figure, another example of the application of world knowledge by the human visual system. In this case, the impression is of a white triangle partly obscuring the view of a black triangular outline and three black squares. Of course, the white triangle does not exist. The effect is caused by the alignment of the breaks in the other figures. The visual system in effect postulates the white triangle to explain the peculiarities in the other figures. After all, on this particular planet we don't normally find shapes like these aligned in precisely this way. It is much more likely that something is obscuring the view of a set of simple objects. Hence the perception of the triangle.

These illusions make a very important point. The human visual system is using much more information than just the patterns of brightness and colour detected by the eye. A great deal of other data is being brought to bear on the problem. Some of this information relates to the general arrangement of things in the world and the way light behaves when it strikes them. Other parts of the information are very specific, for example the arrangement of lines which make up the letters of our alphabet. This latter kind of information is sometimes known as **domain knowledge** because it relates closely to one particular problem domain, in this case reading words. It might be wholly inappropriate for other tasks, such as fleeing from a predator, unless of course the words involved are the instructions for escape.

Given that the human visual system brings so much additional knowledge to bear when analysing the images captured by our eyes, and especially when attributing features in those images to objects in the real world, we should not be surprised to discover that efforts to interpret images by computer based solely on image processing have had but limited success. However, a number of approaches to the problem are available, and research is in progress to try to combine methods to improve the overall reliability of the techniques.

There are several basic approaches to segmentation. Some are based on trying to find regions in the image in which the pixels are in some sense similar to one another. This might be because they have a similar colour or brightness or because they form part of a consistent, repeating pattern or texture. Other techniques are based on trying to identify image features which are consistent with the boundaries between regions or objects. If a complete boundary can be found, it delineates one region from others.

Segmentation for some types of application is easier than for others. Medical applications are particularly challenging as organs and tissues are not regular geometric shapes and rarely have any simple linear features. There are many segmentation techniques and some of them are discussed in section 9.1. The challenge is to find methods which consistently produce image segmentations which are as good as those regularly performed by human beings.

2.5 IMAGE ANALYSIS

The goal of almost all image processing applications is some kind of analysis of the image data. In some applications, identification of one or more objects may be the goal. In the inspection of manufactured items, for example, the goal may be to ensure that all the components of the finished unit are present and are in the correct place. That information might be used to deduce that the item has been properly assembled. The image system performing this task needs to examine the areas of the image in which each particular part should appear, and detect its presence. If all the expected parts are in place, the system registers that the unit is correctly assembled. Notice how, in this example, the image processing operations have reduced the data in the hundreds of thousands of pixels of the image down to the simplest choice. The assembly either passes or fails inspection.

Other applications require not only the detection of one or more objects but their measurement as well. In medical applications it is frequently necessary to measure the size of objects. For example, to determine if a particular course of treatment is having a beneficial effect, it might be necessary to follow the size of a tumour, say, over a period of weeks or even months. Images taken at appropriate intervals can be analysed and the size of the tumour measured from them. The important information here, from the patient's point of view, is not the images themselves. It is the change in size of the tumour with time. The images are simply a means of deducing that information. Of course, in a practical situation things are not as clear cut as this. There may be additional information which the physician can deduce from the appearance of the tumour in the images. However, the provision of quantitative information is of major importance in many applications.

Image analysis is discussed in chapter 9.

2.6 SUMMARY

In this chapter we have seen the basic components which go to make up any image processing application. The goals of image applications are, frequently, the detection of objects and the measurement of some of their characteristic features. Applications normally consist of acquisition, enhancement or restoration, segmentation and analysis. Each of these steps is composed of one or more image processing functions, the basic building blocks of all image applications.

In the chapters which follow, we will look in more detail at the components of image applications and at the functions used to implement them.

3

Conventional Functions

In this chapter we will cover some of the basic functions which can be useful in image processing. Many, such as the standard arithmetic and mathematical functions and simple logical operations, will be familiar to most readers. They are included for completeness. Others, such as those for manipulating brightness and contrast or for thresholding, are much more specific to image processing.

A number of issues arise when applying even quite simple operations to images. Some of these issues relate to situations in which images of differing type or size are involved. We will look at these issues first, in this chapter, then move on to arithmetic, basic mathematical functions, and logical operations before considering thresholding, grey level re-mapping and gradients. The chapter concludes with a discussion of how of look-up table hardware can be used to implement some useful functions.

3.1 COMPUTATIONAL RULES

When performing computations with conventional numerical values, we need to apply rules which govern what happens in unusual circumstances. For example, in typical programming languages there are rules which govern the action taken when performing **mixed mode arithmetic**. This is the term used to describe what happens when an expression to be evaluated contains variables of different type. This happens when an integer is added to a floating point number, for example. As well as rules for mixed mode arithmetic, in image processing we also need rules for the action taken when images of different size are involved in an operation. As an extreme example, we must know what happens when a constant is added to an image.

There is no single right answer for rules like these, and different image processing systems may use different conventions. The rules described here are those embodied in one particular image processing system (Lewis and Ibbotson (1989).) They have been found to be both useful and easy to understand. The rules embody very practical aspects of image processing. It is important to understand ' ᵥ the particular system you use behaves in these situations.

3.1.1 Data Type Conversions

Conversion between data types is often required when mixed mode arithmetic is being performed. We can compare the situation in image processing with that in conventional programming languages, which deal with similar problems. When mixed mode arithmetic occurs one, or sometimes both, of the variables concerned is converted into a data type in which the arithmetic can actually be carried out. For example, in the 'C' programming language the addition of a floating point number to an integer results in both the values being converted to double precision floating point form before the calculation is performed. Sometimes these conversions are required to maintain precision as when multiplying a fractional floating point number by an integer. Sometimes they may be used to prevent a value from overflowing the available range of the data type. The APL language automatically changes the data type of a variable if the value it is required to hold would cause overflow or underflow.

In most programming languages, only a small amount of additional storage is required when variables are converted in this way. This is because in general such conversions only occur for variables which hold a single value, such as an individual integer. These variables are known as **scalars**. APL is an exception because its rules can cause entire arrays to be converted. In typical usage, however, the additional storage needed for conversion to a more accommodating data type is still modest as most applications use only limited size arrays.

In image processing systems, however, large arrays are the norm rather than the exception and conversion of data type may require a significant increase in storage, if an entire image needs to be converted. It is for this reason that automatic type conversion is usually performed only when absolutely necessary, for example to preserve precision. In particular, automatic type conversion is almost never performed on 8-bit unsigned integer data and this leads to some rather bizarre rules for its arithmetic.

3.1.2 Rules for 8-bit unsigned integer arithmetic

The aims of the arithmetic rules for 8-bit unsigned integer data are to avoid vast increases in storage requirements and to ensure that results are also 8-bit unsigned integers. This means that results can be displayed as grey scale images on conventional display devices. To achieve this, the action taken for overflow and underflow is to clip the value to keep it within the range which can be represented. Internally, during a computation, each pixel in turn is held either as a 32-bit signed integer or a floating point value. Which is used depends on the precise nature of the calculation being performed. Use of these internal data types protects the precision of the result during the computation. Clipping takes place as the pixel is written to the output image. Any result pixel value greater than 255 is replaced by 255. Any value less than 0 is replaced by 0. Clearly this arithmetic has shortcomings. Sometimes these will be unimportant. However, if greater precision is required and the storage is available, the data can be explicitly converted to other integer or floating point types before undertaking the computation. This way, a user can decide whether the 8-bit unsigned integer arithmetic is appropriate or whether greater precision is required.

The other data types behave conventionally for mixed mode arithmetic. When the computation involves values of different type, the smaller is effectively converted to the type of the larger. For example, when an integer and a floating point value are combined, the integer image is effectively converted to floating point for the calculation. Actual conversion of the whole image is not normally necessary, pixels being converted during the computation. The result image, however, will be of the larger type, floating point in this case.

3.1.3 Image Size Conversions

As images are arrays, it is possible to specify operations between images which contain different numbers of pixels. We need to define the effect, for example, of adding an image which is 512 pixels square to one which is 256 pixels square. Again, this is a purely practical problem and different image processing systems may choose different approaches.

Lewis and Ibbotson (1989) shows one way to deal with the problem of operations between images of differing size. Basically, the images are aligned at their origins. The image which has the smaller number of pixels per row is then effectively padded to the right with zero pixels. Similarly, the image which has the smaller number of rows is effectively padded at the bottom with zeros. The operation can now be carried out between the two identically sized images. Of course, the implementation of such a rule does not necessarily require that the padding has actually to be carried out explicitly.

There is one important exception to this rule. The exception is when the operation involves a scalar value and an image. If we applied the padding rule in this case, we would perform the operation only on the very first element of the image. This is rarely what is desired and there are usually other ways of achieving that particular result. Instead, an operation involving a scalar and an image is carried out for every pixel in the image. This makes it easy, for example, to add 5 to every pixel in an image or to divide all pixel values by 3.14159.

3.1.4 Edge Effects

One problem, encountered specifically in image processing, is the inability to calculate certain values near the edge of the image. As we shall see, many image processing operations require groups of adjacent pixels in order to calculate the result. Near the edge, not all of the required pixels may be available as they would be beyond the boundary of the image itself. In this situation there are really only two alternatives. Either we do not calculate a result for those pixels too close to the edge of the image, or we make up the missing values from the image data which we do have. For example, we can construct the missing data by copying rows and columns of the data we do have. The first row above the image could be the same as the top image row. The next row above could be the second image row and so on. We have reflected the data in a mirror placed along the top of the image. Another alternative is to make the first row above the image the same as the last image row, the second row above the image the last but one image row and so on. We have effectively wrapped the image round on itself. Either of these techniques can be applied to any boundary of the image.

If we do not calculate pixels for which we have no data, the result image will be smaller than the original, by an amount depending on the particular operation. If we make up the missing data, the results for the edges of the image will be less reliable than those for the rest of it. The approach taken will vary from system to system and may differ for different image operations. Once again, it is important to understand what the particular system you use does in these circumstances in order to avoid unexpected results.

3.1.5 Restrictions on Input Values.

Many of the functions which we will look at in this and other chapters have a restricted range over which they are valid. This means that there are input values for which the function has no meaningful result. A good example is the logarithm function which is not defined for the value 0. When an image processing function encounters an invalid value like this, it must react in some way. The precise action taken will depend on the particular system in use. One solution is to refuse to continue the operation. Another is to place some special error value in the pixels of the result which could not be computed and to issue some kind of message. Whatever your particular system does, you do need to be aware of the consequences of passing invalid input values to a function. In general, this problem is worse in image processing systems simply because of the quantity of data involved. After all, it takes only a single negative value in a 250 000 pixel image to cause a problem with a square root function. Matters are made more difficult when the offending image is the result of a sequence of previous calculations. It may be quite a task to deduce the physical significance of the erroneous value in order to take appropriate action to solve the problem.

3.2 ARITHMETIC OPERATIONS

The conventional arithmetic operations of addition, subtraction, multiplication and division ($+ - \times /$) are carried out on pairs of images on a pixel by pixel basis. Corresponding pixels are retrieved from each of the input images, the computation is carried out and the result placed in the equivalent pixel position of the result. Any size or type conversions necessary are carried out during the operation as described in 3.1.

For addition and subtraction the operations are equivalent to those used in conventional **matrix** arithmetic. Matrices are particular kinds of 2 dimensional arrays. There are specific mathematical operations and properties associated with them. Matrices are of fundamental importance in mathematics. Consequently they are dealt with in many standard mathematics text books (see for example Kreyszig (1972).) It can sometimes be useful to treat images as matrices as we will see in later chapters. For now it is sufficient to point out where image operations are equivalent to matrix ones and where they differ. In particular, the kind of multiplication used for images, where corresponding pixels are multiplied to produce the result pixel, is quite different from matrix multiplication. As a result, a specific matrix multiplication operation has to be defined for images. It is discussed in section 3.3.10.

It is worth noting that the rule, discussed in section 3.1.3, about computations involving a scalar and an image, is entirely compatible with matrix arithmetic for all common operations.

3.2.1 Arithmetic Operations
There are many uses for the normal arithmetic operations on image data. A couple of examples illustrate typical usage.

When using an interactive system for image processing, it can be necessary to modify the contrast range of an image manually, perhaps to match some specific limits. For example, if we wish to apply a logarithm function (see section 3.3.8) to an 8-unsigned integer image, we need to remove any zero values from the data. As we have seen, the logarithmic functions are undefined for values of zero. A common way to remove the zeroes is to add a small positive constant to the entire image. The visual effect of this operation on the resulting image is negligible, though of course, if the resulting image is to be used in further computation, the effects of the addition must be thought about carefully.

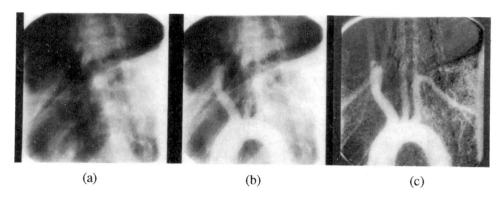

(a)   (b)   (c)

Figure 3.1. Digital subtraction angiography of the aorta. (a) before arrival of contrast medium, (b) after arrival of contrast medium, (c) difference image showing just the contrast medium in the blood vessels. (Original X-ray images acquired at St. Thomas' Hospital, London)

Some applications make use of the digital subtraction of two images to improve the visibility of the important features. In medical imaging with X-rays it is common practice to introduce a contrast medium into the patient to help visualisation of soft tissue structures. Whilst bone scatters X-rays and shows up well in the images, most soft tissue does not. The contrast medium, for example barium meal which is used for investigations of the stomach and intestine, does scatter X-rays and can be seen in the image. Of course, if there are normal body structures in the field of view, they will appear in the image as well. They may obscure the detail being sought. By taking two images, one before the contrast is introduced and one after and then subtracting them, an image is created which contains essentially just the contribution of the contrast medium. In this subtraction technique, it is obviously important that the patient does not move significantly between the two frames. Actually, the X-ray images are recorded on cine film. The contrast is introduced into the patient and the images are recorded. The frames to be used are chosen from the sequence of images. One of them is the last frame which shows no contrast medium in the vessels of interest. The other is the first frame in which the vessels are full of contrast medium. Figure 3.1 shows the technique applied to the imaging of the major blood vessels. When contrast medium is introduced into the blood stream the technique is known as angiography. It has been used routinely for many years, though the digitisation of the images and their digital subtraction is a fairly recent introduction. Figure 3.1(a) shows the situation before the contrast arrives. Figure 3.1(b) shows the vessels full of contrast medium. Figure 3.1(c) shows the result of subtracting the two frames. The arch shaped structure is the aorta which takes high pressure blood from the heart to the rest of the body. Leading upwards from the aorta are the carotid arteries which supply the brain and branching downwards from them are the subclavian arteries leading into the arms. The difference image does illustrate the appearance of additional noise which always accompanies the subtraction of two similar signals.

The particular example of Figure 3.1 was recorded as part of a project looking at the possibility of building three dimensional models of blood vessels from stereoscopic X-ray images (Mol (1984).) Whilst the particular images shown are, on their own, not of any great diagnostic significance, the same basic technique can be applied in a wide variety of medical imaging situations, wherever a contrast medium can be introduced into a relatively static organ or other biological structure. It is particularly valuable for studying fine detail which would otherwise be lost due to the presence of the other scattering structures.

3.3 BASIC MATHS FUNCTIONS

In this section we examine some basic mathematical functions which can be applied to images. Many of these functions are so basic that it is sometimes difficult to find real examples of their use in specific applications. Rather than solving an application in their own right, it is much more likely that a combination of these functions could constitute part of the solution to a particular problem. It is particularly valuable to have access to these basic functions when working with an interactive image system and trying out the effect of various operations. Many of these functions are not only useful with images but are also needed when manipulating the other parameters used by image processing functions. Image systems which treat all their data as self defining objects allow their functions to be used with images, vectors and scalars giving great flexibility of operation.

3.3.1 Sum

The sum of an image is the value computed by adding all its pixels together. It is a scalar value. Because images tend to have large numbers of pixels, the sum of even an 8-bit unsigned integer image is often very large. Consequently, the sum is usually represented as a floating point number.

The sum of all the pixels of an image is used as a scaling factor, for example in histogram computations (see section 4.4) and in some convolution based image filtering (see section 6.1.)

3.3.2 Maxima and Minima

It is possible to define two kinds of maxima and minima when dealing with image data. The first kind is the maximum pixel value and minimum pixel value within the image. The second is the maximum or minimum image constructed from of 2 or more input images. We will look at each of these in turn.

3.3.2.1 *Maximum and Minimum Pixel*

The maximum pixel value in an image is a scalar of the same type as the image itself and containing the maximum value which appears in the image. Likewise, the minimum pixel value in an image is a scalar of the same type as the image itself and containing the minimum value which appears in the image. Together, these quantities define the **dynamic range** of the image, that is the total range of values which it contains. This range is important in many operations, for example when re-mapping the brightness range of the image (see section 3.6.)

3.3.2.2 *Maximum and Minimum Image*

This form of maximum and minimum arises from a comparison of 2 or more images. For a maximum image operation, corresponding pixels are selected, from the set of images being processed, to form a group. From this group, the largest value is found and placed in the corresponding position in the output image. Each pixel position is processed in turn. The minimum image operation is identical, except that the minimum value of the group is used.

   The maximum image and minimum image functions provide one form of comparison between images. They could be used, for example, to discover the maximum and minimum values which occur through a sequence of images taken of the same object over a period of time.

3.3.3 Absolute Value and Sign

The **absolute value** of a variable is its value regardless of its sign. So the absolute value of −42.42 is just 42.42. The absolute value of a positive number is just that number itself. The absolute value of a given image, is an image of the same size and shape and in which each pixel is the absolute value of the corresponding pixel in the original image.

   The **sign** of a variable is a value indicating whether it is positive, negative or zero. The sign is 1 if the value is positive, 0 if the value is zero and −1 if the value is negative. The sign of an image is an image of the same size and shape as the original and in which the value of each pixel indicates the sign of the corresponding pixel in the original image.

   With this coding for sign, the absolute value of an image multiplied by its sign is equal to the original image.

3.3.4 Negative

The **negative** of a value is simply the same value but with its sign reversed. The negative of a given image is an image of the same size and shape in which each pixel is the negative of the corresponding pixel of the given image. There is one important exception to this definition. It applies to 8-bit unsigned integer images. We have seen that 8-bit unsigned integer image data can hold only positive values between 0 and 255. The negative function, as just defined, will lead to pixel values between 0 and −255. Using the arithmetic rules for this data type, described in 3.1.2, all negative values are converted to zero. So the new image is entirely zero, a rather uninteresting result. Because of this, the negative of an 8-bit unsigned integer image is usually taken to be the result of subtracting each of its pixels from 255. This has the pleasing consequence that the resulting image looks like the photographic negative of the original image when displayed.

3.3.5 Ceiling and Floor

The **ceiling** of a variable is the smallest integer which is greater than the variable. The ceiling of 38.12 is 39. The ceiling of −132.67 is −132. The ceiling of a given image is an image of the same size and shape and in which each pixel is the ceiling of the corresponding pixel in the original image.

The **floor** of a variable is the largest integer which is less than the variable. The floor of 38.12 is 38. The floor of −132.67 is −133. The floor of a given image is an image of the same size and shape and in which each pixel is the floor of the corresponding pixel in the original image.

The ceiling and floor functions used on maximum pixel and minimum pixel values respectively, provide integer bounds on the dynamic range of a floating point image.

3.3.6 Modulus

The modulus of two values is essentially the remainder after subtracting the second value from the first an integer number of times. For example, the modulus of 7 and 4 is 3. The modulus of 6.13 and 2.5 is 1.13, which is the remainder after subtracting 2.5 twice from 6.13. The equation which governs the computation of the modulus of x and y is $(x - R)/y = n$. In this expression, R is the modulus and n is an integer. Some definitions of modulus require that R be positive, whilst others allow either sign when either x or y is negative.

The modulus of two images is an image in which each pixel is the modulus of the corresponding pixels taken from the input images.

3.3.7 Powers and Roots

Powers and roots are computed for an image by computing the power or root of each of its pixels. For example, the cube of an image is an image of the same size and shape as the original in which each pixel is the cube of the corresponding pixel in the original image. The square root of an image is an image of the same size and shape as the original in which each pixel is the square root the corresponding pixel in the original image. Non-integer powers and roots are, of course, quite valid.

The usual restrictions apply for the computation of even roots. Negative pixel values in an input image will cause some kind of error condition.

(a)   (b)   (c)

Figure   3.2. Scaled log and exponential. (a) Original image, (b) scaled log image, (c) scaled
exponential image.

3.3.8 Trig, Log and Exponential Functions

The common trigonometric, logarithmic and exponential functions can all be applied
to images. As with other basic mathematical functions, the result of applying one of
these operations to an image is another image of the same size and shape as the
original and where each pixel is the result of applying the particular function to the
corresponding pixel of the original image.

The common trigonometric functions are **sine** and its inverse **arcsine, cosine** and
its inverse **arcosine, tangent** and its inverse **arctangent**. The common logarithmic
functions are **logarithm to base 10, natural logarithm**, and **logarithm to base 2**.
The **exponential** function is the inverse of the natural logarithm. These functions are
all well known. However, there are two further functions which are useful in image
processing, namely **scaled logarithm** and **scaled exponential**. These functions first
perform a logarithm or exponential function and then re-scale the range of values in
the result to match those in the input image. The advantage is that, for example, if
the input image is an 8-bit unsigned integer the scaled logarithm or exponential will
also be in a form for direct viewing. Without the re-scaling operation the values in
the logarithm image, for example, would range from 0 (the logarithm to base 10 of
1) to about 2.4 (the logarithm to base 10 of 255) and would be quite unsuitable for
direct display. Figure 3.2 shows examples of the scaled logarithm and scaled exponential. We will look at how the values are re-scaled in section 3.6.

The logarithmic functions are useful for compressing the dynamic range of an
image. This may allow fine detail to be seen in data which is otherwise dominated
by a few large values. In particular, the scaled logarithm function can be used to
reduce the dynamic range of Fourier spectra and to match them to the grey scale

capabilities of a particular display device. This can allow additional detail to be seen. We will cover this topic in section 7.1.1.2. Conversely, the exponential function can be used to exaggerate differences in otherwise rather uniform data.

Trigonometric functions are often needed when performing geometric operations on images. However, they tend to be used with scalar data rather than entire images. One use for the sine and cosine functions is in the generation of images used for certain kinds of psychophysical experiments into human vision. Many such experiments exploit so-called sine wave gratings as the basis of visual stimuli. Quite complex combinations of individual gratings are often required and these can conveniently be generated using the trigonometric functions applied to suitable images. Figure 3.3 shows examples of some simple gratings created this way.

A number of restrictions about valid input values apply when the trigonometric, logarithmic and exponential functions are used on images. For example, the logarithms of values less than 1 are undefined. The exponential of a relatively modest number may exceed the capability of the machine to represent it. The tangent function has singularities at 90° and 270°, meaning that its value cannot be computed for those angles. As with other functions, these restrictions need to be understood if the operations are to be applied successfully.

3.3.9 Functions for Complex Data

Complex images are images where each pixel is a complex number. We will see how complex images arise and how they may be used in chapter 7. In this section we discuss how some conventional functions used for manipulating complex numbers are applied to complex images.

3.3.9.1 Separating the Real and Imaginary Parts

We saw in section 1.1.2.2 that a complex number has a real part and an imaginary part. Often we need to separate the complex image into two images, one containing the real part and the other containing the imaginary part of the original image. In each case, the resulting image is the same size and shape as the original image. In the case of the real part, extracted by the **real** function, each pixel contains the real component of the corresponding pixel in the original image. In the case of the imaginary image, extracted by the **imaginary** function, each pixel contains the imaginary component of the corresponding pixel in the original image.

3.3.9.2 Magnitude of a Complex Image

The magnitude of a complex number is the square root of the sum of the squares of its real and imaginary parts, ignoring the j. It is a real value. The magnitude of the complex number $3 + 4j$ is 5 .

The magnitude of a complex image is a real image of the same size and shape in which each pixel is the magnitude of the corresponding pixel in the original.

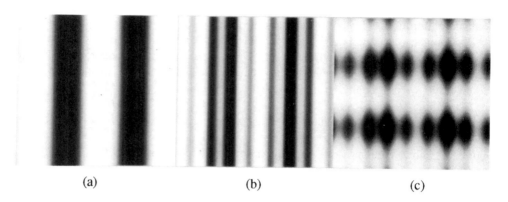

(a)   (b)   (c)

Figure 3.3. Sine wave gratings. (a) Simple horizontal grating, (b) two horizontal gratings of different frequency, (c) horizontal and vertical gratings.

3.3.9.3 Complex Conjugate

The complex conjugate of a complex number is the complex number with the same real part but in which the imaginary part has changed sign. The complex conjugate of $4 + 2j$ is $4 - 2j$. The complex conjugate of a given image is an image of the same size and shape as the original and in which each pixel is the complex conjugate of the corresponding pixel in the original image.

3.3.10 Matrix Multiplication

We have already seen that it is possible to treat images as matrices. We have also seen that the normal definition of image multiplication is incompatible with that for matrix multiplication. Although this is not the place to discuss the details of matrix multiplication, it is defined here in terms of the indexing scheme used in image processing, in contrast with that used in standard texts on mathematics. Though a deep understanding of the theory involved is not necessary here, there are many standard texts on mathematics which cover matrix techniques in detail (for example Kreyszig (1972).)

Two matrices can only be multiplied together if the number of columns of the first is equal to the number of rows of the second. Also, the order of the matrices in the multiplication is important. Reversing the order can change the result. Given two images A and B to be matrix multiplied, the result R is given by:

$$R_{ij} = \sum_{k=0}^{p-1} a_{kj}\, b_{ik} \tag{3.1}$$

Here, i is the x coordinate and j the y coordinate of the pixel being computed. R is the result image and p is the number of columns in A and the number of rows in B .

This equation uses an image style indexing scheme, which is why it might appear a little strange to readers familiar with matrix methods. We have already seen that it is conventional to give the x coordinate of a pixel first and to follow it with the y coordinate. The pixel R_{20} is the second pixel on the top row of the image. Unfortunately this is precisely the opposite of the way in which indices are assigned in matrix methods. In addition, mathematics texts always index beginning at 1 and not 0. As this is a book about image processing and not about mathematics, it uses the image style of indexing. The results are, of course unaffected. All that changes is the form of the equations. It is, however, worth being aware of these differences in notation when referring to texts on mathematics.

Although it is unusual to multiply two images together using matrix multiplication, the technique is commonly used in graphics applications. We will meet it again in section 5.5.1 when we look at perspective transformations applied to images. In this case the matrix multiplication is used to convert three dimensional coordinates in various ways.

3.3.11 Matrix Inversion

The inverse of a matrix is that matrix which when post multiplied with the input matrix yields the unit matrix. It is just like the inverse of a scalar, which when multiplied by the scalar yields 1. Inverse matrices are of great importance in mathematics in general and, as we shall see, have a number of applications in image processing. The importance of the inverse matrix is that it allows certain equations to be solved by calculation. For example, matrix inversion is involved in the computations which allow Principal Components Analysis (see section 7.2.)

The computation of a the inverse of a matrix is rather involved. It has been the subject of a great deal of study and fast, precise methods exist, though they tend to be rather involved. Fortunately it is not necessary to understand the details of the implementations in order to be able to use the results.

3.4 LOGICAL FUNCTIONS

Logical functions deal with the truth or falsehood of expressions. For example, the expression $a>b$ is **true** if a is indeed greater than b and **false** otherwise. The result of such an expression can be represented as a value, commonly 1 for TRUE and 0 for FALSE. We will use capitalisation, like this, when referring to the values which represent truth or falsehood. In this section we will look at some common logical functions and see how they can be applied to images.

3.4.1 Comparison

The normal comparison operators can all be used when dealing with image data.

$=$	equal to
$>$	greater than
$<$	less than
$\geq$	greater than or equal to
$\leq$	less than or equal to
$\neq$	not equal to

The result of comparing two images, using one of these operators, is an image of the same size and shape as the original and in which each pixel represents the truth or falsehood of the comparison between corresponding pixels.

3.4.2 Any and Every

The comparison functions record the truth or falsehood of pixel by pixel comparisons between images. Sometimes, however, we may need to ask questions such as 'Are any of the pixels in this image equal to 42 ?' The function **any** allows us to answer this kind of question. This function returns a single value which is TRUE if any of the pixels of the image to which it is applied have the value TRUE, and FALSE otherwise. To answer the question just posed, we would compare the given image with 42 and then apply **any** to the result of that operation.

The **every** function returns a single value which is TRUE if every pixel in the given image is TRUE and FALSE otherwise. It can be used in a similar way to **any**. For example, to discover if every pixel in image I is greater than the equivalent pixel in image J we can apply the **every** function to the result of comparing I and J using the $>$ operator.

3.4.3 Bitwise logical operations.

Just as standard arithmetic operations can be defined on a pixel by pixel basis for images, so can the usual bitwise logical operations. These include **and, or, exclusive or**, and **not**. In each case, the operation is applied to each pixel in turn and the result is placed in the corresponding position in the result image.

The bitwise operators are effectively applied to each bit of their input pixels in turn. Consequently, they are appropriate only for unsigned integer images. The resulting bit in the equivalent position of the appropriate output pixel is defined by the rules for the particular operation.

and	Result bit is 1 if the same bit in both operands is also 1. It is 0 otherwise.
or	Result bit is 1 if the same bit in either one or both operands is also 1. It is 0 otherwise.

exclusive or   Result bit is 1 if the same bit in only one of the operands is also 1. It is 0 otherwise.

not   Result bit is 1 if the same bit in the operands is 0. It is 0 otherwise.

These are the standard definitions for the usual bitwise logical operations. As an example consider an **and** operation on 8-bit unsigned integers with values 9 and 3. The binary representation of these values is **00001001** and **00000011** respectively. We can see immediately that only the rightmost bit is 1 in both values so the result of the **and** operation is the bit pattern **00000001**, which has the value 1.

3.4.4 Masks

We can use logical operations to build images which can subsequently be used as masks. Masks can restrict the region over which an operation is carried out. They can also be used to remove or insert pieces of image. As a simple example, consider the problem of adding some grey scale text to an 8-bit unsigned integer image. The operations are illustrated in Figure 3.4. Assume, for the sake of simplicity that the image of the text and the image in which it is to be placed are the same size. First we create a mask from the image of the text. We can do this in a variety of ways. In this example we use a comparison operation. Using a ≠ (not equals) comparison of the text image with zero gives us a resulting image in which the pixels have the value TRUE (i.e. 1) wherever there is text and FALSE (i.e. 0) everywhere else. Multiplying this result image by 255 gives us a mask image with values 0 and 255. If we now subtract this mask image from the original image, we create a hole into which we can place the text. All pixels in the original image which are in positions which will be occupied by the text are set to 0. The subtraction exploits the clipping inherent in 8-bit unsigned integer arithmetic and which we discussed in section 3.1.2. Finally, we simply add the text image to the original image. The text overlays the hole created in the original image, merging the text and image as desired. This operation will work whatever grey level is used for the text. It will also work if the text contains a variety of different grey levels or even when colour is involved.

3.5 THRESHOLDING

Thresholding is an operation in which the value of each pixel in the result depends on the value of the corresponding input pixel relative to one or more values known as **thresholds**. There are a number of different ways in which thresholds can be applied to an image. We'll consider the simplest case first. In this situation we have a grey scale image and a single threshold value. Each pixel of the image is examined and if it has a value less than the threshold the corresponding output pixel is set to one particular value, for example 0. If the input pixel is greater than or equal to

      (a)   (b)   (c)

Figure   3.4. Using simple masks.   (a) Text, (b) masked image, (c) image and text combined

the threshold, the output pixel is set to a different value, for example 255. We can define the operation as follows for the ith input pixel of image I .

$$R_i = \begin{cases} H, & I_i \geq T \\ L, & I_i < T \end{cases} \qquad (3.2)$$

Here, R_i is the resulting pixel, T the threshold value, L the below threshold result value and H the above or equal to threshold result value. You can see from this that the simplest threshold is a generalisation of the the comparison operator $\geq$ (greater than or equal to), which we have already covered. However, the threshold operation is more flexible than the simple comparisons. Even in this simplest case, we can specify the output values associated with pixels above and below the threshold. With the comparison operators we are restricted to the values used to represent TRUE and FALSE. Figure 3.5(a) shows the result of thresholding the train image at a value of 102 using 0 for pixels below this value and 255 for those equal to it or above.

    This kind of thresholding is often used to try and separate an object from its background. It is one of the simplest forms of segmentation and we will meet it again when we look at segmentation in section 9.1.1. However it is not a generally useful segmentation technique in grey scale images of typical scenes. Figure 3.5 should be enough to convince you of this. There is no simple threshold which, when applied to this image, will discriminate between, for example, the locomotive and the background.

    Thresholding is usually only successful as a segmentation technique in situations where the lighting is carefully controlled and can be adjusted to make the resulting grey level of the object significantly different from the background. We will examine techniques which exploit special lighting in section 9.1.1.

(a)   (b)   (c)

Figure   3.5. Thresholding.   (a) Train image thresholded at a value of 102, (b) image thresholded at a value of 102 within a range of 75 to 175, (c) original image merged
with another using a threshold of 127.

Thresholding can be applied to the whole of the range of values in an image, as
just described, or it may be restricted to only a small part of the range. Values
falling outside the range being considered are left unchanged. Consider a range of
values $S \leq T \leq U$ where T is the threshold as before, S is the lower limit of the range
over which we want to perform a threshold and U is its upper limit. We want to
threshold those pixels falling between S and U and leave the rest unchanged. The
definition of this threshold operation is:

$$R_i = \begin{cases} I_i, & I_i > U \\ H, & U \geq I_i \geq T \\ L, & S \leq I_i < T \\ I_i, & I_i < S \end{cases} \qquad (3.3)$$

The top and bottom lines of the right hand side handle the cases when the input pixel
value is outside the range over which the threshold is being applied. The middle 2
lines specify the threshold operation within the range. Figure 3.5(b) shows the result
of thresholding an image at a value of 102 within the range 75 to 175. Values
outside the range are unchanged.

So far, we have assumed that the threshold T and the values to be used for the
output, H and L, are simply scalars. However, in a more general case all these
values could themselves be images of the same size as the input image I. The simple
threshold operation is exactly as before except that the threshold value applied can
vary over the input image as can the values used for output. The definition of this
operation is:

$$R_i = \begin{cases} H_i, & I_i \geq T_i \\ L_i, & I_i < T_i \end{cases} \tag{3.4}$$

Instead of a fixed value, the threshold used is the pixel from the threshold image in the corresponding position to that of the input pixel. Instead of fixed output values, the corresponding pixel from the relevant image image is selected. It is possible to view this operation as the merging of images H and L. Pixels are selected from either H or L depending on the relationship between the input pixel and the threshold. Of course, a fixed threshold could also be used for this merge, and this is just what has been done in Figure 3.5(c). Alternatively, we could make H and L constant, in which case the resulting image would be a visual indication of the comparison of image I and the threshold image T allowing us to highlight the differences between them.

There is one further generalisation of thresholding which is noteworthy. We have considered only those situations in which the whole or part of the grey level range of an image is divided into two portions, that below the threshold and that equal to or above it. We could instead establish a whole series of such threshold values and assign the output pixel value depending on the range into which a particular pixel falls. This operation is sometimes known as **grey level slicing**. It is actually a crude way of **classifying** the pixels of the input image based on their value. We will cover classification more fully in 9.1.4.

3.6 GREY LEVEL RE-MAPPING

The general topic of contrast and brightness manipulation is known as **grey level re-mapping**. One common reason for manipulating the contrast and brightness of an image is to compensate for a less than ideal image capture system. Images which are low in perceived contrast can be enhanced by increasing their contrast. This action on its own may be sufficient to reveal additional detail. Another reason for this modification may be to bring two or more images to some common range of brightness values. This may aid, for example, in obtaining the correct colour balance from separate images digitised through standard colour filters (see section 1.3.1.6).

We will cover the basic operations of grey level re-mapping here though we will meet the subject again in section 4.1.1, when we look at alternative ways of expressing these mappings.

3.6.1 Linear Re-mapping
There are two simple ways to alter the grey level of an image. One is to add a constant value to each pixel, thereby altering the overall brightness of the image. This constant is known as the **bias**. The other is to multiply each pixel by a constant value, affecting the contrast in the image but altering the brightness as well. This

constant is known as the **gain**. The linear re-mapping operation applies both these modifications together. It can be written:

$$R_i = gain\ I_i + bias \qquad (3.5)$$

I_i represents the ith pixel in the input image and R_i the ith pixel in the result. You have probably already realised that this expression is in the form of the equation of a straight line. There is a linear relationship between R_i and I_i, hence the name of the mapping. The terms gain and bias are derived from electronics. They refer to parameters of circuits which can be used to carry out this transformation on electrical signals.

If *gain* is larger than 1, the result will have more contrast then the original. If it is less than 1, the result will have less contrast. Likewise, if *bias* is positive, the result will be brighter than the original, whereas if it is negative, the result will be darker.

3.6.2 Image Re-ranging

A different and often more convenient way of expressing a linear re-mapping operation is by specifying the range of values desired in the resulting image. By comparing the desired range of values with the actual range, we can compute a suitable gain and bias to use in a linear re-mapping operation.

We can see how the re-ranging takes place by considering an example. Suppose we have an image with pixel values between 100 and 171, and that we want to stretch the contrast to cover the range 0 to 255. Clearly, in the new image a value of 0 represents the lowest value from the original image, that is 100, and 255 represents the highest value from the original image, that is 171. First of all, we subtract 100 from each pixel of the original image so that its range is 0 to 71. We have the correct value for the smallest pixels in the image. Now we multiply each pixel by 255/71 to stretch the values to lie on the 0 to 255 span. In general we can define this operation on the ith pixel of input image I as:

$$R_i = (I_i - I_{min}) \left[\frac{H - L}{I_{max} - I_{min}} \right] + L \qquad (3.6)$$

where R is the result image, H is the largest value in the new range and L its lowest value, I_{max} is the largest pixel value in I and I_{min} is its smallest value. These can be determined using the maximum and minimum pixel functions described in section 3.3.2.1. In our example, L is 0.

At first sight, this may not seem to be a linear expression. However, for a given image and a given new range of values the terms H, L, I_{max} and I_{min} are all constants. The expression is linear for I_i and is just another way of expressing a linear grey scale re-mapping. The advantage of this form of the equation is that the re-mapping is specified in terms which are easier to envisage than the raw gain and bias values themselves.

3.6.3 A More Robust Image Re-ranging

There are occasions when the normal image re-ranging operation does not yield the desired result. Suppose that, in the example we just considered, the input image contained a single pixel with value 0 and another with value 255. Though they may have no visual importance at all, they will prevent any contrast stretch taking place, since now the input image covers the entire 0 to 255 range.

We can overcome this problem by making an assumption that small numbers of pixels probably contribute little to the visual appearance of the image. Actually this is frequently the case, though it is possible to construct pathological cases in which small numbers of pixels are of great visual significance. Having made the assumption, we exclude the 5% of pixels with the largest values and the 5% of pixels with the smallest values. The central 90% of the pixels are mapped to the central 90% of the available output range. The remaining pixels are mapped to the remainder of the available range of output. Although the mapping is non-linear (actually it is piecewise linear), it can be very useful when trying, to get an increase in contrast in an image to help discern detail visually.

This particular computation requires knowledge of the range of values in the input image, and in particular which values are occupied by the top and bottom 5% of the pixels. To do this, the image's **histogram** must be computed. We will look at histograms and their applications in section 4.4.

3.7 GRADIENTS

Gradients measure how quickly pixel values change when we move across an image. If a particular part of the image is smooth with gently changing grey level, the gradients will be small. On the other hand, if it contains texture or is noisy the gradients will be large. The gradient is also known as the **first derivative** of the image, terminology which originated in calculus. Other derivatives can be calculated for an image. The second derivative is just the gradient of the first derivative, and so on. In this section we are interested in just the image gradient though we will meet the second derivative again in section 6.2.2.

A gradient has both a magnitude and a direction. Two values are required to define it at each pixel position. One convenient way to store this information is as a complex image. The real part holds the gradient in the x direction and the imaginary part holds the gradient in the y direction. In this form, only one image is required to hold the gradient information. The components of the gradient are written $(\partial I/\partial x)$ and $(\partial I/\partial y)$ respectively where, as usual, I represents the image. The two component

(a)   (b)   (c)

Figure   3.6. Gradients. (a) Gradient of train image in x direction, (b) gradient in y direction, (c) magnitude of gradient

gradients can be extracted from the complex representation using the real and imaginary functions described in section 3.3.9.1. Instead of representing the gradient in terms of its magnitude in the x and y directions of the image, we can instead compute it as a magnitude and an associated direction. This is just a different way of expressing the same information. The magnitude and direction are related to the x and y components by the expressions

$$m = ((\partial I/\partial x)^2 + (\partial I/\partial y)^2)^{1/2}$$
$$\theta = \tan^{-1}\left(\frac{\partial I/\partial y}{\partial I/\partial x} \right) \tag{3.7}$$

where, m is the magnitude of the gradient and θ is its direction.

Computation of gradients is inherently error prone. We will see why shortly. Also, gradients are usually computed by a simple approximation. While this is often adequate, it can introduce additional errors which may become a problem. It is important to be aware of the difficulties which gradients may introduce when applying them in imaging applications.

For simplicity, consider the one dimensional case of a single row from an image. The definition of the gradient of the image along the row is:

$$\frac{\partial I_i}{\partial x} = \lim_{\delta x \to 0} \frac{I_{i+1} - I_i}{\delta x} \tag{3.8}$$

I_i represents the ith pixel in a particular row of image I and δx represents the distance between one pixel and the next. The equation means that we take the difference in value between neighbouring pixels on the row and divide by the distance between them to get an estimate of the gradient. This is an approximation which gets nearer and nearer to the true gradient as δx gets smaller and smaller, or alternatively as the number of samples for a given distance gets larger and larger. Normally, in image processing, the pixels are all the same size and unless we need to have the gradient expressed in some particular unit of real spatial measurement, δx is set to 1. This is equivalent to saying that our unit of distance measurement within the image is the pixel. The gradient is very simply the difference in value between one pixel and the next. The approximation applies equally when computing the gradient down a column of the image.

The problem with this approximation is that we are subtracting two potentially large and similar numbers, namely the grey scale values in adjacent pixels. The error in the result is approximately the sum of the error, or noise, in the pixel values themselves. However, because the actual difference between the adjacent values will often be small, the resulting error will often be a much larger proportion of the result. A gradient image is typically much noisier than the image from which it was computed.

There are other methods of computing gradients which rely on using more than just two adjacent points. These techniques may alleviate some of the noise problems by reducing artifacts introduced by the simpler approximation. These techniques do, however, suffer from worse problems at the edge of the image than does the simple approximation. Their need for additional points means either that the gradient cannot be calculated as near the edge as it can by the simple approximation or that more data needs to be extrapolated to provide the missing points. We will see some other techniques for computing gradients when we look at edge detecting filters in section 6.2.3.

In Figure 3.6 the gradients for the train image have been calculated using the simple approach of subtracting neighbouring pixel values. Figure 3.6(a) shows the gradient of the train image computed along its rows, Figure 3.6(b) shows the gradient computed down the columns and Figure 3.6(c) shows the magnitude of the total gradient, computed from equation (3.7). It is clear from the figure that the gradient along the rows tends to show up vertically oriented brightness discontinuities. Likewise, the gradient down the columns shows up horizontal discontinuities. The magnitude of the gradient resembles a line drawing or sketch of the original. We will see how this effect can be exploited when segmenting an image when we look at the technique of **edge detection** in section 9.1.2.

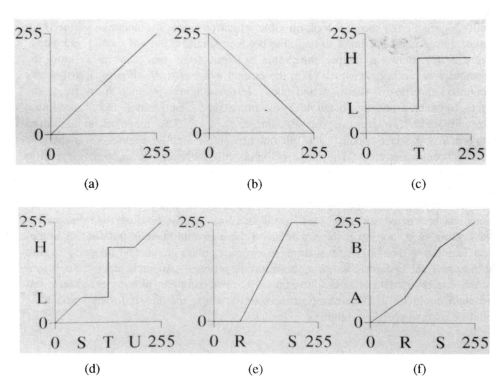

Figure 3.7. Look-up tables. (a) No change, (b) negative image, (c) threshold, (d) bounded
threshold, (e) simple contrast stretch, (f) modified contrast stretch.

3.8 EXPLOITING LOOK-UP TABLES

Look-up tables are hardware facilities in display devices. They provide a mapping
between the pixel value in the image and its representation on the display. They
were introduced in section 1.2. We can use look-up tables to implement a variety of
simple image functions including contrast manipulation and thresholding. By using
the tables we avoid the computation associated with calculating the values on a pixel
by pixel basis. Only the table entries need to be computed. This can often be done
quickly enough to allow interactive modification to be carried out under user control.
The hardware of the look-up table does, however, limit the range and precision of the
data which can be processed this way. Often, only 8-bit unsigned integers are supported.

Figure 3.7 shows some examples of look-up tables. Each is illustrated as a graph
showing the mapping of input to output values. Assume that the input and output of

the table are 8-bit unsigned integers. Figure 3.7(a) shows a look-up table which does not affect its input in any way. The output value for a given input is the input value itself. Figure 3.7(b) shows a look-up table which produces the negative of the input image. Large values of input to the table produce small output values and vice versa. Figure 3.7(c) shows a simple threshold. Output from the table is L until the threshold T is reached, at which point the output switches to H. Figure 3.7(d) shows a bounded threshold. Below S and above U the output is simply the same as the input. Between S and the threshold T, the output is L. Between T and U the output is H. Figure 3.7(e) shows a simple contrast stretch. The range of input values between R and S is mapped to the full output range. Finally, Figure 3.7(f) shows a modified contrast stretch. The range of input values between R and S is mapped to the range of output values between A and B. The residual input and output ranges are mapped accordingly.

Many grey scale re-mapping (section 3.6) and thresholding (section 3.5) operations can be carried out using look-up tables. Importantly, because the computation and loading of a look-up table is a relatively fast operation, it is possible to implement interactive threshold specification or contrast enhancement and hence to exploit the user's visual system in choosing appropriate settings. An input device, such as a mouse, can be used to alter the look-up table. For example, moving the mouse left and right could be used to change the contrast whilst moving it forward and back could be used to change brightness.

3.9 SUMMARY

In this chapter we have covered some basic functions which can be useful in image processing. Some are useful in their own right, others form part of more complex operations. All can be considered building blocks from which image applications, or at least parts of image applications, are built. We have seen how many standard arithmetic and mathematical functions and simple logical operations can be applied to images and looked at the issues associated with mixed mode arithmetic, operations involving images of differing size and at edge effects. We have also looked at contrast and brightness manipulation, at thresholding and at gradients. Finally we have seen how look-up tables can be used to implement certain functions requiring simple mappings whilst avoiding much of the computation.

4

Statistics and Probability

Statistics is the study of ways in which data can be analysed. In particular, statistical methods are often used for **data reduction**. In data reduction, a large set of experimental data is processed to produce a small number of values which adequately represent the entire set. A simple example is the computation of the average value from a set of individual observations during some experiment. The average is used in subsequent calculations to represent all the individual observations which were actually made.

Some statistical methods can be useful even in simple image processing operations. We will look first at the application of statistical operations on the entire image and will then see how similar operations can also be applied to small areas or neighbourhoods of the image.

Probability is the study of chance occurrences, as for example when a coin is tossed before a cricket match and one captain is asked to guess on which side it will fall. Probability is important in statistics and also in image processing. In this chapter we will look at how probability can be applied to image processing in the form of **histogram** based techniques.

4.1 IMAGE MEAN AND STANDARD DEVIATION

A **mean** and a **standard deviation** can be calculated for any collection of values. An image is no exception. The mean is a measure of the overall brightness of a grey scale image. Comparing two grey scale images, the one with the larger mean value will often appear brighter. It is not always case, however, as the mean value takes no account of the range of variation of individual pixel values or of their spatial arrangement. It is quite possible for images which appear very different to have very similar mean values. The mean value is computed by summing all the pixels of the image into a single value and then dividing it by the number of pixels in the image. It can be expressed as:

$$\mu = \frac{1}{n} \sum_{i=0}^{n-1} I_i \tag{4.1}$$

Here, μ is the mean value and I_i is the ith pixel of the input image I, which has n pixels in all.

The standard deviation of an image is a value which characterises the extent to which any particular pixel value is likely to vary from the mean value. The larger the standard deviation, the greater the proportion of pixels which lie further from the mean value. For a grey scale image, a high standard deviation may imply an image with more contrast. It may, however, simply imply an image with a higher noise content. The standard deviation can be expressed as:

$$\sigma = \left[\left(\frac{1}{n} \sum_{i=0}^{n-1} I_i^2 \right) - \mu^2 \right]^{1/2} \tag{4.2}$$

Here, σ is the standard deviation and μ is the mean, as computed above. Once again, I_i is the ith pixel of the input image I, which has n pixels in all. To be strictly accurate, both the mean and standard deviation are actually defined as limits when the number of values being considered is infinite. So in practice what we compute from the formulae just given are estimates of the mean and standard deviation. When we deal with entire images, we usually have a large number of pixels and the estimates are very good. They are still useful even when small areas of the image are considered, as we will see in section 4.2.1.

The mean value and standard deviation of an image often indicate its perceived brightness and contrast. It is not always possible to predict how an image will appear, just from its mean and standard deviation. The spatial arrangement of the pixels is critically important in the process of human visual perception. However, for a wide variety of images the mean and the standard deviation are useful indicators.

The square of the standard deviation, written σ^2, is known as the **variance** of the image.

4.1.1 Modifying Image Means and Standard Deviations

We have already seen that the mean and standard deviation of an image are a measure of its overall brightness and contrast. Consequently, it is possible to specify brightness and contrast changes in terms of mean image value and standard deviation. This can be easier than trying to use gain and bias, as we did in section 3.6.1. The problem of computing the resulting image, given a target mean and standard deviation, is that of distributing the change in the overall value to each individual pixel.

In the case of the mean, the computation is very simple. If we want the mean value of the image to become μ_{new}, we add $\mu_{new} - \mu$ to each pixel. We can show this very easily. If the assertion is correct, the new mean is given by:

$$\mu_{new} = \frac{1}{n} \sum_{i=0}^{n-1} (I_i + \mu_{new} - \mu) \qquad (4.3)$$

which can be re-arranged to:

$$\mu_{new} = \left[\frac{1}{n} \sum_{i=0}^{n-1} I_i \right] + \mu_{new} - \mu \qquad (4.4)$$

From equation (4.1), the term in brackets is just the original mean μ. The two terms μ cancel out and the equality is clearly valid, demonstrating that we can achieve the desired mean value this way. In the terms used in section 3.6.1, we are applying a bias of $\mu_{new} - \mu$.

We can set the standard deviation of the image by multiplying each pixel value by the ratio of the desired standard deviation to the existing one.

$$R_i = I_i \frac{\sigma_{new}}{\sigma} \qquad (4.5)$$

Once again, R_i represents the ith pixel of the result image and I_i the ith pixel of the input image. This computation, however, causes the result image to have a different mean value from the original image. A similar calculation allows us to vary the standard deviation without altering the mean value of the image. In this case, we multiply the difference between each pixel value and the image mean value by the ratio of the desired standard deviation to the existing one.

$$R_i = \mu + (I_i - \mu)\, \frac{\sigma_{new}}{\sigma} \tag{4.6}$$

Using the expressions for mean and standard deviation given earlier, it is quite easy to show that these two methods do indeed lead to the desired standard deviation.

The modifications to individual pixel values to achieve desired means and standard deviations are just forms of the linear re-mapping, as discussed in 3.6.1. The difference here is in the way in which the gain and bias values are determined from quantities which are closely related to brightness and contrast and which are consequently easier to envisage.

4.2 OPERATIONS USING LOCAL STATISTICS

4.2.1 Local Mean and Local Standard Deviation
We have seen the computation of the mean and standard deviation of entire images. It can also be useful to compute these quantities over small parts of an image. In particular, we can compute a local mean value or standard deviation at each point in the image by considering the value of the pixel and its immediate neighbours. This is the first time we have encountered an example of a **neighbourhood operation** . We will illustrate the approach by considering the local mean operation.

Figure 4.1 shows a 5 pixel square region from an image. The highlighted values within that region show one particular 3 pixel square neighbourhood. There is a central pixel, which has the value 23, surrounded by its 8 nearest neighbours. The local mean computation is a normal mean calculation but, in this example, includes only the central pixel and its 8 neighbours. The resulting value, in this case 53, is placed in the output image at the position equivalent to that of the central pixel of the neighbourhood. This computation is performed with each pixel in the input image in turn being the centre of the neighbourhood. There are some exceptions, near the edge of the image. For a 3 pixel square neighbourhood, the mean cannot be calculated when the central pixel is on one of the edges of the image. Part of the neighbourhood then lies outside the image. As we saw earlier, individual image processing systems deal with this situation in different ways. Some will produce a result which does not include the incalculable pixels, and is therefore smaller than the original image. Others will set the pixel values to 0 or may notionally extend the input image by re-using values from elsewhere to allow the computation to take place. Whatever the scheme employed, it can be important to understand what the system used actually does in this circumstance. The problem of computation of neighbourhood operations at the edge of the image affects every function which is implemented this way.

42	57	38	71	85
65	**88**	**59**	**42**	41
18	**21**	<u>**23**</u>	**26**	31
98	**76**	69	**73**	81
22	28	19	17	11

Figure   4.1. Neighbourhood.   A small neighbourhood around a particular pixel in an image

The local mean operation is an example of a smoothing function. Neighbourhood operations which perform this kind of function are often known as **smoothing filters**. We will meet some more smoothing filters shortly. We will look at a more general approach to filters, based on a specific kind of neighbourhood operation, in chapter 6.

Because, in the local mean operation, we replace each pixel by the mean of its neighbours, we produce an image in which the variation between successive pixels is damped out. This simple operation can be effective in noise reduction. The amount of smoothing which takes place depends on the size of the neighbourhood used. For smoothing, it is normal to use a square neighbourhood, but not essential. Figure 4.2 shows examples of images smoothed by local averaging. It also illustrates how a threshold can be applied to the smoothing operation to help prevent real detail from becoming blurred.   The local mean operation is carried out as before, but if the resulting value differs from the central pixel value by less than the threshold, the central pixel itself is copied to the result image instead of the computed value. The effect of the threshold is to reduce the blurring. However, the best value to use for the threshold can often only be deduced by inspection of the resulting image.

The assumption underlying the use of the threshold is that noise in the image will tend to perturb a pixel a long way from the value of its neighbours. So smoothing is applied when this situation occurs but is suppressed when the pixel value is close to the mean.   Detail tends to be preserved because smoothing is suppressed when unnecessary. This use of the threshold in the local mean is one example of a class of methods which are defined by their goal rather than their implementation. The goal is **edge preserving smoothing** which, as its name implies, seeks to smooth out noise whilst preserving the real detail in the image and in particular the boundaries between areas.

(a)   (b)   (c)

Figure   4.2. Local mean for smoothing. (a) Train image smoothed with 7 by 7 pixel local
          mean, (b) image smoothed with 15 by 15 pixel local mean, (c) image smoothed
          with 15 by 15 pixel local mean with a threshold.

The local mean operation can be used directly to reduce noise in an image. The
local standard deviation, on the other hand, can provide information which might be
used in other kinds of image algorithm. It gives information about the degree of
variation of pixel value within the neighbourhood. As with the local mean, it is
computed in the same way as the normal standard deviation but over the neighbourhood rather than the entire image. The local standard deviation can be used to vary
the behaviour of another image operation at different places in the image. Algorithms which are sensitive to the local characteristics of the image and which can
vary their behaviour as a consequence are known as **adaptive**. Local image statistics
are very important for this class of algorithms.

In the next section we will look at an example of a technique which is adaptive
and which uses local standard deviation to modify its behaviour.

4.2.2 Statistical Differencing

Statistical Differencing is basically an adaptive form of the standard deviation modification which we covered in section 4.1.1. The computation is adaptive in the sense
that the adjustment is based on the local standard deviation of the input image rather
than its overall standard deviation. Each pixel is adjusted individually based on the
standard deviation of the neighbourhood in which it exists. The effect is to bring the
standard deviation, and hence the contrast, of each local area to the same value. This
is not true of the normal linear re-ranging technique and as a result statistical differencing is capable of revealing detail not visible using simpler methods.

Statistical differencing enhances detail in the image regardless of the local brightness. The operation is particularly useful for images which have a high dynamic

(a)   (b)   (c)

(d)   (e)

Figure   4.3. Local area smoothing operations. (a) Original image, (b) original image treated
        by statistical differencing, (c) original image with spot noise added, (d) noisy
        image smoothed with 7 by 7 median filter, (e) noisy image smoothed by a 6
        nearest neighbour filter.

range and in which detail is present throughout the range of brightness. The simplest
form of statistical differencing is formulated as follows:

$$R_i = \mu_{local} + (I_i - \mu_{local}) \frac{\sigma_{new}}{\sigma_{local}} \tag{4.7}$$

The subscript $local$ here refers to the locally computed values of mean and standard
deviation within the neighbourhood being considered. Apart from this, you should
note that the expression is essentially identical with that for computing a new overall
image standard deviation and which was introduced in 4.1.1. Values of μ_{local} and
σ_{local} are computed for each neighbourhood. Then the transformation in equation (4.7)
is applied to the central pixel in that neighbourhood. The variable factors are the

new desired standard deviation σ_{new} and the size of the neighbourhood. Figure 4.3(b) shows the effect of treating an image by statistical differencing. Notice how detail in shadow areas is much easier to see after processing.

4.2.3 Median Filtering

The median of a set of values is the value for which half of the values in the set are larger and half are smaller. For example, consider the set of numbers 9,32,28,23,6. If we rearrange these in ascending order we find 6,9,23,28,32. The middle value of the sequence is clearly 23 and this is indeed the median. There are 2 values greater than the median and 2 less than it. By contrast, the mean value of this set is quite different from the median and in this case is 19.6. The median is always one member of the set of values whereas the mean is computed and therefore may not be. As with the definition of mean and standard deviation, the definition of the median shows it to be an approximation which gets better and better as the number of values in the set gets larger and larger. However, it turns out to be a useful concept even when the number of values involved is small, as in the neighbourhood operation of median filtering.

In median filtering, the median value of each neighbourhood is determined. In the example of Figure 4.1, the median value is 59. This value is placed in the result image at the position equivalent to that of the central pixel of the neighbourhood. Just as for local averaging, the computation is performed with each pixel in the input image in turn being the centre of the neighbourhood. The same problems occur at the edges of the image as they do in local averaging and are solved in similar ways. Again, as with the local mean, a threshold can be applied so that the median value is only used if it differs from the central pixel value by more than a predetermined amount. Median filtering is particularly effective at reducing spot noise. This kind of noise is manifested by a relatively infrequent but high amplitude random fluctuation. Figure 4.3 shows an example of the use of median filtering. Figure 4.3(c) shows the train image with spot noise added. Figure 4.3(d) shows the result of filtering this noisy image using a 7 by 7 median filter. The noise has been almost entirely removed. The median filter is very effective, though it does tend to be quite a slow operation. This is because the pixels in each neighbourhood must be sorted in order to find the median value. As the number of elements to be sorted increases as the square of the neighbourhood size, it is important that a good sort algorithm be used to prevent filters with large neighbourhoods taking excessive time to compute.

The median filter is one of the better edge preserving smoothing filters.

4.2.4 Nearest Neighbour Filtering

k nearest neighbour filtering is yet another neighbourhood operation. It is similar to the local mean operation. However, in this case the resulting value is not the mean of the whole neighbourhood, but the mean of the k neighbours of the central pixel whose values are closest to its value. The value of k depends on the size of the neighbourhood. For the 3 by 3 pixel neighbourhood of Figure 4.1, 6 would be an appropriate figure. The pixels with values 21,23,26,42,59,69 are the k nearest neighbours of the central one. The value of the filter in this case is 40 . This filter possesses something of the characteristics of median and local mean smoothing and is another successful edge preserving smoothing filter. Figure 4.3(e) shows the result of filtering the noisy image, of Figure 4.3(c), with a 6 nearest neighbour filter.

4.2.5 Sigma Filtering
Sigma filtering is an adaptive form of k nearest neighbour filtering. We have already seen that adaptive filters modify their characteristics based on the local image statistics of each neighbourhood. The sigma filter is so named because it is based on the standard deviation σ of the pixels in the neighbourhood. As with the k nearest neighbour filter, the sigma filter replaces the central pixel with an mean computed from some of the pixel values of the neighbourhood. However, instead of using a fixed number of neighbours, sigma filtering uses only pixels whose values which fall within a particular range of that of the central pixel. The range used is computed from the standard deviation of the neighbourhood. If the standard deviation is very small, the resulting value will be very similar to, if not identical with the central pixel value. On the other hand, if the standard deviation of the neighbourhood is large, a significant amount of averaging will take place. The sigma filter is an attempt to produce an edge preserving smoothing filter which improves its performance by adapting to the local conditions in the image.

4.2.6 Choosing a Smoothing Filter
We have now seen a number of basic smoothing filters. The question which remains is which one to choose for a specific application. In probable ascending order of computation time, the filters we have looked at are:

1. Local Mean

2. Median Filter

3. k Nearest Neighbour Filter

4. Sigma Filter

This is also approximately the order of increasing quality, though that is a very difficult term to define and is very application dependent. There is no hard and fast rule about which of these filters to use in any particular case. This kind of rather non-specific smoothing constitutes an image enhancement. As we saw in chapter 2, about the only way to choose between comparable enhancement techniques is to try them out on the particular data. Trial and error may not be an academically attractive technique, but it is about all that is available in the absence of a good model of the particular degradation which we are trying to correct. When applying smoothing filters, the degradation involved is almost always noise. If a model of the degradation is available, a more rational choice of smoothing filter can be made. The filter can be made to compensate for the specific properties of the noise. We will look at this approach, known as image restoration, in chapter 8.

4.3 PROBABILITY

Probability is the study of chance events, for example, the result of throwing an ordinary dice. It is not possible to predict which number will be uppermost when the dice stops moving. If an occurrence is an absolute certainty, we say it has a probability of 1. We will assume that it is absolutely certain that the dice will come to rest with one of its faces uppermost, so the sum total of the probabilities of each particular face being uppermost must be 1. The dice has 6 faces and, unless someone is cheating, each has an equal probability of appearing uppermost. Consequently each face has a probability of 1/6 of appearing at the top. In this case, a probability of 1/6 means that if we throw the dice a large number of times, each number will appear on top on about 1/6 of the throws. The larger the number of throws, the better will be the approximation to 1/6.

The situation is similar when tossing coins. Discounting odd events such as the coin landing on its edge, it will fall head side up about 1/2 the time and tail side up for the remainder.

We really should address the question of what we mean by an odd event. An example of an odd event is the coin landing on its edge or the dice landing on one of its corners. We tend to discount these spectacular events because they are so improbable. The probability of such an event is so low, in comparison with the normal situation, that we can safely ignore it from the point of view of our calculations. Another way of looking at this is to say that we would have to throw the coin a very large number of times indeed to have any hope of seeing such a peculiar event. The probability of an event can be used to determine an expectation that the event will occur. This can be used to deduce a number of attempts after which we might become suspicious if the event had not occurred. For example, if we throw the dice 36 times, we expect the value 4 to appear on top about 6 times, as this event has a probability of 1/6. Of course, there is no guarantee that it will, but if 4 has not appeared at all after that number of throws, we might suspect the interference of some external agent.

4.3.1 Probability and Images

The random selection of pixels from an image can be treated very much like throwing a dice. We can ask questions about the probability that a particular value pixel will occur, just as we can about how often a particular face of the dice will appear uppermost. The more often a specific value occurs in an image, the more likely it is that we will pick that value by random selection of a pixel. We can determine the probability of finding any particular pixel value by counting the number of pixels in the image with that value and dividing by the total number of pixels in the image. For example, suppose we have a 10 000 pixel image having 5000 pixels with value 0 and 5000 with value 255. The probability of finding a pixel with value 255 is one half, just the same as of tossing a coin and having it come down heads. The probability of finding a pixel with value 1 is, of course, zero. There simply aren't any.

4.4 THE HISTOGRAM

A graph showing the probability of each particular pixel value in an image is known as a **histogram**. Histograms have a variety of uses in image processing. In this section we will look at the accumulation of histograms and their use in grey level re-mapping and thresholding.

4.4.1 Accumulating Histograms

To accumulate a histogram we need first to count the total number of pixels with each possible value which occurs in the image. Then we divide each of these counts by the total number of pixels in the image to obtain the probability value. The counting process is simple. Notionally, we set up a counter for each possible value which a pixel could contain. For an 8-bit unsigned integer image, we need 256 such counters. We then traverse the image looking at each pixel in turn and adding 1 to the counter for that particular pixel value. Each resulting count is effectively the expectation for that pixel value. Dividing each count by the total number of pixels in the image gives the probability. We can write this as:

$$Pr(v) = \frac{\text{Count}(v)}{n} \qquad (4.8)$$

where $Pr(v)$ is the probability of a pixel having value v, Count(v) is the total number of pixels with value v, and n is the total number of pixels in the image. Actually, it is often possible to work directly with the counts rather than the probabilities. Indeed, it is common for histograms to be computed as counts by image processing systems. However, if we want to compare the histograms of two images of different size, we need to use probabilities to remove any differences due simply to the different total numbers of pixels.

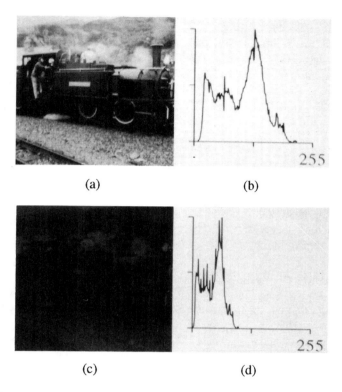

(a)   (b)

(c)   (d)

Figure   4.4. Images and histograms. (a) Original image, (b) histogram of original image, (c)
low contrast and darkened image, (d) histogram of dark, low contrast image

4.4.2 The Cumulative Histogram

A slight modification of the method for accumulating a standard histogram yields
another useful form. Rather than determining the probability of a pixel having a
particular value, we determine the probability of it having being less than or equal to
that value. Since the required probability represents the cumulative total of the probabilities for all pixel values less than or equal to the one in question, this histogram is
termed **cumulative**. We can write the operation as follows:

$$CPr(v) = \sum_{j=0}^{v} Pr(j)$$ (4.9)

We can accumulate this form of histogram almost as easily as the standard one. We look at each image pixel in turn, as before, and increment the counter corresponding to its value and also the counters for every pixel value less than its value.

The cumulative histogram has a specific use in the technique known as **Histogram Equalisation** which is covered in section 4.5.

4.4.3 Evaluating Histograms

Figure 4.4(b) shows the histogram of the train image of Figure 4.4(a). The shape of this histogram is typical of many real world scenes. There is a preponderance of pixels in the middle value range. Relatively few pixels have very large or very small values. The histogram shows that there are pixels in the image with just about the full range of brightness. Because of this we would not expect much visible change to occur in the image if we were to apply a grey level re-mapping operation, like those discussed in section 3.6. The histogram gives us a way of evaluating the image to see what kinds of basic faults it may have and also to see what kind of modifications might be appropriate. For example, the image in Figure 4.4(c) is clearly lower in contrast and darker than that in Figure 4.4(a). The error is so gross that it is easy to decide what is wrong with the image. A quick look at the histogram, shown in Figure 4.4(d) confirms the diagnosis. In situations where the nature of the error is less obvious, it is often easier to deduce the cause of the problem from the histogram than from the image itself.

Histograms are particularly valuable when digitising images. They show whether or not the full dynamic range of the digitisation system has been exploited. Changes in camera settings or lighting can quickly be deduced by inspection of the histogram. Histograms are especially useful in colour digitising when individual primary colours are being acquired separately. We discussed the basic procedure in section 1.3.1.6. Differences in overall light transmission between the different standard colour filters can easily be seen in the image histograms. Alteration to camera or to lighting can be made on the basis of the histograms to correct the colour balance of the resulting image.

4.4.4 Histograms and thresholding

In section 3.5, we saw that thresholding commonly does not separate distinct objects in an image. It is rare to find an image in which one part of the brightness range is occupied by one object to the exclusion of all others. This kind of partitioning can occur, however, and once again the histogram of the image may indicate the situation and can be used to deduce a suitable threshold value. In fact, the image of the train, which we have been using, does show this property. Figure 4.4(b) shows the histogram. It has two distinct major peaks with a trough between them. This kind of histogram is known as **bi-modal**. In fact, the pixels below grey level 102 are predominantly part of the train itself whilst the remainder are in the rest of the scene.

Figure 3.5(a) shows the effect of thresholding the train image at grey level 102. The value was chosen after inspection of the histogram. How well such a threshold partitions the image depends very much on the scene being viewed and on the conditions. In a controlled environment, it may be possible to arrange the lighting to achieve the desired discrimination. However, under normal lighting conditions it is rare to encounter a situation in which thresholding provides satisfactory segmentation.

Histograms with a larger number of peaks can also occur. Once again, the grey level values of the troughs between the peaks are the best candidates for thresholds. It is also possible to devise methods for automatic location of likely threshold values from a histogram. Such methods need to be able to identify the major peaks and troughs in the histogram and ignore the small local variations.

4.5 USING HISTOGRAMS IN RE-MAPPING

This section looks at the application of histograms in grey scale re-mapping. The main techniques involved are **histogram equalisation** and **histogram specification**. Before we look at these techniques in detail, we need to cover a small amount of introductory material on functions and their inverses.

4.5.1 Functions and their Inverses

We have already seen a number of functions which can be applied to images. At this point we need to take a slightly more formal look at functions in preparation for the discussion on histogram based techniques. A function is a rule which converts some input value to an output value. There can be one and only one value of the output for a given value of input. The square root is an example of a function. There are many examples of functions which have inverses. A function which is the inverse of another function, undoes that function's effect. The exponential function and the natural logarithm are inverses of each other. Applying the exponential function first followed by the natural logarithm yields the initial value. In other words

$$\ln(e^x) = x$$

Functions which can be expressed algebraically are known as **analytic**. They can be computed to arbitrary precision for any valid input value. The natural logarithm and exponential functions are analytic. Although many analytic functions have inverse functions, it is by no means generally the case.

From the definition above, it is possible to consider tables of values as if they were functions. After all, the table provides a rule for mapping an input value to an output value. Of course, it is not possible to retrieve an output value for any arbitrary input value. Only those in the table can be used. For example, Figure 4.5 shows a table which can be used to evaluate e^x. We can look up discrete values of e^x

x	1	2	3	4	5
e^x	2.72	7.39	20.09	54.60	148.41

Figure   4.5. Tabulated values of the exponential function.

so long as the table contains them. Actually, we can estimate values e^x, even if they are not in the table. We look up values of the function either side of the one required and make some estimate from them. In the following discussion, we will assume that it is a good enough approximation to choose the nearest value which actually occurs in the table.

A very important property of the table of values of a particular function is that we can use it to estimate the inverse function as well. For example, if we look up the value 54.60 in the second row of Figure 4.5, the corresponding value of 4 from the first row is its natural logarithm. We can treat any arbitrary tabulation of values, such as a histogram, in this way. The table gives us a completely general way of approximating inverse functions, regardless of their form. We will use this property shortly to modify the shape of the histogram of an image and thereby to alter its brightness and contrast. The technique is known as histogram specification.

4.5.2 Histogram Equalisation

Histogram equalisation can be used to enhance the appearance of an image and to make certain features more visible. It is a means of re-mapping the pixel values in an image in an attempt to equalise the number of pixels with each particular value. The effect of this is to tend to allocate more grey levels where there are most pixels and to allocate fewer levels where there are few pixels. This tends to help increase the contrast in parts of the histogram which are most heavily populated. This often reveals detail previously hidden.

One approximation to ideal histogram equalisation combines adjacent levels which have too few pixels into a single level. Consequently, some pixel values in the result will be unoccupied. It can be shown that the mapping function required to equalise the histogram is just the cumulative histogram which we saw in section 4.4.2. Gonzalez and Wintz (1977) show a simple proof of this. It is not necessary to understand the proof in order to follow how histogram equalisation is carried out.

The histogram equalisation is performed using equation (4.9). First, we calculate the value $CPr(v)$ for a given pixel value v. This calculated value will be between 0 and 1 because it is a probability. To convert this into a new pixel value w we need to map it into the range of pixel values we are using. The general expression for this is:

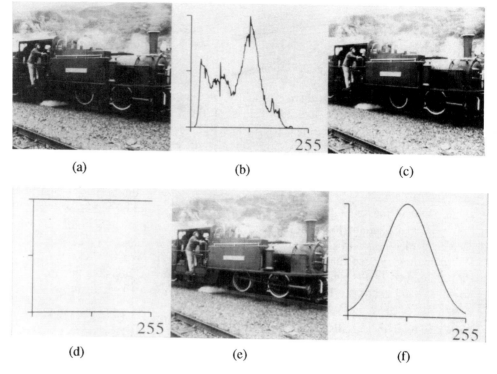

Figure 4.6. Histogram equalisation and histogram specification. (a) Original image, (b) histogram of original image, (c) histogram equalised image, (d) histogram of histogram equalised image, (e) image after histogram specification, (f) histogram after histogram specification

$$w = CPr(v)\,(W_{max} - W_{min}) + W_{min} \tag{4.10}$$

where W_{max} and W_{min} are the largest and smallest pixel values we want to use in the output image. For example, for an 8-bit unsigned integer image where we want to use the entire available grey scale, W_{max} is 255, W_{min} is 0 and so we simply multiply $CPr(v)$ by 255. Since our image can represent only whole numbers, we need to round the resulting value to the nearest integer. This integer is the new pixel value for all pixels in the input image which have value v. Repeating this simple calculation for all pixel values in the input image, we obtain a mapping relating input image pixel values to output image pixel values. Applying this mapping to the input image yields the histogram equalised result. Of course, the equalisation is approximate. The occupied pixel values in the result will each have about

$n_{he} = n/(W_{max} - W_{min})$ pixels, where as usual n is the total number of pixels in the image. However, there may still be levels which are very different. In particular, as stated, the technique can never reduce the number of pixels in a given level. Any pixel value which originally had many more than n_{he} pixels, will still have that number, though of course the pixel value itself may have been modified as a result of the equalisation. More sophisticated implementations are available which can split a single pixel value and map the pixels into more than one other level. Of course, the difficulty then is to decide which pixels to move to other values and which to leave at the existing value. Rosenfeld and Kak (1982) describe two possible techniques. One is based on random redistribution of the pixels. The other looks at the pixels to be distributed and at their spatially nearest neighbours. It moves particular pixels to be most consistent with the values of those neighbours.

A couple of additional points are worth noting. First, there is no reason why the result image has to be of the same data type as the original, though it usually is. Second, since the result of equation (4.10) is a mapping, it can often be expressed as a look-up table. This means that the result of the histogram equalisation can be viewed without updating the pixels of the original image, reducing the time taken to complete the operation. For a look-up table to be used, the data type of the result image must be compatible with the image display in use. This often means that 8-bit unsigned integer images must be employed.

Figure 4.6(a)-(d) show the train image and the results of a histogram equalisation operation. The technique used splits single levels where necessary, mapping the pixels into other levels by random redistribution of the pixels. The resulting image has a perfectly equalised histogram. It is a horizontal line.

4.5.3 Histogram Specification

Histogram specification goes one stage beyond histogram equalisation. Rather than modify the image to obtain a uniform histogram, this re-mapping changes the image to match a specified histogram shape. To do this, it uses the idea of the inverse of a function introduced in section 4.5.1. In histogram equalisation we use the cumulative histogram of an image as a mapping to modify the image and make its histogram uniform. The reverse operation is also possible. We can take an image with an equalised histogram and map it to have any desired histogram. The mapping in this case is the inverse of a cumulative histogram. The required cumulative histogram can be easily computed from the desired histogram itself. We now have two mappings. We can go from any image to one which is histogram equalised. Also, we can go from a histogram equalised image to one with any desired histogram. Putting these two mappings together allows us to change the histogram of any image to any desired shape. The calculation proceeds as follows.

Suppose we have an image I and a desired histogram H. First we perform histogram equalisation on the image to obtain the equalised image I_{he}. Then we form the cumulative histogram C_H of the desired histogram H using equation (4.9). Finally we use a tabulation of C_H and apply its inverse to I_{he} to evaluate the result. This is just the same as using a table of values of a function to look up its inverse, as we did in section 4.5.1. Figure 4.6(e)-(f) show a particular histogram applied to the train image. The histogram is a Gaussian curve centred on grey level 128 and dropping nearly to zero at grey level 0 and 255.

Histogram specification can be applied to images to try and normalise them for comparison purposes. Two images taken on different occasions may differ in overall brightness or other illumination based properties. By performing a histogram specification operation on both images to bring them to a common histogram, much of the variation can be removed allowing a more useful comparison of the detailed differences. Alternatively, certain types of image may tend to have characteristic histograms which mean that much detail is still hidden even after histogram equalisation. Better discrimination of detail can be achieved by specifying a particular histogram shape. For example, Cocklin et al. (1983) suggests using the finite Rayleigh Distribution as a target histogram shape when viewing digital chest X-ray images. The particular form of the distribution chosen is not important here. It was selected after study of the particular characteristics of the histograms of chest X-rays, which are in general heavily weighted towards higher grey level values. The important point is that by modifying the histogram in some application specific way, significant details in the image may be easier to see.

4.6 ENTROPY

Entropy is a concept which originally arose from the study of the physics of heat engines, and of the steam engine in particular. In that connection it has often been described as measuring the amount of disorder in a system. A living organism, such as a plant, is very highly organised and consequently has a low entropy. When it dies, it decays and becomes completely disrupted. From the point of view of the plant, its entropy has increased. Another way of expressing entropy, which is useful when thinking about image data, is as the spread of possible states which a system can adopt (Dugdale (1970).)

In the case of an image, these states correspond to the possible values which individual pixels can adopt. For example, in an 8-bit unsigned integer image, there are 256 such states. If all the states are equally occupied, as they are in the case of an image which has been perfectly histogram equalised, the spread of states is a maximum, as is the entropy of the image. On the other hand, if the image has been thresholded, so that only two states are occupied, the entropy is low. If all the pixels have the same value, the entropy of the image at its minimum value of zero. Notice how, in this progression, as the entropy of the image is decreased, so is its effective information content. We have moved from a full grey scale image, with high entropy, via a thresholded image, with low entropy, to a single valued image, with zero entropy.

Entropy can be computed from equation (4.11) under the assumption that the pixel values used are not correlated with one another. This assumption holds reasonably well for many types of image.

$$E = -\sum_{j=0}^{M-1} Pr(j) \log_2 Pr(j) \tag{4.11}$$

In this equation, $Pr(j)$ is the probability of pixel value j occurring. It is given by equation (4.8). M is the number of different values which pixels can adopt. In our example, of an 8-bit unsigned integer image, M is 256.

We can investigate the limits of equation (4.11) to see how we arrived at the earlier figures for image entropy. Suppose we have an image in which every pixel has the value k. The only non-zero term in the summation will be for $Pr(k)$, whose value is 1. Since $\log_2 1$ is zero, so is the entropy. At the other extreme, if all pixel values are equally occupied, the value of $Pr(j)$ for every value of j is the same. Since there are 256 different levels, each $Pr(j)$ is 1/256. The sum then evaluates to $\log_2 256$, which is 8. In fact for any value of M, the maximum value which the entropy can attain is $\log_2 M$.

Given the histogram of an image, we can compute equation (4.11) and determine the entropy. Entropy calculated by equation (4.11) is defined in terms of bits per pixel. One way of thinking about this value, which is particularly relevant to image compression, is that an 8-bit unsigned integer image with an entropy of less than 8 bits per pixel, is capable of being represented in a more compact form. The entropy indicates the average number of bits per pixel needed to represent the image without information loss. Choosing a representation which can achieve such a compression is not necessarily simple. Some of the techniques commonly employed are discussed in section 7.3.1.3.

4.7 SUMMARY

In this chapter we have covered the use of some basic statistical functions in image processing. We looked at computation of statistics for the entire image and saw how brightness and contrast modification could be specified in terms of them. We also saw how local neighbourhood operations could use local statistics to allow them to be adaptive. We have seen a number of algorithms for smoothing images based on local statistics and an adaptive algorithm for improving visibility of detail. We saw some simple applications of probability in image processing and in particular how histograms can be used in thresholding and in contrast and brightness modification.

Finally, we looked at the notion of entropy, in relation to images, and in particular at how it can measure information content.

5

Geometric Functions

In this chapter we will look at a number of ways of modifying images spatially. We will see the effects of re-ordering pixels within the image. We will look at operations to combine images together and to remove specific parts from an image. We will also see how the size and shape of an image can be modified in various ways ranging from simple enlargement to perspective transformations which present the image as if painted onto a three dimensional surface.

5.1 CHANGING THE PIXEL ORDERING

Some simple spatial effects can be achieved by re-ordering the pixels within an image. There are four common re-orderings which, together with their obvious visual attraction, are also sometimes useful for treating data which may not be in the desired sequence.

5.1.1 Mirror

The **mirror** function returns an image in which the pixels have been reversed in order along each row. The order down the image columns is unaltered. The effect is that of viewing the image in a mirror placed next to one of its vertical edges. Figure 5.1(a) shows the effect of applying the mirror function to the train image.

(a)   (b)   (c)

(d)

Figure 5.1. Pixel re-ordering. (a) mirrored image, (b) vertically mirrored image, (c) transposed image, (d) image rotated 90° clockwise

The mirror function is sometimes useful when data is ordered inappropriately. The optics of an image acquisition system may, for example, cause the image to be reversed during capture. Another use for the mirror function, in medical image processing, is for comparison of pairs of organs in a single individual. For example, we might want to compare left and right lungs to look for differences. An image of the left lung can be mirrored, aligned with, and finally subtracted from an image of the right lung to highlight any differences. Similar techniques can be employed when mammograms (breast X-rays) are being examined.

The mirror function can be used for recovering from simple mistakes. I can admit to having used it on more than one occasion after digitising a transparency mounted the wrong way round in front of the camera!

The mirror function can also have useful effects when applied to things other than images. For example, in systems which treat look-up tables as images with a small number of rows (Jackson(1984), Lewis and Ibbotson (1989)) the effect of mirror on a normal grey scale look-up table is to produce its inverse. The negative image look-up table of Figure 3.7(b) is related to the no change table of Figure 3.7(a) by a simple mirror operation.

5.1.2 Vertical Mirror

The **vertical mirror** function returns an image in which the pixels have been reversed in order down each column. The order along the image rows is unaltered. The effect is that of viewing the image in a mirror placed next to one of its horizontal edges. Figure 5.1(b) shows the effect of applying the vertical mirror function to the train image. As with mirror function, the vertical mirror is useful when data is ordered inappropriately. It can also be used to re-order non-image data, such as colour look-up tables.

5.1.3 Transpose

The **transpose** function returns an image in which the rows have been converted to columns and vice versa. The first row of the original image becomes the first column of the new image. If the original image was not square, the new image has an x size equal to the original image's y size and a y size equal to the original image's x size. Figure 5.1(c) shows the effect of applying the transpose function to the train image.

The transpose operation is often useful when dealing with the matrices and vectors involved in some of the geometric operations which we will look at in section 5.5. It is also useful for manipulating the vector representation of separable **convolution** masks, as we will see in chapter 6.

5.1.4 Rotation by Multiples of 90°

Rotation of an image by 90°, 180° or 270° can be achieved simply by re-ordering the pixels in the image array. We will see a more general method of image rotation which can cope with arbitrary angles in section 5.4. In a 90° rotation, the first row of the image becomes the last column, the second row becomes the penultimate column and so on. In a 180° rotation, a mirror image of the first row becomes the last row, a mirror image of the second row becomes the penultimate row and so on. Some image systems provide only these simple rotations. They are much simpler and faster to compute than generalised rotations. Figure 5.1(d) shows the effect of applying a 90° rotation to the train image.

As well as rather obvious uses, such as enabling images to be displayed in a different orientation, perhaps to match sideways printing of a document, this simple form of rotation has a specific use in connection with the orientation of **convolution** masks prior to computation, as we will see in chapter 6.

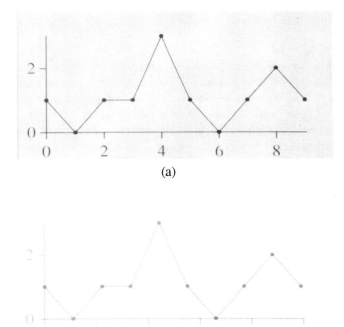

(a)

(b)

Figure   5.2. Re-mapping pixel coordinates.   (a) Part of one row of an image in the original
         coordinates. (b) Part of the same row in the new coordinates.

5.2 CHANGING SIZE

The physical size of an image is determined by the number of pixels it contains and
the size of each pixel.   When we talk about changing the size of an image, we
usually mean altering the number of pixels in each image row and the number of
rows in the image. We can't normally affect the size of an individual pixel. It is a
property of the device on which the image is being displayed. Indeed, one common
reason for altering the size of an image is to make it compatible with some particular
display or printing device. For example, when preparing the figures for this book it
was necessary to alter the sizes of the images so that they would be of the particular
physical size which the page layout demanded.

   Images can, of course, be made bigger or smaller. The degree of size change
does not have to be the same along the rows and down the columns. Indeed it is
quite possible to make an image bigger in one direction and smaller in the other at

the same time. If we are increasing the size of the image we have to create pixels in
the result image which have no counterparts in the original image. We have to estimate the values to use for these new pixels from the pixels nearby. The general
name for this operation is **interpolation**. When we are reducing the size of an image
we need to discard pixels. Some techniques simply ignore the discarded pixels.
Others modify the pixels in the result image to take account of those discarded.
Whatever the technique, the aim is to change the number of pixels in the image
whilst retaining its original appearance, brightness and contrast. Of course, there are
limits to how well this can be achieved and the greater the difference between the
initial and final size the less faithful will be the representation. Also, some techniques are better than others in retaining the information in the original image,
though at the cost of additional complexity and computation.

5.2.1 Coordinate Mapping and Re-sampling.

Techniques for changing the size of an image are based on two operations. First, a
mapping has to be established between the pixel coordinates of the original and result
images. This allows us to relate the position of pixels in the result image to their
position in the original image. Figure 5.2(a) shows a few pixels from one row of an
image which is going to be enlarged by 10%. Figure 5.2(b) shows the same pixel
values but plotted on the coordinates of the enlarged image. Each pixel has moved
along the row to the right by 10%. After the transformation, many of the pixels have
fractional coordinates. This is a problem for our normal image representation which
requires integer image coordinates. To solve this difficulty, we need a second operation, known as **re-sampling**. We met the idea of sampling a photograph or scene in
section 1.1.1.2. Re-sampling an existing image is rather different. The source of the
data is not a continuous function, like the intensity of light reflected from an object,
but is a set of discrete values. We have a function sampled with a particular grid and
now we are changing the grid size. In the example of Figure 5.2, we cannot directly
obtain the brightness of the pixel at the new coordinate 5. We have no sample from
the original image which corresponds to this position in the result. We must interpolate its value from the nearby values which we do know, such as those at coordinates
4.4 and 5.5. It is the particular method of interpolating the new pixel value which
distinguishes the various methods of changing the size of an image from each other.

5.2.2 Nearest Neighbour Interpolation

In nearest neighbour interpolation, the value for any pixel in the result is selected
from the closest available known pixel value. Figure 5.3(a) shows the result of this
technique applied to the data of Figure 5.2. Throughout this figure, the bold line
indicates the values of the pixels from the original image, transformed into the coordinates of the result image and joined by straight line segments. The solid circles,
joined by the narrower lines, represent the actual pixel values for the result image as

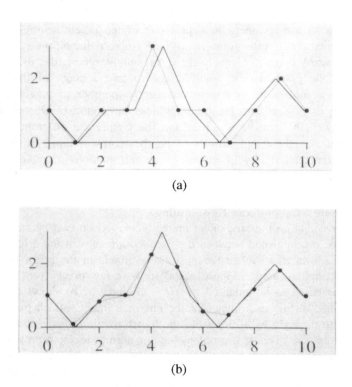

Figure   5.3. Comparison of different interpolations.   (a) Nearest neighbour interpolation, (b)
          linear interpolation.

computed by each interpolation technique.   The closer the symbols are to the line, the
better is the approximation provided by the re-sampling.   Consider the value at coordinate 5.   The nearest known value is that at coordinate 5.5, namely 1.   Consequently, the pixel at coordinate 5 in the result has a value of 1.

   In this example, we have deliberately only considered pixels in a single row and
only considered transformation of their x coordinate.   However, the same technique
extends directly to two dimensions.   In the general case, we alter both the width and
the height of the image simultaneously.   Both x and y pixel coordinates are transformed to new values and we find the nearest neighbour by rounding them to integers.

5.2.3 Pixel Replication and Deletion
Nearest neighbour interpolation is commonly known as **pixel replication**, when the
image is being made larger, and **pixel deletion**, when it is being made smaller.

Figure 5.2(a) shows an example of pixel replication at new coordinates 5 and 6. In both cases, the nearest known pixel is the one at 5.5, so that is the value used. Effectively, we have added a new pixel to the result by duplicating an existing value in the original image.

Similarly, when we are making an image smaller, we need to reduce the number of pixels. In this case, nearest neighbour interpolation will simply ignore some pixels. They will not qualify as being the nearest neighbours of any of the pixels in the result. This is pixel deletion. Effectively, we are producing the result image by deleting selected pixels from the original image.

5.2.4 Linear Interpolation

So far we have looked at techniques which simply select a value from the original image to use in the result. The only question has been which value to select. Linear interpolation uses two values from the original image to construct the value at the desired coordinate. Figure 5.4(a) shows the approach. Suppose we know the values g_1 and g_2 of two pixels at coordinates x_1 and x_2 and we wish to estimate the value g_3 at coordinate x_3. In linear interpolation we assume that the unknown value lies on a straight line between the known values. Simple geometry leads to the result

$$g_3 = \left(\frac{x_3 - x_1}{x_2 - x_1} \right)(g_2 - g_1) + g_1 \tag{5.1}$$

Figure 5.3(b) shows the result of applying linear interpolation to the data of Figure 5.2. As an example, the value at coordinate 5 is about 1.9. It is computed from the values at coordinates 4.4 and 5.5 by applying equation (5.1). Since the bold line in the figure was constructed by joining the known pixel values with straight line segments, it should come as no surprise to see that every point computed by linear interpolation lies on the solid line. However, this does not mean that this interpolation faithfully reproduces the original data. In particular, the peak at coordinate 4.4 has been lost altogether. A peak is present at coordinate 4 but it is broader and lower than that in the original image.

Despite the differences between the original data and approximations based on linear interpolation, these techniques are frequently used in image processing with excellent results. Application to images requires a generalisation to two dimensions, the resulting technique being known as **bi-linear** interpolation. Figure 5.4(b) shows how it works. In this figure, A, B, C and D are the pixels in the vicinity of pixel P, whose value we need to establish. First, we interpolate along the x direction by applying equation (5.1) between points A and B to obtain the value of point Q. Similarly we can use points C and D to obtain the value at R. Finally we apply the equation again, this time in the y direction, between points Q and R to get the value at P.

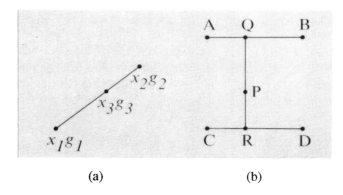

(a)   (b)

Figure   5.4. Linear interpolations.   (a) Linear interpolation, (b) bi-linear interpolation.

All re-sampling techniques distort the pixel values of the original image to some degree. This does not stop them being useful in modifying the size of images, particularly when the reason for the change is to allow the image to be viewed.   In general, techniques based on some kind of computed interpolation produce smoother images than those based on methods such as nearest neighbour selection. They do, however, take longer to compute.   Figure 1.3(b) shows part of the train image enlarged using bi-linear interpolation. The resulting image is smooth and free from pixelation artifacts despite the problems associated with re-sampling and despite the fairly gross assumption that the pixel values change in a linear fashion along the rows and down the columns of the image.

5.2.5 Curvilinear Interpolation
In order to use linear interpolation we have made a significant assumption about the way that the brightness of the original, continuous image varied between the points at which we sampled it.   We have assumed linear variation and have been able to derive equation (5.1) on that basis. Though the assumption is fairly crude, the technique works reasonably well, particularly if we have a large number of small pixels. Effectively, we have assumed a linear variation between pixels and, using the known pixel values, we have established the equation of the line joining the brightness values of a particular pair. Knowledge of this equation allows us to compute the value a pixel should have at any intervening point. More sophisticated approximations are possible, however and often give smoother results.   In **curvilinear interpolation** the brightness is assumed to vary between pixels along some particular kind of curve, for example

$$v = V_0 + V_1 x + V_2 x^2 \tag{5.2}$$

where we are considering just the x coordinate of the pixel and v is its brightness. From the known pixel values in the region of the image around the point at which we want to interpolate, we establish the particular equation by determining the values of the coefficients V_n. Then from equation (5.2) we can calculate the value of the particular pixel we are interested in. The whole process needs to be repeated for each pixel in the result.

The procedure for finding the coefficients in equation (5.2) is known as **curve fitting**. This operation is commonly used when trying to find the best line to plot through a set of data resulting from a scientific experiment. The **least squares** technique is often used to perform this kind of fit. In our example, it would find the values of V_n which minimised the square of the distance between the actual pixel values and the curve. This is considered to be the best fit curve. A detailed understanding of the technique is not required here. However, it is described in standard works on statistics (for example Bevington (1969).)

Curvilinear interpolation requires more known pixel values than does linear interpolation. We need to have at least the same number of known values as there are coefficients in the particular curve chosen. Polynomials, like equation (5.2) are often used. Of course, equation (5.2) deals with only one dimension. Approaches similar to the one already described for linear interpolation can be employed to extend the technique to two dimensions. Because of the greater complexity involved in curvilinear interpolation, it will take considerably longer to compute the resulting pixel value than does the bi-linear technique.

Curvilinear interpolations can be used advantageously when the image to be re-sized is noisy. The greater smoothing implied by the technique is advantageous. An alternative approach is to smooth the image by some other means first and then to use bi-linear interpolation to perform the size change.

5.2.6 Heterogeneous Size Change

It has already been mentioned that it is feasible to change the size of an image along its rows by a different amount from that used down its columns. This kind of size change will, of course, also change the shape of the image. One particularly important use for this kind of size change is when an image capture or display device has rectangular rather than square pixels. We mentioned this problem in section 1.3.1 in connection with image acquisition systems. Basically, it is a problem of image representation. It is normal for image algorithms to assume that the pixels of the images they process are square. This avoids the need to carry explicit size information with the image and simplifies and speeds up the algorithms which then do not need to cope with non-square pixels. The disadvantage is that, before being processed, an image captured from a device with non-square pixels must first be converted so that its pixels are square.

Suppose we have captured an image from a television camera and the resulting image has pixels which are 1.33 times as wide as they are high, reflecting the 4:3

overall aspect ratio used. To convert this image so that it has square pixels, we need to increase the number of rows in the image by 1.33. We could use any of the techniques for changing image size, though in this case linear interpolation would be the most appropriate of those we have discussed. Actually, when dealing with source data like this it is worth using the most sophisticated technique available consistent with the inherent quality of the image data. Any distortions introduced at this stage will be present throughout the subsequent processing of the image.

5.3   CUT AND PASTE OPERATIONS

It is often desirable to be able to remove part of an image and to deal with separately. Also it can be very useful to combine two or more images together spatially. These operations are commonly known as **cut** and **paste** respectively. Cut operations extract an area of a given image according to some geometric specification. The result is known as a **subimage**. Paste operations combine two or more images or subimages to create a new image. Cut operations can be used to remove a region of particular interest from a larger image. The reduction in size can be useful in reducing processing times form any operations to be applied to the image. Paste operations are usually most useful for presenting images. For example, many of the figures in this book were created by pasting together sets of individual images in appropriate combinations.

5.3.1   Rectangular Cut Operations

In the simplest case, the area to be extracted from an image is itself rectangular. This means that the resulting subimage can be represented as another image. The only question which remains to be answered is how to specify the area to be extracted. Clearly we can use a pair of coordinates to define this area. Jackson(1984) suggested a useful notation based on pixel coordinates and employing a syntax suitable for use in language driven interactive image processing systems. At least two implementations of this image processing language currently exist, namely IBM IAX Image Processing (Jackson(1984)) and the IMPART Image Processing System (Lewis and Ibbotson (1989)), both of which were developed at IBM's Scientific Centre in Winchester, England.

The notation for subimages is based on coordinate ranges. Two ranges are specified, the first for the x coordinate and the second for the y coordinate. For example

$$I_{i:j,k:l} \quad i \geq j,\ k \geq l$$

is the subimage of I whose top left corner is the pixel I_{ik} and whose bottom right corner is I_{jl}. The usefulness of the notation is in its shorthand forms. For example, *

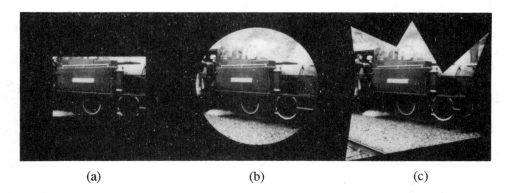

(a)   (b)   (c)

Figure 5.5. Extracting subimages.   (a) Rectangular subimage, (b) circular subimage, (c)
irregular subimage

is used to indicate a complete row or column or the remainder of a row or column.
So, the expression

$$I_{*,k:l}$$

specifies the rows of I starting with k and ending with l and

$$I_{j:*,k:l}$$

specifies the same rows but starting from an x coordinate of j. It is possible to form
cut and copy operations using this notation. For example

$$R_{j:*,k:*} = I_{n:m,o:p}$$

copies the specified subimage from I into R with its top left corner positioned at R_{jk}.
Figure 5.5(a) shows a rectangular subimage extracted from the central area of the
train image.

5.3.2 Concatenation Operations
One form of paste operation is known as **concatenation**. Concatenation is the
placing side by side of two images to form a new, larger image. Two forms of
concatenation are possible. Horizontal concatenation allows one image to be placed
to the right or left of the other. Vertical concatenation allows one image to be placed
above or below the other.

When the images are of the same size in the dimension along which they are being joined, the concatenation is straightforward. However, if they are of unequal size, a decision has to be made about how to align them and how to pad the smaller image. The most useful way to do this is to align the top edges , in horizontal concatenation, and the left edges, in vertical concatenation, and to pad the smaller image using the size conversion rules already described in section 3.1.3.

As already mentioned, many of the figures in this book were produced by suitable horizontal and vertical concatenation of the component images.

5.3.3 Generalised Cut and Paste Operations

Cut and paste operations involving rectangular areas are sufficient to meet most, common image processing requirements. However, occasionally it may be necessary to perform these operations using non-rectangular areas. The problem of describing non-rectangular areas of an image is not restricted simply to cut and paste operations. It can be encountered in a variety of applications. Non-rectangular areas demand additional information to describe the size and shape of their boundary. The nature of the information required to describe the boundary depends on its shape. If the shape can be defined geometrically, the boundary definition can be stored in **parametric** form. This means that only the values (parameters) required to regenerate the shape need be recorded. For example, a circular boundary can be described by three parameters, namely the x and y coordinates of its centre and its radius. The circular subimage consists of the full image together with these three parameters. Cut and paste operations involving this subimage use only those pixels within the boundary. Figure 5.5(b) shows a circular subimage extracted from the train image.

Although we have not considered it quite this way before, standard rectangular images actually have their boundary stored in parametric form. The x size and y size of an image define its boundary when used with the assumption that the image origin is in the top left hand corner.

Sometimes, the boundary cannot be described by a simple geometric figure. It may, for example, have been drawn by hand. In this case the coordinates of every pixel on the boundary must be recorded. The definition of the subimage consists of the full image together with the list of all boundary coordinates. The list contains substantially more data than the parametric definition, of course, and the larger the subimage the more data is required to describe it because the larger is the number of pixels in its boundary.

There is one further way to represent a non-rectangular subimage. This technique tends to be used in image synthesis systems and paint programs used for creating video artwork. First, the rectangle which completely encloses the desired subimage is determined. This is simply a matter of finding the maximum and minimum x and y coordinates of the pixels in the boundary. This rectangular area is copied from the original image to form a new image. Then, all pixels outside the desired area are given a special value which marks them as not being part of the area. Figure 5.5(c) shows an irregular subimage defined this way and extracted from the train image. The disadvantage of this technique is that one pixel value must be reserved to act as the marker. Image synthesis systems usually allow the pixels outside the desired area to be treated as opaque and of a particular colour. In this case the cut and paste operations are similar to the rectangular ones we have already looked at. Alternatively, the pixels outside the area can be treated as transparent, allowing the background to show through and so providing the non-rectangular versions of the operations.

Whereas most image processing systems store rectangular images defined by their x size and y size, there is little commonality about non-rectangular images and indeed many systems do not allow them at all.

5.4 PLANE ROTATION

We saw in section 5.2 that changing the size of an image required re-mapping of the pixel coordinates followed by a re-sampling operation. Plane rotation is similar but the coordinate re-mapping is a rotation rather than a change of size. The rotation takes place in the plane of the image about some arbitrarily defined point.

This kind of rotation can be used to correct deficiencies in the alignment of an image during digitisation of photographs or negatives. It can be difficult to ensure precise orientation when digitising photographic material. Small differences in orientation may be very significant if the objective is, for example, to compare pairs or sets of images with one another. Also, computations involving sets of images may be adversely affected by small mis-alignments. Often a simple rotation can be used to correct the problem. Determining precisely what the rotation needs to be is usually the difficult part. However, when images which have to be aligned precisely are captured it is usual to arrange for some obvious alignment markers with known geometry to be present in the field of view. These are commonly called **fiducial marks**. Knowledge of the true position of these marks allows the correcting rotation to be applied.

As with the size change operation, the rotation is calculated in two steps. First, we compute the new position of the pixels of the original image. In general these will not be at integer coordinates in the rotated image. Some form of interpolation is required to obtain pixel values at integer coordinates in the new image. Once again, nearest neighbour and bi-linear interpolation are often used.

The mapping of coordinates from the original image to the new image uses the standard formulae for rotation of axes.

$$D_x = d_x \cos \theta + d_y \sin \theta$$
$$D_y = d_y \cos \theta - d_x \sin \theta$$

$$(5.3)$$

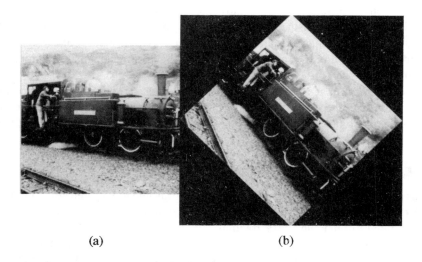

(a)   (b)

Figure   5.6. Plane rotation.   (a) Original image, (b) image rotated 45°

Here, d_x and d_y are the distances of the pixel from the centre of the rotation before
the rotation takes place. They can be computed from the pixel's coordinates and the
coordinates of the centre of rotation. D_x and D_y are the distances after the rotation.
Again, they can be converted to the new pixel's coordinates using the coordinates of
the centre of rotation. θ is the angle of rotation. It is positive for an anticlockwise
rotation.

One interesting consequence of a plane rotation is that the result image is larger
than the original unless the rotation is an exact multiple of 90°. As an example,
Figure 5.6 shows shows the train image rotated by 45°. The train image is 512
pixels square. The rotated image is some 1.4 times bigger in each direction, at 724
pixels square.

5.5 CHANGING SHAPE

In this section we will look at various ways of changing the shape of an image. One
reason for wishing to change the shape of an image is to illustrate how it would look
if painted or draped over some arbitrary, three dimensional surface. One application
is in the provision of eye catching artwork, particularly for advertising material.
Many home computers are now capable of running so-called 'paint' programs
capable of generating this kind of synthetic image. However, less ephemeral uses for

these operations also exist, particularly when the image represents some physical property of the surface onto which it is painted. One particular application, where the image represents the results of processing satellite images of the earth and the surface is taken from ground survey data is discussed in section 5.5.2.

We have already seen that image rotation can be used to correct for mis-alignment between pairs or sets of images. Some types of variation in viewing or digitisation condition cannot be corrected by rotation alone, however. A more general modification of the image data is required. This kind of operation is needed in a variety of image applications including remote sensing. It is discussed in section 5.5.3.

5.5.1 Perspective Transformations

To form a perspective view of an image we need to undertake three operations. First, we must compute the 3D coordinates of each pixel in the image. These coordinates are defined by the position and shape of the object on which we are draping the image. Next we must transform the 3D coordinates into a set of 2D coordinates representing the way in which the 3D coordinates would appear from a particular viewpoint. Together, these two transformations determine where any given pixel from the original image appears in the result image. As with the plane rotation and size change operations, an interpolation is also required because, in general, the transformation will lead to fractional pixel coordinates. Again, nearest neighbour or bi-linear interpolation is commonly used to establish the pixel value in the result image.

We will use a simple example to illustrate the steps. Figure 5.7(a) shows the arrangement. Point E represents the eye viewing a plane, P, positioned obliquely to the viewing direction. P is not parallel with the x axis but instead is at an angle ϕ to it. The z axis defines the viewing direction and the eye is at the origin of the coordinate system being used. Line AE is a ray from point $A(x_a, y_a, z_a)$ in the plane P to the eye. It intersects the display plane B at point $C(x_c, y_c, z_c)$. The display plane B is the plane $z = z_b$. For the eye to see point A in proper perspective, its image must appear at point C on the display. The perspective transformation we are looking for is the one which relates the coordinates of A and C. From the diagram, it is easy to see the relationship between the y coordinates. A similar relationship holds for the x coordinate. The relations are

$$
\begin{aligned}
y_c &= y_a \, (z_b \, / \, z_a) \\
x_c &= x_a \, (z_b \, / \, z_a)
\end{aligned}
\tag{5.4}
$$

Equation (5.4) allows us to map known 3D coordinates onto our display. Actually, a small modification is required to get directly to image coordinates as in our images the y axis increases downwards. As yet we have not tackled the problem of

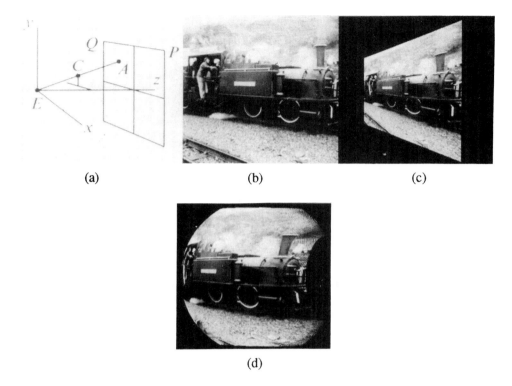

(a)   (b)   (c)

(d)

Figure 5.7. Perspective transformation. (a) Diagram showing perspective geometry, (b) original image, (c) perspective view, (d) mapping onto sphere

describing plane P. Strictly speaking, P is not really a plane, which is an infinite object. It is actually a bounded region of size x_s by y_s lying in a plane which cuts the z axis at $z = z_p$ and rotated by an angle ϕ about the y axis. The z axis passes through the centre of the region. We need to specify the coordinates of the region's corners and indeed of every pixel of the image which we want to map onto it. If P lay in the plane $z = 0$, rather than where it actually is, it would be a simple matter to define the corners of the region. To convert these coordinates to those of the corners of P where it is actually positioned, we need to rotate the region about the y axis by angle ϕ and then move its centre to $z = z_p$.

Operations like moving coordinates along an axis, usually known as **translation**, rotating them about an axis and scaling dimensions along an axis, are very common in 3D computer graphics. The operations are usually represented as matrices. A coordinate is written as a column vector containing four elements. The top three are the x, y and z values and the bottom element is always 1. The appropriate transfor-

Translation by t_x,t_y,t_z	Scaling by s_x,s_y,s_z	Coordinate as a column vector
1 0 0 t_x 0 1 0 t_y 0 0 1 t_z 0 0 0 1	s_x 0 0 0 0 s_y 0 0 0 0 s_z 0 0 0 0 1	x y z 1

Rotate about x axis by θ	Rotate about y axis by ϕ	Rotate about z axis by ψ
1 0 0 0 0 $\cos\theta$ $\sin\theta$ 0 0 $-\sin\theta$ $\cos\theta$ 0 0 0 0 1	$\cos\phi$ 0 $-\sin\phi$ 0 0 1 0 0 $\sin\phi$ 0 $\cos\phi$ 0 0 0 0 1	$\cos\psi$ $\sin\psi$ 0 0 $-\sin\psi$ $\cos\psi$ 0 0 0 0 1 0 0 0 0 1

Figure   5.8. 3D Transformation matrices.   The matrices governing the standard 3 dimensional
coordinate transformations.

mation matrix is used to premultiply the coordinate vector and the resulting vector is
the transformed coordinate.   Figure 5.8 shows the matrices used for translation,
scaling and rotation of coordinates. The individual matrices can be combined to form
a single matrix actually applied to the coordinate.   In our example, we can premultiply the translation matrix by the rotation matrix to get the combined transformation
matrix. It is important to get the order of the matrices right when forming the combination. Swapping the order of the matrices is equivalent to performing the translation first followed by the rotation. This does not give the same result since the
rotation is about the y axis, not about a line in the plane itself.

In summary, the steps needed to generate our perspective view of the image are
as follows. First we define the plane on which we want the image to lie in a convenient position and orientation. Then we compute the transformation matrix which will
position the plane so that we will get the desired view. We use the transformation
matrix to convert the coordinate of each pixel of the image to its true 3D coordinate
and then we map the 3D coordinate to the 2D viewing position using equation (5.4).

Finally we interpolate to find the appropriate pixel value. Figure 5.7(c) shows the train image mapped onto a plane oriented in a manner similar to the diagram of Figure 5.7(a). The plane is rotated by $-25°$ about the y axis. Nearest neighbour interpolation was used.

So far, we have only considered mapping an image onto a planar object. Indeed we have assumed implicitly that the image does not even need to be scaled when being mapped onto the plane. In the more general case where the underlying object is non-planar, some additional mapping must be devised to specify where on the surface a particular pixel will be positioned before the perspective transformation is applied. This mapping is dependent on the nature of the surface and on the desired effect. For example, imagine mapping an image onto a upright cone. The bottom edge of the image must map to the circumference of the base of the cone. However, the entire top edge of the image maps to the single point at the cone's apex. We can of course set up a mapping for this situation in terms of the relevant geometric transformations.

Figure 5.7(d) shows the train image mapped onto a hemisphere. This image was created as follows. First, the hemisphere was placed with its base in the plane $z = 0$ and with its convex side towards the negative z axis. The image was positioned on the hemisphere simply by giving each pixel a z coordinate based on its x and y coordinates and using the equation of a sphere, namely

$$r^2 = x^2 + y^2 + z^2 \tag{5.5}$$

where r is the radius. The hemisphere was then rotated and translated rather like the plane in Figure 5.7(c) and the image was re-sampled using the overall coordinate transformation.

In practical image synthesis systems, things are a good deal more complex than in the two examples just given. In particular, in our examples, the coordinate system is fixed with the eye as the origin. This can be very inconvenient and so most computer graphics and image synthesis systems introduce another set of coordinates for defining the viewing position. Converting coordinates between these systems is done using the transformation matrices we have already seen. This additional set of coordinates allows the viewing position to be altered independently of the orientation of the objects being viewed. A detailed discussion of the techniques employed in 3D computer graphics would be inappropriate here. There are a number of introductory texts available on the subject, for example Angell (1988), which has a very clear description of the geometry used in 3D computer graphics and discusses the additional complexities. However complex the particular transformation used, the overall method remains the same. First we compute the transformation which re-maps the coordinates and then we re-sample the image based on that transformation.

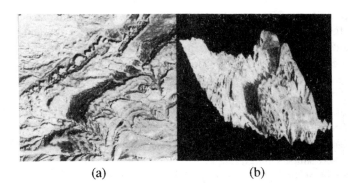

(a)   (b)

Figure   5.9. Visualisation using a digital terrain model.   (a) Original Landsat image, (b)
          image painted on digital terrain model

5.5.2 Painting a Digital Terrain Model

As high-performance workstations become more affordable, and as the technology of
high resolution, full colour displays improves, the means by which information is
presented to users is becoming increasingly sophisticated. A subject known as **scientific visualisation** has emerged in recent years. It aims to exploit technology to
allow people more easily to assimilate the results of experimentation and observations. Frequently, it involves the display of three dimensional surfaces painted or
textured in accordance with their underlying properties. Some visualisations depict
matter which cannot be observed directly, such as individual molecules or sub atomic
particles. Others show more accessible objects, perhaps rendered in new ways.

An example of a fairly common visualisation used in remote sensing is the combination of data recovered from satellite images with a **digital terrain model**. This
kind of model is derived from surveys of the earth's surface. Extensive databases of
this type of data exist for much of the land surface of the earth. If the data from
satellite images is first transformed into a terrestrial coordinate system it can then be
painted onto a surface derived from the digital terrain model. Views of such a model
can depict both the ground properties detected by the satellite and the geography of
the area in question.   This kind of visualisation is often aimed at helping the
geological interpretation of the area in question.

Figure 5.9 illustrates a satellite image and the result of transforming it to lie over
a digital terrain model. The original image is from one of the NASA Landsat earth
observation satellites and shows a region of the state of Wyoming in the USA.

5.5.3 Generalised Image Warping

We have now seen three specific ways of modifying an image all based on the same underlying operations. The modifications are size change, plane rotation and perspective transformation. The underlying operations are the re-mapping of the pixel coordinates and the re-sampling of the image. Indeed, the only factor which distinguishes the three kinds of image modification is the particular re-mapping employed. So far we have looked at mappings which are specified geometrically and which have precise definitions independent of the image data. However, there are situations in which more complex mappings need to be employed and where those mappings may not be precisely known and may have to be inferred from the image data itself. This more general geometric manipulation is known as **image warping** and often combines size and shape change.

One of the most complex situations in image acquisition is that of a satellite sensor viewing the earth. We will use this as an example of the application of image warping. Rarely is the desired terrestrial area directly under the track of the satellite, so the sensor is usually pointing to the right or left and a perspective transformation is involved. Also, it is normal to correct satellite images to produce plane views which correspond to one of the standard cartographic coordinate systems, used in map making. The curvature of the earth is, in effect, a distortion which must be removed. The goal is to allow images collected at different times from different satellite positions to be compared directly. Again, a transformation is involved. If the position of the satellite and the shape of the earth were known with sufficient precision and if the distortions inherent in the sensors being used were also known, it would be possible to correct the images directly. A transformation, like this, derived from knowledge of the properties of the objects being viewed and of the image acquisition system is known as a **scene/sensor model**. Unfortunately, as well as being extremely difficult to obtain, it is often the case that this model is only an approximation. For example, all satellites wobble in their orbits. The wobble introduces a degree of uncertainty about the satellite's position and orientation and makes the scene/sensor model imprecise. In the absence of precise independent definitions of the transformation required to correct the images, the only alternative is to try to use the image data itself to help.

In order to use the image to define a transformation, we need to locate in it points whose real positions are known. These points are termed **control points**. In our example of the satellite, the control points would probably be easily recognisable geographic features such as mountains or rivers which have been surveyed on earth and for which accurate positional data is available. If we have the real 3D locations of these points and also their positions in the image, we can construct a mapping which can then be used to transform the coordinate of any pixel of the image into the desired cartographic coordinate.

The transformation consists of two equations. One relates the x and y coordinates of a pixel in the image to its cartographic x coordinate whilst the other relates the image coordinates to the pixel's cartographic y coordinate. Commonly, polynomials are chosen to represent the transformation. For example, the following pair of degree 2 may be sufficient.

$$x = C_0 + C_1 i + C_2 j + C_3 ij + C_4 i^2 + C_5 j^2$$
$$y = D_0 + D_1 i + D_2 j + D_3 ij + D_4 i^2 + D_5 j^2 \qquad (5.6)$$

Here, x and y are the cartographic coordinates and i and j are the pixel coordinates from the image. The coefficients C_n and D_n are the unknown quantities. We take each equation independently and find values for its coefficients using the control points. The method is exactly the same as for fitting a polynomial curve through a set of experimental data and we can use the method of least squares so long as we have at least as many control points as there are coefficients to find. It is not necessary to understand how the least squares method is used to appreciate the overall approach. However, readers interested in the technique will find information on its use for some types of line and curve fitting in Bevington (1969). Its application to derivation of polynomials for transforming pixel coordinates is described in Niblack (1986), where the matrix equations are also given.

Up to this point, we have assumed that finding the control points is simple. If we are taking control points from a map, there is little choice other than to use an operator to identify the appropriate geographical features in the image. However, if we are trying to warp one image to match another and the images are not too different there are automatic ways in which the control points defined in one image may be located in the other image. The technique involved is called **correlation** and it is covered in section 6.3.

Whether we use a scene/sensor model or control points to establish the coordinate transformation, we still need to re-sample the input image. Again, the nearest neighbour and bi-linear interpolation techniques can be used to establish the values of the pixels in the result image.

5.6 OTHER SPATIAL OPERATIONS

We close this chapter with a look at some simple but nevertheless useful spatial operations which do not fit into any of the categories already covered.

5.6.1 Shifting an Image
The shift operation changes the positions of pixels in the image array without losing any data. For example, shifting the image by 10 pixels in the x direction takes the first 10 pixels of each row and makes them the last 10 pixels, preserving their order. Shifting in the y direction takes rows from the top of the image and moves them to

(a)   (b)   (c)

Figure   5.10. Other spatial operations.   (a) Train image after shifting, (b) image showing
position of cross-section, (c) image cross-section

the bottom. Shifting effectively changes the pixel origin of the image. Figure 5.10(a)
shows the train image after being shifted in both x and y directions.

As we will see, in section 7.1.1.2, the shift operation is useful in converting
between the two common forms of Fourier spectrum.

5.6.2 Image-Cross Section

An image cross-section is a graph of the brightness of the image along any arbitrary
line drawn on the image. It can be useful when examining closely the values in the
image in some particular region. It shows how the brightness or colour varies as we
traverse the image along the chosen line and can often show up details difficult to
see from the image data itself. For example, an underlying brightness trend from one
side of the image to the other may be visible in the cross-section though it is not
apparent from viewing the image itself. Such a trend may have been caused by
uneven illumination when the image was digitised. Figure 5.10(b) shows the train
image marked with a line indicating where a cross-section will be taken.
Figure 5.10(c) shows the cross-section itself. In this case it shows the brightness of
each pixel plotted against its position in the marked line. There are 255 pixels in the
cross-section.

5.7 SUMMARY

In this chapter we have looked at a number of ways in which image data can be
manipulated spatially. We have seen how cut and paste operations can be carried
out, how the size and shape of an image can been modified and how images can be
rotated. We have also seen how images can be made to appear painted on various

3D surfaces and how more general geometric corrections can be applied. Many of these techniques are based on the fundamental steps of computing a coordinate transformation and then re-sampling the image.

6

Convolution and Correlation

Convolution and correlation are closely related operations in image processing. Though the functions serve entirely different applications, as we shall see, the computations involved are very similar. Both are neighbourhood operations. However, convolution is used for filtering images, to reduce noise or to enhance the visibility of certain features, whereas correlation is used to measure how similar two images are. Indeed, correlation is often used to position one image relative to another at a position of maximum similarity.

Convolutions and correlations can be computed directly on images. Alternatively, they can be computed after the image has been transformed into a different domain. We will concentrate on the direct or **spatial domain** computations in this chapter and look at implementations in the **Fourier domain** in section 7.1.2. As well as looking at the computation, we will look at the importance of these techniques and see applications of them. Some of the linear systems theory underlying the functions is also presented, but it is not necessary to understand it to appreciate the results of the techniques.

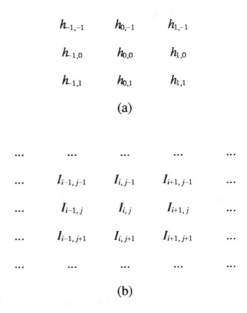

Figure 6.1. Spatial convolution. (a) A 3 x 3 convolution mask, (b) a 3 x 3 neighbourhood
within an image

6.1 COMPUTING SPATIAL CONVOLUTIONS

Spatial convolution is a neighbourhood operation. We first saw neighbourhood operations in section 4.2.1 when we looked at the local average function. In a neighbourhood operation we compute a result at each output pixel using the corresponding
input pixel and its neighbouring pixels. For a convolution, the calculation is a sum
of products. Figure 6.1 shows a three pixel square **convolution mask** and a neighbourhood from an image. The individual elements in the mask are called **weights**.
The data in the mask determines the effect of the convolution by defining the filter to
be applied. The values are derived from the **point spread function** of the particular
filter. This function is a definition of the filter. We shall see examples of particular
point spread functions, masks and their effects in section 6.2. For the moment we
will concentrate simply on the calculation itself.

The index used in the mask has its origin at its central pixel. The image is
indexed from its top left corner in the usual way. Using the terminology of
Figure 6.1, we can write the equation describing the computation as follows:

$$R_{i,j} = \sum_{k=i-1}^{i+1} \sum_{l=j-1}^{j+1} I_{k,l}\, h_{i-k,\, j-l} \tag{6.1}$$

Each pixel is taken in turn from the neighbourhood of the image and multiplied by one of the elements of the mask. The sum of these individual products constitutes the result pixel. Each pixel participates in exactly one multiplication, as does each mask element.

We will see why this particular computation is useful shortly. Before we do, however, there is one pattern in the computation which is worth exploring. It is not particularly apparent from equation (6.1) but can be seen if we expand the summations explicitly.

$$
\begin{aligned}
R_{i,j} = \;& I_{i-1,\,j-1}h_{1,1} &+&\; I_{i,\,j-1}h_{0,1} &+&\; I_{i+1,\,j-1}h_{-1,1} \\
& I_{i-1,\,j}h_{1,0} &+&\; I_{i,\,j}h_{0,0} &+&\; I_{i+1,\,j}h_{-1,0} \\
& I_{i-1,\,j+1}h_{1,-1} &+&\; I_{i,\,j+1}h_{0,-1} &+&\; I_{i+1,\,j+1}h_{-1,-1}
\end{aligned}
\tag{6.2}
$$

Equation (6.2) is arranged so that the individual terms contain the pixels in the neighbourhood in the sequence from top left to bottom right. The corresponding mask elements in each term are sequenced in precisely the opposite direction, starting at the bottom right and moving to the top left. An interesting consequence of this is that if the mask is rotated by 180° the sequence of terms in image and mask is exactly the same. It is as if the rotated mask is being placed over the image and the multiplications are being performed between a mask element and the image pixel which lies under it. Some implementations may take this approach to the computation as it can simplify the indexing into the image and mask. Indeed, some implementations automatically rearrange the mask elements so that users can specify masks as if the ordering in the image and mask are the same. Many convolution masks are symmetric. Consequently there is no change when the mask is reordered. However, for asymmetric masks it is important to know how the image system in use interprets the data and what rearrangement, if any, is carried out.

The example of Figure 6.1 shows a three pixel square mask. Masks do not have to be square, but often are. They are normally an odd number of pixels in width and height so that the origin of the mask is in its geometric centre. As with other neighbourhood operations, it is not possible to compute values for the convolution near the edges of the image. The calculation requires pixel values which are outside the boundaries of the input image. As a consequence, it is normal to set a strip of pixels around the edge of the image to zero. The width of the strip along the top and bottom of the image is $floor(y_m/2)$ and along the sides it is $floor(x_m/2)$. Here, x_m is the width of the mask and y_m is its height. The three pixel square mask of the example will leave a one pixel wide strip, which cannot be computed, around the entire image. It can be important to know what a particular image processing system does in these circumstances. It may be that the result image is smaller than the input image by the number of rows and columns which cannot be computed. Alternatively, the image may remain the same size and merely have zero placed in the strips around the edge. This second course of action is quite popular as it means that the result can be directly compared with the original and can participate in further computations whilst retaining its alignment. However, the zeros in the edge strips will affect the result image's statistics to some degree and may have adverse effects on other image processing functions.

Some systems may offer ways to complete the computation right up to the edge of the input image by using data from elsewhere as if it were the additional rows and columns of pixels outside the boundary of the input image. One such technique uses rows from the bottom of the image to supply the required data at the top and vice versa. Similarly, the extra columns on the left are copied from those on the right and vice versa. There is no physical justification for techniques like this, for the most part. They merely offer ways to invent data that is not actually present in the input image. They do, however, allow the result to be of the same size as the input image whilst avoiding the potential difficulty posed by the strip of zero pixels.

Sometimes it is useful to **normalise** the result of the convolution computation. Since it is a sum of products calculation it is quite possible for the result to be too large to store in the same type of data as the original image. This is particularly true of 8-bit unsigned integer images. If the weights of the mask do not add up to -1, 0 or 1, it is usual to normalise the result by dividing it by the sum of the mask weights. This guarantees that the result will fit into the data type of the input image. Naturally, during the computation for an individual pixel, larger data types are used to maintain precision. Conversion to the output data type is made as the pixel is written to the result. The ability to maintain the same data type, and therefore range, as the original image is useful when further calculation involving the images is involved. It is also useful when the original image is an 8-bit unsigned integer as it means that the result of the convolution can be directly displayed along with the original.

6.1.1 The Computational Load

Convolution is quite an expensive operation in terms of the amount of computation involved. In the example of the previous section, it needs nine multiplications, nine additions and a single division to compute a normalised convolution for each pixel of the input image. Considering square convolution masks, the number of additions and multiplications is equal and goes up as the square of the size of the mask. Figure 6.2 shows the number of operations involved for a number of different mask sizes and an input image which is 512 pixels square. The first column shows the

Mask Size	Mask Elements	Adds and Multiplies	Divisions	Total
3	9	2 359 296	262 144	4 980 736
5	25	6 553 600	262 144	13 369 344
7	49	12 845 056	262 144	25 952 256
9	81	21 233 664	262 144	42 729 472
11	121	31 719 424	262 144	63 700 992
15	225	58 982 400	262 144	118 226 944
25	625	163 840 000	262 144	327 942 144

Figure   6.2. Computational load.   Computational load for various square convolution masks. Number of operations calculated for an image which is 512 pixels square, having 262 144 pixels in all.

size of the convolution mask. The second gives the number of weights in the mask. The third column shows the number of multiplications required. An equal number of additions is also needed. The fourth column gives the number of divisions required if the convolution result needs to be normalised. The final column shows the sum total of all the numeric operations needed to perform the convolution. The values in the table assume computation right to the edge of the image. These masks are relatively modest in size when compared with the 512 pixel square image, yet the number of computations rapidly becomes enormous. It must be noted that the table shows only the number of computations. It does not take into account other operations which must be performed. These include extracting the correct pixels from image and mask, writing the result pixel to the output image and maintaining the various indexes and counts which control the whole operation. The overall number of instructions executed is typically several times larger than the count in the totals column of Figure 6.2.

Whilst there are special case algorithms, which can exploit properties such as symmetry in the convolution mask to speed up the computation, it is clear from Figure 6.2 that unless a very powerful machine is available or special hardware assistance is provided, spatial convolution rapidly becomes prohibitive in terms of computational cost. Convolution filtering is almost invariably carried out with small masks because of this. This is not always desirable. For larger masks there is considerable benefit to be gained by performing the convolution not in the spatial domain of the image but in the **Fourier domain**. The Fourier transform is discussed in chapter 7. The benefit of computing the convolution in the Fourier domain arises because although there is an additional burden of computing the necessary transformations of the image, the computation of the convolution itself is much simpler. The particular mask size above which the Fourier domain implementation is worthwhile depends to a large extent on the particular machine in use. It also depends on the data type of the original image. As we shall see in chapter 7, the Fourier transform requires floating point calculations whereas many spatial convolutions can be performed as integer calculations. The relative performance of the integer and floating point calculations on the available machine becomes an important factor. On machines with fast floating point hardware, it may be worth performing the calculation in the Fourier domain with masks as small as 9 elements square. We will look at this alternative approach to convolution in section 7.1.2.2.

6.1.2 The Practical Importance of Spatial Convolution

Convolution is a technique for filtering images. Individual filters are defined by the convolution masks used. However, the fundamental algorithm remains the same regardless of the particular filter. Consequently, there is much benefit to be gained by providing highly optimised algorithms and specialised hardware to support convolution. An investment in speeding up this one computation pays dividends in the performance of a wide range of filters.

Many image processing systems have special purpose hardware for implementing spatial convolutions. There are two sources of improved performance when comparing special hardware with general purpose machines. First, the multiplication and addition operations can be overlapped. After the initial multiplication, the accumulation of the product into the sum can take place in parallel with the next multiplication. Integrated circuit solutions to this overlapped computation are widely available. Second, it has already been mentioned that the maintenance of various counts and indexes which allow the retrieval and storage of the correct elements of the images and mask can require more instructions than the computation itself. Convolution hardware usually maintains all this associated control information automatically whilst the computation is taking place.

Special purpose hardware allows a relatively restricted set of spatial convolutions to take place at high speed. Limitations are usually in the range of data types supported and in the maximum size of mask allowed. Despite the restrictions, this approach allows the most commonly required convolutions to be carried out rapidly. A more cynical observation might be that these common convolutions are the ones most frequently used because they are the only ones which can be computed quickly. Convolution hardware can speed up the computation to the point where a 3 by 3 mask can be applied to a 512 by 512 pixel image in a small fraction of a second.

6.1.3 The Theory behind Convolution

In this section we will look briefly at the theory which underpins the notion of spatial convolution for filtering. Though the theory may be of interest, it is not necessary to understand it to appreciate the practical results of this kind of filtering. This section can be safely omitted if desired.

Convolution is a result of **linear system theory**. For our purposes, a system is some object or process which transforms an image in some way. For example, the lens on a camera constitutes an optical system. We can write this as

$$R = \Psi[I] \tag{6.3}$$

R is the resulting image, I is the input image and Ψ is the effect of the system. The system is said to be **linear** if a linear combination of input images produces the same combination of outputs as its result. We can write this as

$$\Psi[aI + bJ] = a\Psi[I] + b\Psi[J] \tag{6.4}$$

In this case there are two input images I and J. The values a and b are arbitrary constants. Equation (6.4) basically says that the effect of applying two separate images to the system together is the sum of applying them individually. Essentially, the images do not interfere with one another as they pass through the system. This is a very convenient situation and it turns out that the equation holds for a large number of imaging systems. The result is often known as **linear superposition**.

One particularly interesting property of a linear system is its **point spread function**. This is the image which results from an ideal point source being applied to the system. In the case of a lens, the resulting image will probably be a somewhat blurred version of the point source, the degree of blur depending on the quality of the lens and on how accurately it is focused. We can express the point spread function as

$$h(i - k, j - l) = \Psi[\delta(i - k, j - l)] \tag{6.5}$$

In this equation, δ denotes the two dimensional Kronecker delta function. This function has the following property

$$\delta(m,n) = \begin{cases} 0, & m \neq 0, n \neq 0 \\ 1, & m = 0, n = 0 \end{cases} \tag{6.6}$$

Equation (6.5) relates the response of the system to a point source located at position (k,l), showing how it varies with position in the result. If the region in the system's output over which h is non-zero is finite and closed, the system is said to have a

finite impulse response (FIR). This is the normal case for the systems we are interested in. The commonly encountered systems for which this is not precisely true, approximate the situation well.

The point spread function for a linear system determines how that system affects its input images. We can see this by considering an input image in a slightly unusual way. The linear superposition property says that when we apply multiple images to the system they do not interfere with one another. As a consequence, we can consider a single input image as a large number of input images, each of which is a point source at just one particular location. It may help to think of extracting each pixel in turn from the input image and putting it into the equivalent position in an otherwise zero image. Linear superposition says that applying this vast number of images to the linear system is just the same as applying the input image itself. This independence of the input pixels from one another makes it quite easy to derive the overall effect of the system on the input image. First, let us express the notion of considering the input image to consist of a large number of independent point sources. We need an expression which relates one particular point source to the entire input image.

$$I_{i,j} = \sum_k \sum_l I_{k,l}\, \delta(i-k, j-l) \tag{6.7}$$

Equation (6.7) uses the Kronecker delta to select individual entries from the image I. The only time that the product within the summations is non zero is when $k = i$ and $l = j$. This is the only occasion on which the Kronecker delta is anything other than zero. Equation (6.7) may, at first, seem a rather contrived way of extracting pixels from image I. However, because of the summation which it contains, we can use the linear superposition property when considering how the linear system affects the image. We start by applying the effect of the linear system to both sides of equation (6.5).

$$\Psi[I_{i,j}] = \Psi\left[\sum_k \sum_l I_{k,l}\, \delta(i-k, j-l) \right] \tag{6.8}$$

Because of linear superposition, the response of the system to a set of sources is identical to the sum of the responses to each individual excitation and we can rearrange the right hand side of equation (6.8).

$$\Psi[I_{i,j}] = \sum_k \sum_l I_{k,l}\, \Psi[\delta(i-k, j-l)] \tag{6.9}$$

Finally, we can recognise that the term involving the Kronecker delta is just the same as the right hand side of equation (6.5) and so we can substitute the point spread function giving:

$$\Psi[I_{i,j}] = \sum_k \sum_l I_{k,l}\, h(i-k, j-l) \tag{6.10}$$

This is the convolution equation. Equation (6.1) is a special case of this equation in which particular limits have been placed on the summations because the size of the point spread function is known. Of course, there has been a terminology change too. We now recognise that the convolution mask which defines the effect of the system on its input is in fact the system's point spread function. More correctly, the mask is the sampled version of the continuous point spread function.

In summary, if a system or process can be considered to be linear, its effect on an input image can be computed directly from its point spread function by applying equation (6.10). The theory is just as relevant in the application of filters to an image as it is in analysing the degradations introduced by an optical system We will meet this idea again in chapter 8, when we consider ways of correcting for the degradations introduced during image acquisition. For the purposes of the present chapter, however, we are more concerned with how convolution can be applied to filtering images to achieve desired changes in their characteristics.

6.2 FILTERING USING CONVOLUTION

Convolution provides a way to filter images. The precise nature of the filter is determined by the values in the convolution mask. This mask is, in fact, a sampled form of the **point spread function** of the filter. The point spread function is the image which results from applying the filter to an ideal point source of light. An approximation to an ideal source is an input image with just one, non zero pixel.

Using different masks we can provide a wide range of filters including those which help reduce noise, enhance sharpness, or highlight certain kinds of feature. Before we look at some specific examples, we need to understand in more detail what we mean by a filter, when the term is applied to images. To do this we will start by considering the more commonly encountered situation of filtering signals, such as sound.

The notion of frequency is well understood when applied to sound. Sound is carried by vibration of the air and its frequency is a count of the number of vibrations which occur each second. Frequency is directly related to the way in which we perceive sound. The higher the frequency of a musical note, for example, the higher is its pitch. Equipment for reproducing music is often fitted with filters so that the sound can be adjusted to suit the listener's preferences. Usually, there is a

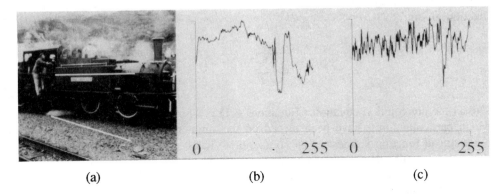

(a)　　　　　　　　　　(b)　　　　　　　　　　(c)

Figure   6.3. High and low spatial frequencies.   (a) Original image marked with two cross sections.   The upper is through a fairly smooth region, whilst the lower is through a region exhibiting considerable texture.   (b) Cross section through smooth region, (c) cross section through region containing high spatial frequencies

bass control which affects the low frequency notes and a **treble** control for the high frequencies. Turning up the bass increases the proportion of low frequency component in the overall output. Likewise, turning up the treble increases the higher frequency content.

Whereas sound frequency is a measure of changes occurring with time, frequency, when applied to images, is a measure of changes occurring in space. Consequently it is known as **spatial frequency**. Spatial frequency is a measure of how quickly brightness or colour variations occur in an image as we traverse it. Areas of an image which have a large amount of visible fine detail or texture contain high spatial frequencies. The brightness or colour vary quickly as we traverse the area. If we plot a cross section (see section 5.6.2) through such an area, the plot shows rapidly varying brightness or colour levels. An area which consists of smoothly changing brightness or colour has little high spatial frequency component, and its cross section looks correspondingly smoother. Figure 6.3 shows cross sections through smooth and textured parts of the train image.

This description of spatial frequency is of necessity vague. We will see more precisely what it means when we look at the Fourier transform in chapter 7. However, the analogy with frequency when applied to sound should lead us to expect that it is possible to perform operations which are similar to turning up the bass or treble on audio equipment. Indeed it is. Increasing the low spatial frequency component of an image is equivalent to smoothing it. This is usually done to reduce noise, but can tend to blur detail. Increasing the high frequency component makes the image appear sharper, but can lead to an increase in noise.

Now that we understand the basic approach, it is time to look at some real examples of smoothing filters, sharpening filters and filters which can be used to help locate object boundaries. These are known as **edge detectors**. We will also see an example of an adaptive filter, where the weights in the convolution mask change as it moves across the image, altering the effect which the filter has.

6.2.1 Smoothing Filters

Smoothing filters reduce noise in an image by lowering the proportion of its high frequency components. Because of this they are also known as **low pass** filters. They allow low frequencies to pass unchanged but attenuate high frequencies. We have already seen some methods of smoothing which are not based on convolution but which are, nevertheless, neighbourhood operations. In section 4.2 we saw local averaging, k nearest neighbour and sigma filtering which are all based on computing some mean value from pixels in the vicinity of the one in question. In those filters, the value of each chosen neighbour pixel was used unchanged. No weighting was applied. In contrast, in **Gaussian Smoothing**, a convolution mask is used which is a two dimensional Gaussian curve. This weights some neighbouring pixels more than others. Figure 6.4 shows the effect of applying a Gaussian smoothing filter to the train image. There is a noticeable blurring with the particular filter used. Figure 6.4(b) shows the point spread function of the filter. The high central values in the mask smoothly drop towards the edges. Figure 6.4(c) shows the actual convolution mask used to smooth the image.

The Gaussian filter is circularly symmetric. Any cross section through the centre produces the same familiar, bell shaped curve. A one dimensional, Gaussian with a maximum value of A is given by:

$$G_r = Ae^{-\left(\frac{r^2}{2\sigma^2}\right)}$$

(6.11)

Here, r represents the distance from the origin of the curve to the point being computed. The curve has its maximum value A at the origin, as can easily be seen by substituting $r = 0$ into equation (6.11). The value σ is a measure of the width of the curve. When $r = \pm\sigma$ expression in parentheses evaluates to -1/2. The curve has dropped to $e^{-1/2}$ or about 60% of its maximum value. The bigger the value of σ the wider is the curve and the more smoothing is applied. One interesting consequence of the form of equation (6.11) is that the Gaussian curve does not have a finite impulse response. The exponential term continues getting smaller but never reaches zero. However, for most practical purposes, the function can be considered zero beyond about 3σ from its centre, when its value is little more than 1% of the maximum. Indeed it is possible to use small Gaussian smoothing masks reasonably successfully even though they have a half width of less than 2σ. The mask shown in

(a)   (b)   (c)

Figure   6.4. Gaussian smoothing.   (a) Smoothed image, (b) point Spread Function (not to
        scale), (c) convolution mask

Figure 6.4(c) has this property.   In some applications, however, it may be necessary
to use masks which go significantly further than 3σ.

It is important to note how small a convolution mask is being used in Figure 6.4
The small size of the mask necessarily means that the sampling of the point spread
function of the filter is rather coarse.   Although we could have used a larger filter
with the same value of σ, there would have been little improvement.   There is no
way to improve the sampling fidelity of the central portion of the point spread function, which contains the largest values.   This region has the most significant effect on
the output.   It is inevitable that filters with a small value of σ will be more coarsely
represented than those with a larger σ.   This limitation is common in convolution
based techniques and it can sometimes be important to consider how the practical
implementation of the filter mask may affect the quality of the result.

Because the weights in the masks used for Gaussian smoothing are all positive,
the typical value resulting from the convolution operation will be many times larger
than the value of the input image.   Consequently, it is usual to normalise each result
pixel by dividing it by the sum of the weights, as was described in section 6.1.   This
ensures that the result can be represented by the same data type as that of the original
image.

As with the other smoothing techniques we have seen, convolution with a
Gaussian mask is an enhancement technique.   It is non-specific in that it reduces the
strength of the high frequency components of the image regardless of whether they
are due to noise or not.   As with all enhancement techniques, the applicability of
Gaussian smoothing to a given application can only be assessed by trials.   For some
applications, it may be difficult to detect differences between the results produced by
the various smoothing techniques we have covered here and in section 4.2.   Again, as
with other enhancements, the choice of the particular smoothing technique used may

be governed more by what is available than by any obvious superiority of one technique over the others.

6.2.2 Sharpening Filters

Sharpening filters help reduce blur in an image by raising the proportion of its high frequency components. Because of this they are also known as **high pass** filters. They allow high frequencies to pass unchanged but attenuate low frequencies. Actually, the term is still applied even when the filter actively boosts the high frequency components of the image. Operations based on derivatives are high pass filters. The amplitude of the derivative of a signal gets larger as the frequency of the signal increases, even if its own amplitude remains constant. Unfortunately, because derivatives record only changes in the image, areas in which there is no change in the input image become zero in the result. This is ideal for detecting brightness discontinuities, as we will see shortly. However, for image sharpening, the bias towards high frequencies is rather too much when using derivatives alone. To redress the balance, sharpening filters can be constructed by combining a derivative filter with the original image.

A common derivative used in sharpening is the **Laplacian**. This is a two dimensional second derivative operation. It computes the magnitude of the total second derivative of the image at each point. It is not directional. The equation which defines the Laplacian is:

$$\nabla^2 I = \frac{\partial^2 I}{\partial x^2} + \frac{\partial^2 I}{\partial y^2} \qquad (6.12)$$

Here, ∇^2 is the notation used to denote the Laplacian. The right hand side of the equation is the sum of the second derivatives of the image in the x and y directions respectively.

It is probably easier to visualise the effect of this operator in its one dimensional form. Figure 6.5 shows the Laplacian applied to a brightness discontinuity. Figure 6.5(a) shows the idealised discontinuity and Figure 6.5(b) shows the effect of applying the Laplacian operation to it. Note how the Laplacian has a positive hump as the gradient of the brightness increases, is zero in the middle of the discontinuity and has a negative hump as the gradient again falls to zero. This is all consistent with the Laplacian being the second derivative of the brightness. Figure 6.5(c) is just the inverse of the Laplacian. Finally, Figure 6.5(d) shows the effect of adding the inverse Laplacian to the original image. Naturally, this is just the same result as subtracting the Laplacian itself from the original image. The humps in the inverse Laplacian have the effect of increasing the overall contrast of the discontinuity. As the central portion of the discontinuity is the same width as before but its amplitude

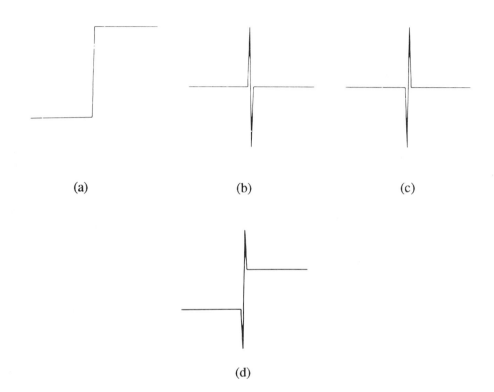

(a)   (b)   (c)

(d)

Figure 6.5. The Laplacian in one dimension. (a) Brightness discontinuity, (b) Laplacian applied to (a), (c) inverse of the Laplacian, (d) (c) added back to original

is higher, its overall rate of change of brightness must also be higher. Another way of saying this is that the edge has been sharpened.

The humps in the filtered image represent places where the output has overshot the values of the original image. So long as the degree of overshoot is not too large, the filtered image will be acceptable. Too large an overshoot, however, could result in additional phantom edges being perceived. These edges are due to the additional brightness discontinuities between the humps and the pixel values in their vicinity.

Figure 6.6 shows an example of a high pass filter applied to an image. Figure 6.6(a) shows the image after filtering. It appears crisper, with better defined object edges and detail. However, the digitisation noise, inherent in the original image, has also been made more obvious. This noise can be seen as horizontal lines across the image. It is particularly visible on the locomotive itself. Figure 6.6(b) shows the filter mask used to sharpen the image. It is the inverse Laplacian added to the original image. The effect of the inverse Laplacian alone is shown in

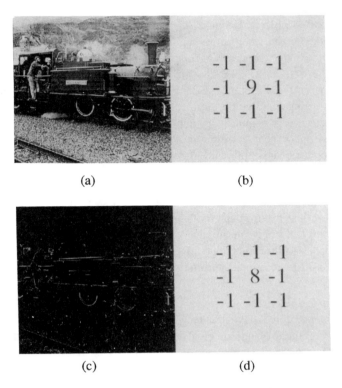

(a)   (b)

(c)   (d)

Figure   6.6. High pass filtering. (a) Sharpened image, (b) convolution mask for sharpening,
(c) result of applying the inverse Laplacian alone, (d) the inverse Laplacian convolution mask

Figure 6.6(c) and the mask is shown in Figure 6.6(d). The only difference between
the inverse Laplacian and the high pass filter is that the central weight is 8 not 9.
The addition of the input image to the inverse Laplacian accounts for the increase of
1. The effect of this, in equation (6.1) (and naturally in equation (6.10) which is the
general form), is to add the input pixel value to the corresponding result pixel. It is
worth noting what a dramatic effect on the result, a small change in the mask can
have.

As with Gaussian smoothing, this kind of high pass filtering is non-specific and is
consequently an enhancement. Whilst it undoubtedly works on a large number of
different images it does not attempt to correct specifically for particular kinds of
degradation introduced into the image. Indeed, as with the noise in Figure 6.6(a), it
may make some degradations worse. We will look at ways of correcting for specific
defects in chapter 8.

6.2.3 Edge Detecting Filters

A discontinuity in the brightness or colour of an image is often associated with the boundary of an object. Because of this, these discontinuities can be of use when trying to divide up the image into regions which correspond to the various objects being viewed. Image processing functions which locate these discontinuities are known as **edge detectors**. We saw, in section 2.4, that the task of segmenting an image is inherently difficult. Edge detection is one of the commonly used approaches in trying to solve the problem.

Edge detection is a complex problem in its own right. The goal is not simply to identify pixels on or near a discontinuity. In its fullest form, edge detection must provide a geometric description of the edge, perhaps in terms of straight line segments or some smooth curve. It must also be robust in the presence of noise and able to discriminate between object boundaries and discontinuities caused by other effects. We will look in detail at edge detection in section 9.1.2. In this section we are interested in just the first stage of the process, namely locating pixels which have a high probability of being on an edge. There are a number of standard, convolution based, approaches to this first stage. Before we look at them in more detail we need to understand a little additional terminology.

6.2.3.1 Intrinsic Images

Up to this point we have dealt with images which represent, in one form or another, the brightness or colour of a real scene, digitised and stored in a computer. This is true even after the image has been filtered to sharpen its edges or to smooth away some of its noise. The image still represents the same basic property as the original. However, when we discuss edge detection, the brightness or colour patterns in the image are no longer its most interesting aspect. The aim of an edge detecting filter is to assign a value to each pixel of the result image based on how likely it is that the corresponding input pixel is part of an object boundary. No longer does the output represent, for example, brightness. It now represents, what we could call, 'edgeness'.

An image which represents something other than a directly observable, physical quantity, like brightness or colour, is sometimes known as an **intrinsic image**. Of course, there is nothing to stop an intrinsic image being displayed in just the same way as any other image, assuming its range of values can be mapped successfully onto that required by a display. Indeed, Figure 6.6(c) is an intrinsic image. It shows the output from an inverse Laplacian filter which in itself can be used as a measure of 'edgeness' (see section 6.2.3.3.) An intrinsic image which depicts the strength of edge points is usually known as an **edge map**.

Intrinsic images tend to require a little more interpretation than straightforward modifications of normal images. Edge detectors are a good example of this phenomenon. When we look at an image, such as Figure 6.6(c) we must remember that each of its pixels represents the likelihood that the corresponding pixel of the original image is part of an object edge. The brighter the pixel, the more probable it is that it forms part of an edge. In the image, each pixel is treated individually. The fact that we, as human observers, see extended edge features is due entirely to our own, very sophisticated visual system joining up the brighter pixels for us. We saw some of this sophistication in section 2.4. In particular, in Figure 2.1 we saw how much image interpretation the visual system carries during the process of perception. This interpretation is in operation when we view Figure 6.6(c).

For a computer based system, the tasks of selecting the candidate edge pixels (called **edgels**) from the amongst the noise in the intrinsic image, joining them into chains and describing the chains geometrically are the difficult parts of segmentation by edge detection. We will discuss them further in section 9.1.2.

6.2.3.2 Simple Directional Edge Detectors

We saw, in section 3.7, that gradients are inherently directional. This is in contrast to the second derivative Laplacian which retains no directional information. The first set of edge detection filters we will look at are based on gradients and consequently are themselves directional. The directionality is expressed by having a pair of filter masks for each filter. One returns the component of the gradient along the x direction and the other its component in the y direction. This requires two separate convolution operations. We have already seen that an alternative representation of the gradient can be obtained from these components by applying equation (3.7). Both representations contain sufficient information to define the gradient completely.

Figure 6.7 illustrates three commonly used edge detectors based on gradients. Each filter is shown applied to the train image. The x and y components of the gradient are illustrated together with the filter masks actually used. Notice how the vertical edges tend to be revealed by the x direction mask and the horizontal ones by the y direction mask. In Figure 6.8 the magnitude of the gradient computed from each of the filters is also given. This was calculated using equation (3.7).

As we might expect, since all three filters are based on computation of gradients, their results are rather similar. In addition, these results are similar to those in Figure 3.6, which was computed using the simplest possible approximation to the gradient. All the methods produce intrinsic images in which bright pixels are good candidates for belonging to the edges of objects. However, all of them also produce responses which are plainly not due to object edges. Some of these are due to other kinds of image feature, such as texture, and some to noise. We saw, in section 3.7, that computation of gradients was inherently noisy. Though the masks used for the directional edge detectors use a larger neighbourhood than the direct computation of gradient (as in equation (3.8)) and are consequently less noisy, noise is still a problem with these simple detectors.

Because these simple, directional edge detectors are easy to compute and not overly taxing computationally, they are frequently used in applications without regard to one of their most important drawbacks. The size of the filter mask determines the

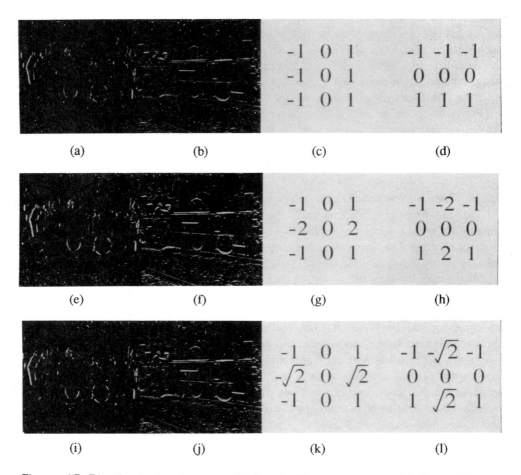

Figure 6.7. Directional edge detectors. (a) Prewitt filter x component, (b) Prewitt filter y component, (c) Prewitt filter x direction mask, (d) Prewitt filter y direction mask, (e) Sobel filter x component, (f) Sobel filter y component, (g) Sobel filter x direction mask, (h) Sobel filter y direction mask, (i) Isotropic filter x component, (j) Isotropic filter y component, (k) Isotropic filter x direction mask, (l) Isotropic filter y direction mask

width of the edges to which these detectors will respond. Edges which are only two or three pixels wide will show very strong responses since the whole of the discontinuity can be covered by the mask. Edges which are broad, however, will lead to a much reduced response. Only a portion of the edge will be under the mask at any one time. Consequently, the difference in pixel values in the image between one side of the mask and the other will be only a portion of the total. Worse still, there will

(a)　　　　　　　　　　　(b)　　　　　　　　　　　(c)

Figure　6.8. Gradient magnitudes from directional edge detectors.　(a) Prewitt filter, (b) Sobel filter, (c) Isotropic filter

be responses to the edge at a whole series of mask positions.　The effect is that whereas a sharp edge will give a strong and very localised response, a broad edge will give a wide and rather weak one.　Note that the terms broad and sharp, used here, are not absolute but relate to the width of the edge in comparison with the width of the mask.　Broad might imply an edge as little as three or four times the mask width, not a large amount on a 512 pixel square image.

There are two difficulties associated with this response to broad edges.　First, the edge localisation is difficult.　Some search must be made of the detector output to try to determine where the centre of the edge actually is.　Additionally, it is common to combat the noise problem in these simple detectors by considering only the strong responses.　If we do this we run the risk of ignoring the weak responses due to broad edges altogether.　Without some sophisticated search of the intrinsic image involving grouping of adjacent weak responses it may be impossible to distinguish the noise from the broad edges.　These kinds of search are notoriously awkward to implement and defeat the object of the essentially simple approach which the filters provide.　Normally the problem is simply ignored and the loss of edge information is accepted or not even considered.

More sophisticated methods of edge detection take specific account of the edge width problem.　The general approach is to use not one detector but several, each of a different size and therefore optimised to detect edges of a different width.　Normally, this involves using several convolution operations with masks of different sizes.　We will see two examples of this approach.　The Marr-Hildreth edge detector is described in section 6.2.3.3.　The Canny edge detector is covered in section 9.1.2.3 where it is used to illustrate the whole process of detecting edges, from identifying the brightness discontinuities through to the generation of geometric descriptions.　One difficulty of generating several different intrinsic edge images from different sized filters is to reconcile them with one another. The same edge may produce a response in two or more filters but it may not be in exactly the same place. Identifying edges common to several intrinsic images can be quite difficult. We will return to this point in section 9.1.2.

6.2.3.3 Omnidirectional Edge Detectors

We have already seen that the Laplacian is an omnidirectional second derivative operator which can be used as an edge detector. Figure 6.6(c) is an example of its output. In the output of the inverse Laplacian, however, the bright pixels are not actually at the centre of the brightness discontinuity. Referring to Figure 6.5 we can see that the peak in the function is on the light side of the discontinuity. If the edge is sharp, the displacement of the peak from the centre of the edge will be small. However, if the edge is rather broad, the displacement will be significant. This problem led David Marr and Ellen Hildreth (Marr and Hildreth (1980), Marr (1982)) to propose using not the brightest pixels in the result image but rather the zero values. The inverse Laplacian contains both positive and negative values. The zero value in the vicinity of the edge represents the place where the gradient is steepest. This point is a good indication of the centre of the edge profile.

Marr and Hildreth did not simply use the Laplacian or the inverse Laplacian by itself. Conscious of the edge width problem, which we looked at in section 6.2.3.2, they combined the Laplacian with Gaussian filters of various sizes to produce a family of filters capable of detecting edges of various widths. Filters using wide Gaussians detect wide, slow edges. Filters with narrow Gaussians detect narrow, sharp edges. Figure 6.9 shows two such filters, one with a narrow Gaussian, the other with a wide one. The use of a Gaussian as part of the filter automatically has a noise reducing effect. The wider the Gaussian, the less the noise. Each filter is tuned to detect edges of a particular scale. Figure 6.10 shows the effect of applying Marr-Hildreth filters of different scale to an image. Bright pixels in these images represent zero values in the filter output. Note how the smallest filter picks up the most detail. Note also how edges in the edge map from the smallest filter are also sometimes present in the maps from the larger filters.

The Marr-Hildreth filter can be written:

$$\nabla^2 G_r = C \left[1 - \frac{r^2}{2\sigma^2} \right] e^{\frac{-r^2}{2\sigma^2}} \tag{6.13}$$

The Laplacian of a Gaussian actually has a minimum at its origin. C is the value of that minimum. It is more usual to specify a Marr-Hildreth filter with a maximum at its origin. Effectively we multiply the entire function by -1 and make C a positive constant. The reason for doing this is that the filter then bears a strong resemblance to certain detectors found in the human retina (Marr (1982)). Once again, in

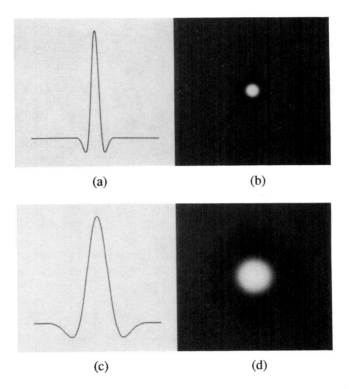

Figure 6.9. The Marr-Hildreth filter. (a) Cross section through narrow filter, (b) Point
spread function for narrow filter, (c) Cross section through wide filter, (d) Point
spread function for wide filter

equation (6.13) the value σ controls the width of the filter by specifying the width of
the Gaussian, as in equation (6.11). In fact, the innermost points where the curve
passes through zero are at

$$r = \pm \sigma \sqrt{2}$$

when

$$r^2 = 2\sigma^2$$

We can see from Figure 6.9 that the overall size of the filter needs to be about three
times the distance to its innermost zero. This has some interesting consequences in

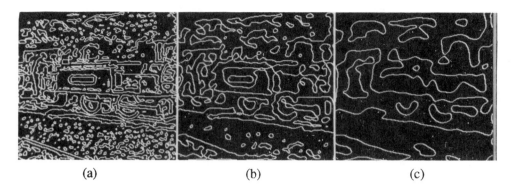

(a)   (b)   (c)

Figure 6.10. The effect of Marr-Hildreth filters. (a) Edge map from narrow filter, (b) edge map from moderate sized filter, (c) edge map from wide filter

terms of the size of convolution mask we might expect to have to use. In Figure 6.4 we smoothed an image using a Gaussian with

$$\sigma = \sqrt{2}$$

To form a Marr-Hildreth filter using the same Gaussian, we would need a mask with a half width of about

$$3 \times \sqrt{2} \times \sqrt{2} = 6$$

This implies a filter of about 13 by 13 elements. Convolution masks for Marr-Hildreth filters with even a modest amount of smoothing tend to be rather large. As with the Gaussian, it is possible to economise a little by not using values near the extremities of the filter. Even so, this particular filter would require at least an 11 by 11 mask to specify it. Figure 6.2 contains values for the number of operations which filters of this size require. Usually, a substantial benefit can be gained, in terms of a reduction in the number of operations required, by performing these convolutions in the Fourier domain.

The convolution is only the first step in using these filters. The centre of the edge is marked by zero values in the filter output. To form the edge map, we need to locate these zeros. In practice, because of noise and sampling effects, the zero value may not appear explicitly as a pixel in the result image. The zero has to be inferred from the values on either side of it. The usual approach is to scan along each image row and down each column. Any pixel which really is zero is marked as an edge point. In addition, any pixels where the sign of the filter output changes are also marked. Of course, if the filter output changes sign between a pair of pixels, a choice must be made about which one to mark as the zero. The simplest approximation is to mark the one with the smaller absolute value. This is the nearest neighbour kind of approximation which we first met in section 5.2.2. It is possible to locate the zero, and hence the centre of the edge, to sub pixel accuracy, using linear interpolation, if necessary. The edge maps in Figure 6.10 were produced using the simple approximation.

The large size of the Marr-Hildreth filters means that they are computationally expensive. Unlike some other filters, it is not possible to use the kind of performance enhancements described in section 6.2.5.2. However, a very good approximation to the Marr-Hildreth filter can be formed by subtracting two Gaussians of different width. Since computation of the individual Gaussian filters can be optimised, this is an attractive alternative. The resulting filter is known as a **difference of Gaussians** or DOG filter.

6.2.4 Adaptive Filters

So far, we have looked at convolution operations in which the same filter mask has been applied over the whole image. For some purposes, however, it may be necessary to modify the filter depending on the local image conditions. A filter which is modified in this way is known as **adaptive**. The adaptation might be based, for example, on the local pixel statistics. We have already seen this kind of adaptation, which is used in the statistical differencing enhancement (section 4.2.2.) Alternatively, the adaptation might be based on the image geometry. The filter's behaviour might depend on which part of the image it is being used on.

An interesting example of this kind of adaptive filter is shown in Figure 6.11. The figure shows a conventional chest X-ray from a patient suffering from the condition **pneumothorax.** This is commonly known as a collapsed lung. In this condition, air has leaked in between the chest wall and the outer surface of the lung. This interferes with normal breathing. In the healthy chest, expansion of the rib cage increases the volume of the lung, reducing the interior pressure and causing air to be drawn in via the nose and mouth. However, if there is air between the chest wall and the lung, as in pneumothorax, the increase in chest volume is not transmitted properly to the lung and it fails to inflate correctly. Instead, the volume of the air between the chest wall and lung varies. Whereas a completely collapsed lung is relatively easy to detect in a chest X-ray, a partial collapse, as illustrated in Figure 6.11(a) can be very difficult to spot. The condition shows up as a faint discontinuity in brightness, roughly the shape of the chest wall but positioned some little way inside it. The edge in question has been marked in the enhanced image shown in Figure 6.11(b) (Cocklin et al. (1982)). The enhancement is a selective edge detector, enhancing edges which might be caused by the pneumothorax but not others. The objective of the enhancement is to make it easier for human observers to detect the presence of the pneumothorax.

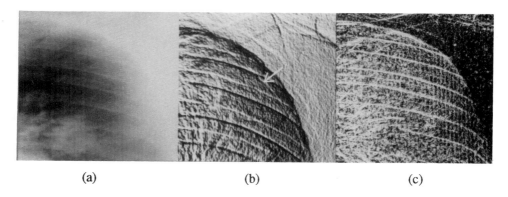

(a)   (b)   (c)

Figure 6.11. Adaptive filtering for detection of pneumothorax. (a) Original chest X-ray
        image, (b) enhanced image showing the pneumothorax, (c) effect of a Sobel
        filter on the original image. (Original X-ray images courtesy of the Brompton
        Hospital, London)

Normal edge detector techniques, such as the Sobel filter (section 6.2.3.2), are not
useful in detecting the pneumothorax. There are many good edge responses and the
rather weak discontinuity caused by the pneumothorax cannot easily be discriminated
from the others. Figure 6.11(c). shows the magnitude of the result of applying the
horizontal and vertical Sobel masks to the chest X-ray image. The pneumothorax
cannot be seen. We really need a filter specially designed to detect only the
pneumothorax. Because of the shape of the lung the approximate direction of the
discontinuity can be calculated once a single position has been identified in the chest.
This important position turns out to be close to the **hilum**, the point where the blood
vessels and air passages enter the lungs. Above the level of this point, the
pneumothorax will lie close to the circumference of a circle centred on the hilum.
To detect it, we need a kind of radial edge detector. Below this level, the
pneumothorax is approximately vertical. Consequently a conventional edge detector,
such as the Sobel y direction mask, can be used. One way to implement a radial
edge detector is by computing a series of directional masks optimised for specific
edge orientations. A convolution can then be carried out and the appropriate mask
selected depending where in the image the convolution is being computed. The aim
of the mask selection is to orient the preferred edge detection direction tangential to
the pneumothorax. Figure 6.12 shows the effect of four masks based on the Prewitt
filter (section 6.2.3.2). As well as the horizontal and vertical masks, two more at 45°
and 135° have been defined. By choosing the most appropriate mask, based on the
geometric criterion already discussed, a reasonable response can be obtained from the
directional filters due to the pneumothorax.

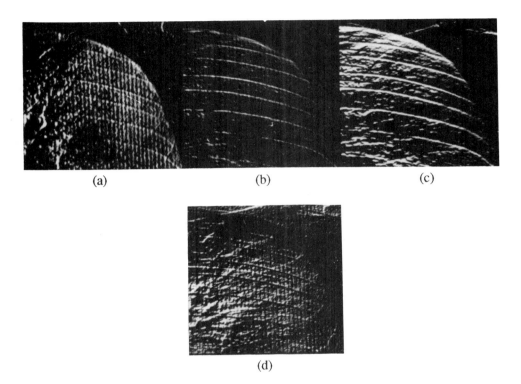

(a)   (b)   (c)

(d)

Figure   6.12. Effect of simple directional edge detectors on a pneumothorax.   (a) Vertical
edge detecting filter, (b) 45° edge detecting filter, (c) horizontal edge detecting
filter, (d) 135° edge detecting filter

In practice, more directional masks than this are needed to give a good, continuous response. In addition they need to be larger than the 5 by 5 masks shown in
Figure 6.12 to allow the necessary improvement in directional selectivity. Continuity
of the edge is important to the performance of human observers locating the
pneumothorax in the enhanced image. In practice, the result shown in Figure 6.11(b)
was obtained with a special purpose computation which, although analogous to the
convolution approach, performed the edge detection in a way which was less expensive computationally than the multiple convolutions would have been. The principle,
however, remains exactly the same.

6.2.5 Implementing Filters

In this section we will look at some practical aspects of the implementation of
convolution masks. First, we will discuss how to sample the filter's point spread

function to create the convolution mask. Then we will look at a property of some convolution masks which allows them to be implemented with a significantly smaller number of operations than normal. This property is known as **separability**.

6.2.5.1 Sampling the Point Spread Function

We have already seen two examples of the process of sampling. The sampling of an image during digitisation was discussed in section 1.1.1.2. The re-sampling of an image during geometric operations was discussed in section 5.2.1. In this section, we extend the notion of sampling to cater for situations when increased precision may be necessary.

First, we need to understand in some detail what a pixel represents. From our original discussion of sampling, a pixel is a value which represents the intensity of the light reaching the detector from a small area of the scene being imaged. In some sense, the pixel value is the average brightness of the area. If we are actually sampling a real scene, we normally make the assumption that the optical system and the detector provide a pixel value which is a good representation of the average brightness. However, when we sample a point spread function, we can be more specific about what we regard as a good representation. Intensity is a measure of the amount of light falling on a particular area of some object. The amount of light is known as the **flux**. We can think of it as being a certain number of photons falling on the area per second. The brighter the light, the higher the flux and the greater the number of photons. The intensity of the light falling on our single pixel is the flux divided by the pixel's area.

The simplest approximation, when sampling, is to use the value of the intensity in the middle of the pixel as the value for the whole pixel. For the case of the point spread function, this just involves computing its value at the coordinate of the centre of the pixel. This approximation is reasonably accurate as long as the value of the intensity does not change much within the pixel. However, we have seen that convolution masks can be quite crude approximations to the point spread function of a given filter. Because of this, it is quite possible for the value of the function to vary significantly within a single mask element. Consequently, we need a sampling method which will give a single value representative of the point spread function despite its variation within the element.

The basic approach to achieving a better representation is to sum the contributions to the total flux through the pixel from each small area of it. When we have the total flux through the pixel, we can divide by the area which will give us the pixel intensity. In mathematical terms, we integrate the point spread function to find the volume under the surface which it represents. This gives us the total flux from which we can derive the intensity. We are computing the average value of the point spread function within the area of the pixel rather than taking one particular value. The resulting values will be very similar to those derived by direct sampling, if the point spread function does not vary much across a pixel. However, there can be significant variations where the function is changing rapidly. Hummel and Lowe (1989) showed that significant improvements in accuracy can be obtained, in techniques involving Gaussians, by using these locally computed average values in the filter masks. In particular, they showed an improvement in the accuracy of edge location from detectors such as the Marr-Hildreth operator.

6.2.5.2 Separable Filters

Large convolution masks require large numbers of computations during filtering. Figure 6.2 shows the numbers of operations involved for a range of mask sizes. For square masks, the number of operations increases as n^2, where n is the width or height of the mask in pixels. For example, a 15 by 15 mask will take approximately 225/9 or 25 times as many operations as a 3 by 3 mask. Some filters, however, can be decomposed into a pair of one dimensional filters. One of these is applied down the columns of the image producing an intermediate result. The second filter is then applied along the rows of this intermediate image. The big advantage in applying these two, one dimensional filters is that the number of operations is proportional to $2n$ rather than n^2. For small masks the benefits are small. However, for the 15 by 15 mask, the separable version takes only 30/225, or about 13% of the number of computations of the full mask.

Unfortunately, not many commonly used masks are separable. The ones that are have only positive values and have certain symmetries. The most commonly used, separable filter is the Gaussian. The one dimensional masks which are equivalent to a particular two dimensional mask are related to it by matrix multiplication. For example, the one dimensional masks for a Gaussian are the transpose of each other. If $\mathbf{v}$ represents the vertical mask for the Gaussian then its transpose $\mathbf{v}^T$ is the horizontal mask. The following equation relates the one dimensional masks and two dimensional masks $\mathbf{V}$:

$$\mathbf{V} = \mathbf{v}\,\mathbf{v}^T \qquad\qquad (6.14)$$

Figure 6.13 shows actual values for horizontal mask $\mathbf{v}^T$ and two dimensional mask $\mathbf{V}$ for a 7 by 7 filter with a maximum value of 1 and a σ of 1. It also shows the effect of smoothing the image using the separable form of the filter and using the conventional form of the filter. The only difference between the results is that the separable form took only about a quarter as long to compute as did the full, two dimensional form.

$1.1 \times 10^{-2} \; 1.4 \times 10^{-1} \; 6.1 \times 10^{-1} \; 1.0 \times 10^{0} \; 6.1 \times 10^{-1} \; 1.4 \times 10^{-1} \; 1.1 \times 10^{-2}$

(a)

$1.2 \times 10^{-4} \; 1.5 \times 10^{-3} \; 6.7 \times 10^{-3} \; 1.1 \times 10^{-2} \; 6.7 \times 10^{-3} \; 1.5 \times 10^{-3} \; 1.2 \times 10^{-4}$
$1.5 \times 10^{-3} \; 1.8 \times 10^{-2} \; 8.2 \times 10^{-2} \; 1.4 \times 10^{-1} \; 8.2 \times 10^{-2} \; 1.8 \times 10^{-2} \; 1.5 \times 10^{-3}$
$6.7 \times 10^{-3} \; 8.2 \times 10^{-2} \; 3.7 \times 10^{-1} \; 6.1 \times 10^{-1} \; 3.7 \times 10^{-1} \; 8.2 \times 10^{-2} \; 6.7 \times 10^{-3}$
$1.1 \times 10^{-2} \; 1.4 \times 10^{-1} \; 6.1 \times 10^{-1} \; 1.0 \times 10^{0} \; 6.1 \times 10^{-1} \; 1.4 \times 10^{-1} \; 1.1 \times 10^{-2}$
$6.7 \times 10^{-3} \; 8.2 \times 10^{-2} \; 3.7 \times 10^{-1} \; 6.1 \times 10^{-1} \; 3.7 \times 10^{-1} \; 8.2 \times 10^{-2} \; 6.7 \times 10^{-3}$
$1.5 \times 10^{-3} \; 1.8 \times 10^{-2} \; 8.2 \times 10^{-2} \; 1.4 \times 10^{-1} \; 8.2 \times 10^{-2} \; 1.8 \times 10^{-2} \; 1.5 \times 10^{-3}$
$1.2 \times 10^{-4} \; 1.5 \times 10^{-3} \; 6.7 \times 10^{-3} \; 1.1 \times 10^{-2} \; 6.7 \times 10^{-3} \; 1.5 \times 10^{-3} \; 1.2 \times 10^{-4}$

(b)

(c)   (d)   (e)

Figure   6.13. One and two dimensional masks for Gaussian smoothing. (a) One dimensional mask for horizontal component, (b) two dimensional mask, (c) original image, (d) image smoothed using one dimensional masks, (e) image smoothed using two dimensional mask

6.3 CORRELATION

There are image processing applications in which it is necessary to measure the similarity between images or parts of images. For example, we might need to locate a particular feature in an image. If we already have an image of the feature alone, at the appropriate scale, we can place it over the image to be searched, moving it around until we find maximum similarity. The position of this maximum indicates the position of the feature itself.

    The measure of similarity between images is known as their **correlation**. The computation of the correlation is very similar to that involved in convolution. Only the indexing scheme is different. We can think of the window, that is the small

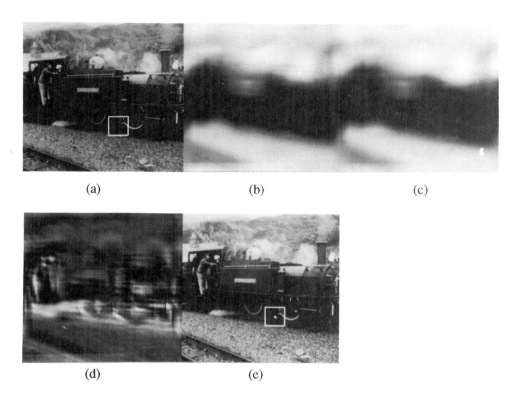

(a)   (b)   (c)

(d)   (e)

Figure 6.14. Locating a feature using correlation. (a) Original image showing feature to be
            detected, (b) result of correlation calculation, (c) result of local sum calculation,
            (d) correlation normalised by local sum, (e) original image showing peaks in
            normalised correlation

image containing the feature to be found, as playing a similar role to that of the mask
in convolution. The window is a small array of pixels being positioned over the
main image at different places and taking part in a sum of products calculation. The
resulting intrinsic image is a correlation map. Its pixel values represent how well
each small neighbourhood of the main image matches the window. If there is a
single, strong maximum value in the correlation map it indicates the location of the
desired feature.

It is usual to normalise the result of a correlation in order to make the resulting
peaks sharper and easier to identify. Consequently, the full equation for a correlation
is a little more complex than that for a convolution.

$$C_{i,j} = \frac{\sum_k \sum_l I_{k,l}\, h(k-i, l-j)}{\sqrt{\sum_k \sum_l I_{k,l}^2}} \tag{6.15}$$

The similarity of the upper term of this equation with the equation for convolution (equation (6.10)) is clear. They differ only in that the ordering of the indexes used for the window in correlation is reversed when compared with those used for the mask in convolution. Consequently, the computational burden of un-normalised correlation and convolution is essentially the same. The figures for the number of operations required to compute various sizes of convolution, given in Figure 6.2, apply also to un-normalised correlation. It should not be surprising, therefore, to find that considerable efforts are employed to reduce the area over which the search must take place when the window to be matched is large. The similarity in the computation also means that the kind of special hardware which can be used to speed up convolution operations can also help with correlations. All that is necessary is a rotation of the correlation window by 180°, before applying the convolution. This rotation corrects for the different indexing schemes used in the two operations. Also, as with convolution, it is possible to compute the correlation in the Fourier domain. Once again, the reason for doing this is simply to reduce the number of operations required. The window size at which it becomes worth computing the correlation in the Fourier domain is essentially the same as that for a convolution. Unfortunately, the normalisation cannot be computed in the Fourier domain. Since the normalisation term has to be computed over the same area as the correlation itself, it alone is more computationally expensive than spatial domain convolution, since it contains a square root term.

An alternative normalisation which, though not rigorously correct, is nevertheless sometimes effective, is illustrated in Figure 6.14. The feature being searched for is part of the image itself and is shown outlined in Figure 6.14(a). This is a particularly characteristic feature, including as it does a portion of a wheel rim, which is light in colour. The result of the correlation calculation is shown in Figure 6.14(b). Figure 6.14(c) shows the result of computing local sums over the same areas as the correlation. This image is cheaper to calculate than the denominator of equation (6.15), particularly as it can be computed in the Fourier domain. It is equivalent to a convolution using a mask of the same size as the correlation window and with every element set to 1. Figure 6.14(d) shows the result of normalising the correlation using the local sum. Finally, in Figure 6.14(e) the position of the best correlations is shown, overlayed on the original image. Two possible matches are shown. Centrally within the white square is a spot marking the highest peak in the normalised correlation. This corresponds to the feature we are looking for. Slightly above this and to its right is another bright spot near the locomotive's cylinder. This marks a secondary peak in the normalised correlation and another possible match. However, this second peak is much lower than the main peak. Consequently, a search for the largest pixel value in the normalised correlation image gives the correct location of the feature. It must be remembered that this perfect result has been obtained under ideal conditions, where the feature to be matched is highly characteristic and is, in any case, part of the image itself. In real correlations, where the correlation window data is synthetic or is taken from a different image it may be less easy to decide which is the appropriate feature from among candidate matches.

Even though the number of operations needed to perform this kind of correlation may be very large, the search only allows us to match features in precisely the same orientation as the window and with precisely the same scale. There are applications for which these restrictions are not a problem. For example, the automatic location of control points in satellite images can be carried out using correlation. The approach is also applicable for features which are circularly symmetric and where orientation is irrelevant. However, when the orientation or scale are important but uncertain it may be better to perform the comparison not directly on the pixels themselves but on some properties which can be derived from the image and the window. We will look at some possible approaches in chapter 9. Properties which are not affected by the orientation of the feature are known as **rotation invariant**. Likewise, properties unaffected by the size of the feature in the image are known as **scale invariant**.

6.4 SUMMARY

In this chapter we have looked at the closely related topics of convolution and correlation. We have seen why they are important and how a wide variety of different functions can be provided by essentially one image processing algorithm. We discussed the linear systems theory on which the convolution technique is based. We saw the large amount of computation which a typical convolution or correlation requires and noted that special hardware support for these operations is sometimes provided. We also noted that the computational burden for large convolutions and correlations can be reduced by performing them in the Fourier domain, a topic covered in the following chapter.

7

Transforming Image Representations

So far in this book, we have considered only one kind of image representation. For the most part, the images we have looked at have recorded brightness as a function of position. We have encountered the notion of colour images (see section 1.1.3) without considering the possible ways in which such data can be encoded. We have also seen that attributes, other than directly observable properties like brightness, can be stored as intrinsic images (see section 6.2.3.1.) Once again the representation has not been discussed explicitly.

In practice, there are many different ways in which image data can be represented. In this chapter we will look at a number of them. Some of the representations are approximations. For example, in section 7.4 we will see how grey scale and full colour images can be approximated when only a small number of bits is available to code each pixel. These changes of representation are useful to allow images to be displayed or printed on devices with restricted capability. Likewise, in section 7.3 we will look at techniques by which the amount of data used to store or transmit an image may be reduced. The representation used in the compressed form of the image is usually quite unlike that in the original. Often, compression implies that the image which results from the decompression of the data is an approximation to the original image.

Other kinds of transformation produce representations which, although different from the original data, are completely equivalent to it in terms of the information contained. These so-called **domain** transforms, of which the Fourier transform is by far the most important, allow images to be treated in ways entirely different from those used on the original data. We will start by discussing domain transformations and looking at some ways in which they can be applied.

7.1 TRANSFORMING DOMAINS

Domain transforms provide alternative ways of describing an image. Instead of recording brightness as a function of position, we can choose a completely different representation of the image. In the Fourier transform, the image is stored as a set of spatial frequency values together with their associated amplitudes and phases. We will see what this means in detail shortly. The point is that instead of brightness as a function of position, the Fourier representation is essentially amplitude as a function of spatial frequency. The normal representation of an image is said to be in the **spatial domain**. The Fourier representation is said to be in the **frequency domain**. The Fourier transform is not the only domain transform, though it is the one most commonly used in image processing applications.

The domain transforms all have the same basic form which can be expressed as

$$T(u,v) = \sum_{x=0}^{M-1} \sum_{y=0}^{N-1} I(x,y) \, g \, (x,y,u,v) \qquad (7.1)$$

Here, T is the transformed image, I the input image, of size M by N, and g is the transformation kernel. The equation expresses the fact that each pixel in the result depends on all the pixels in the input image. Each input image pixel is multiplied by the appropriate entry in the transformation kernel and added to the sum. It should be immediately obvious that direct computation of an equation of this sort takes a prodigious number of operations. As with convolution, the computational load can be greatly reduced if the transformation kernel can be separated. Fortunately, the common transforms, including the Fourier transform, do have separable kernels. In addition, much research has been applied to the development of efficient algorithms for computation of the domain transforms. Again, as with convolution, the variety of tasks to which the transforms can be applied has made it worthwhile developing highly efficient methods for their computation.

7.1.1 The Fourier Transform

We met the notion of spatial frequency when discussing filtering in section 6.2. Areas of an image containing high spatial frequency components vary rapidly in pixel value as we traverse them. Conversely, areas with only low spatial frequency components vary slowly. The French physicist Joseph Fourier, who lived between 1768 and 1830, developed a representation of functions, based on frequency, which has

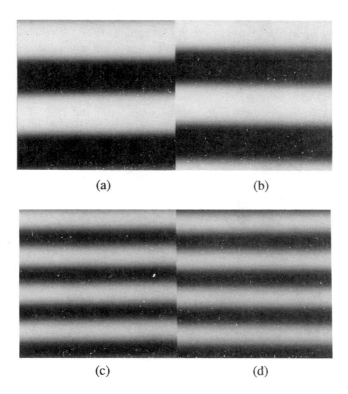

Figure 7.1. Sine wave properties. (a) vertical sine wave with a frequency of two cycles in the height of the image, (b) as (a) but with a phase of 45°, (c) sine wave with twice the frequency and half the amplitude of (a), (d) as (c) but with a phase of –45°

been of considerable importance in many branches of mathematics and science. The representation, which now bears Fourier's name, has been significant because it allows complicated functions to be represented in a way which has very useful properties and which is often much easier to deal with than the original function itself. An image can be regarded as a function of two variables. The variables are the x and y coordinates of a given pixel and the value of the function is the pixel value itself. Consequently, the Fourier transform can be used to generate a new representation of the image, based on spatial frequencies and preserving all the information of the original. It is not appropriate to prove the properties of the Fourier transform in this book. In any case, there are literally dozens of standard mathematical texts which cover the material (for example Kreyszig (1972).) It is possible, however, to demonstrate how an image can be represented in terms of spatial frequencies.

Initially, we'll consider that a particular spatial frequency describes a sine wave which repeats a specified number of times over a given distance. The units in which spatial frequency is expressed are arbitrary. Sometimes they are related to the size of the image, at other times to the size of a pixel. For some applications it is important to have some absolute measure, in which case the actual distance represented by each pixel may be needed. A simple, vertically oriented sine wave is shown in Figure 7.1(a). It has a spatial frequency of two cycles within the height of the image. The pixel values in the image vary between −100 and 100. The sine wave is said to have an **amplitude** of 100. For the purposes of display, black represents -100 and full white represents 100. A mid grey tone represents 0. As well as amplitude and frequency, a third value is required to characterise a sine wave completely. The **phase** of a sine wave represents where, along its length, it passes through 0. The wave in Figure 7.1(a) passes through 0 at the origin and has a phase of 0. The wave in Figure 7.1(b) passes through 0 after 1/8 of a cycle. It is common to represent the phase as an angular measure, one cycle of the wave being equivalent to 360° or 2π radians. The phase of the sine wave in Figure 7.1(b) is 45°. Figure 7.1 also shows a higher frequency, lower amplitude sine wave with a phase of 0° and with a phase of −45°.

The theory, which Fourier developed, proposes that by adding together many sine and cosine waves with different amplitudes, frequencies and phases, it is possible to construct almost any arbitrary function. The set of component waves includes one with zero frequency. This is a constant term, sometimes referred to as the D.C. (direct current) component, reflecting the fact that some terminology in this area is derived from signal processing and electronics. The theory means that by adding together many different sine and cosine waves we should be able to construct any arbitrary image. Looking at the image of the train, which has been used as an example many times, you may not feel comfortable with the idea that it can be represented by a large number of simple waves. Indeed, the spatial frequency representation of such an image is necessarily complicated. The image shown in Figure 7.2(a) is, however, much simpler. As a demonstration of the Fourier technique we will synthesise this image from its spatial frequency components. The images in Figure 7.2(b)-(g) show the effect of adding successively more components. In this case, each component is a sine wave image, similar in form to those in Figure 7.1, with amplitude, frequency and phase chosen in accordance with the Fourier theory. No cosine waves are needed. To get the two dimensional pattern, we use images with the sine waves along the x direction and along the y direction. As we add more and more components, the resulting image appears more and more like the target image in Figure 7.2(a). Indeed, by adding a sufficient number of components we can make the resulting image arbitrarily close to the target. Figure 7.2(h) shows the differences which remain between the synthesised image and the target. In the residual image, mid grey indicates zero difference, white indicates

(a)   (b)   (c)

(d)   (e)   (f)

(g)   (h)

Figure   7.2. Synthesis from Fourier components.   (a) Target image to be synthesised, (b) effect of the first component alone, (c) effect of adding the second component, (d) effect of adding the third component, (e) effect of adding the fourth component, (f) effect of adding the fifth component, (g) effect of adding the sixth component, (h) residual difference.

that the Fourier components are too large and black that they are too small. It is clear that the components give a good representation of the original image.

The particular set of sine waves used for this image is based on the series:

$$S(x) = \sin(\omega \frac{2\pi}{N} x) + \frac{1}{3} \sin(3\omega \frac{2\pi}{N} x) + \frac{1}{5} \sin(5\omega \frac{2\pi}{N} x) + \tag{7.2}$$

$$\frac{1}{7} \sin(7\omega \frac{2\pi}{N} x) + \frac{1}{9} \sin(9\omega \frac{2\pi}{N} x) + \frac{1}{11} \sin(11\omega \frac{2\pi}{N} x)$$

This one dimensional equation shows the situation along a single row of the result image. A similar expression holds for the variation in brightness down a column. The basic brightness pattern is a sum of smaller and smaller amplitude sine waves of increasing frequency. In the equation, N is the number of pixels on a row and ω represents the frequency of the first sine wave component. In Figure 7.2 this was chosen to be 4 cycles in the width of the image. This is the same as the number of pairs of black and white squares along a row of the target image. The factor $2\pi/N$ deserves some attention. A complete cycle of a sine wave takes place over an angle of 2π radians. Consequently, for a single cycle of the sine wave to occur in the length of one row of the image, we need to multiply each pixel coordinate by $2\pi/N$ to convert it to an appropriate angle. This factor gives us the correct scaling for one cycle in the width of the image. We can now multiply it by ω, our desired number of cycles, to get the appropriate mapping between pixel coordinate and angle for the sine function.

Equation (7.2) alone will not lead to the pattern of Figure 7.2(a). If we simply applied the equation to every row, for example, they would be identical. However, Figure 7.2(a) shows a periodic reversal of black and white squares down each column as well as along each row. We need to shift the starting position of the function defined by equation (7.2) periodically. This is equivalent to altering the phase of the sine waves. In fact, the images in Figure 7.2 are 512 pixels square. Each individual square is 64 pixels square. After every 64 rows, the phase of the sine waves in equation (7.2) was changed by adding π to the angle used in the computation. These phase reversed sine waves were used for the next 64 rows, after which the original set were used again. This cycling continued across the image. The same procedure was used to generate the components in the y direction.

In fact, if the computations had actually been carried out this way, a huge number of trigonometric calculations would have been required. In fact, only one row was calculated in each case. It was then copied to produce the set of 64 identical rows. The two sets of 64 rows, representing the zero phase and π, phase sine waves were formed into a complete image by repeatedly using the concatenation operations described in section 5.3.2. Once this image, containing all of the x direction components was finished a simple transpose operation (section 5.1.3) was used to produce the equivalent y direction components.

Whilst it is no way a full justification of Fourier's theory, this illustration shows that it is indeed possible to construct an image from a set if sine waves. The set used here vary in frequency, amplitude and phase. If we want to represent the image in terms of the sine waves we need to record all of these properties for all of the component waves. Using a sufficiently large number of components we can synthesise an image which is arbitrarily close to the target image.

The question of how well a set of sine and cosine waves represents the original image is an interesting one. After all, a digital image is itself an approximation to the pattern of brightness which existed when it was captured. The sampling of the brightness pattern has introduced a limitation in the possible spatial resolution of the image. Changes in brightness which occur within the width of a pixel clearly cannot be directly recorded. This can be thought of as a limit in the spatial frequencies which need to be employed to represent the underlying brightness pattern as faithfully as does the spatial domain image. Sine and cosine waves with periods very much less than the width of a pixel make essentially no contribution to the pixel value. They will pass through many cycles in the width of the pixel and their contribution will be averaged. These averages are very close to zero. However, when the period is about the width of a pixel we reach a limiting condition. At lower frequencies, significant contributions appear. Above this frequency, the contributions are small and diminishing. Consequently, the highest frequency waves normally employed in representing an image are those with a period equal to the width of a pixel. Once again, proof of these results is beyond the scope of this text. However, the results are important for the fidelity of the frequency domain representation and we will return to them shortly.

7.1.1.1 Fourier Transforms as Images

Now that we have seen that it is possible to synthesise an image from a set of components with various spatial frequencies, we need to address the question of how to represent the frequency domain information as an image in its own right. Recall that the components each have an associated amplitude, frequency and phase and that there are two spatial dimensions to account for. The representation of the Fourier transform of an image is another image in which the u axis represents spatial frequency along the original image's x axis and the v axis represents spatial frequency along the original image's y axis. It is conventional to display the transform with its u axis horizontal. We have already noted that the highest frequency component in the transform has a period equal to the width of a single pixel. Its frequency is 1 cycle per pixel. If we choose the transform image to be the same size as the original, we can place the constant term at the origin and the highest frequency term at the other end of the axis. Each pixel in the transform now represents a change in frequency of 1 cycle in the width of the image. The origin holds the constant term, the next pixel holds the 1 cycle per image width, the next the 2 cycles per image width and so on. The last pixel holds the N cycles per image width, or 1 cycle per pixel term, N being the number of pixels along the image dimension of interest.

Now that we know where to place the particular values appropriate to each spatial frequency component, we must decide what information needs to be recorded. We know that there are amplitude and phase values associated with each component. The question is, precisely how should we record them? At this point we need to examine the form of the equations which allow us to compute the Fourier transform. Remember that these are nothing more than equations which allow us to determine the properties of the sine and cosine waves which, when added together, reconstitute the original image. The equations may appear complex at first sight. However, our use of them is restricted to an explanation of the way in which data is stored in the resulting transform image. It is not necessary to have a deep understanding of these equations in order to appreciate the applications of the Fourier transform, which we will cover later. However, it is necessary to know what data is stored in a Fourier transform image and where it is stored in order to be able to interpret these images in some applications. A broad understanding of the equations is helpful in this context.

We can write the two dimensional Fourier transform as

$$F(u,v) = \frac{1}{N} \sum_{x=0}^{N-1} \sum_{y=0}^{N-1} I(x,y) e^{-2\pi j(ux + vy)/N} \tag{7.3}$$

where

$$e^{-2\pi j(ux + vy)/N} = \cos(2\pi(ux + vy)/N) - j \sin(2\pi(ux + vy)/N)$$

and the inverse transform as

$$I(x,y) = \frac{1}{N} \sum_{u=0}^{N-1} \sum_{v=0}^{N-1} F(u,v) e^{2\pi j(ux + vy)/N} \tag{7.4}$$

where

$$e^{2\pi j(ux + vy)/N} = \cos(2\pi(ux + vy)/N) + j \sin(2\pi(ux + vy)/N)$$

Equation (7.3) defines the two dimensional, discrete, Fourier transform. This equation transforms the input image $I(x,y)$ into its transform $F(u,v)$. Equation (7.4) defines the inverse operation which converts the Fourier transform back into the original image. For simplicity, the equations show the case when the image is square and of size N by N pixels. The transform is the same size as the original image. In the equations, x and y represent the coordinates of a pixel in the spatial domain and u and v represent the coordinates of a pixel in the frequency domain. Also, j is the square root of -1.

Comparison of equation (7.3) with the general form of domain transforms, given in equation (7.1), shows that the transform kernel contains an exponential expression involving potentially complex results. The expansion of the term is given with equation (7.3). This term is the origin of the sine and cosine waves which constitute the Fourier representation. Because the exponential term may be a complex number, even though the original image $I(x,y)$ is real, the product is in general complex and we need a complex image (section 1.1.2.2) to represent the transform. This has significant consequences for the amount of storage required.

It is not immediately obvious from equation (7.3) what significance the real and imaginary parts of the transform have, and in particular how they relate to the amplitude and phase of the corresponding sine and cosine wave components. However, it is possible to express equation (7.3) slightly differently and arrive at the quantities which we want. First, we separate the real and imaginary parts.

$$F(u,v) = R(u,v) + jI(u,v) \tag{7.5}$$

Here, $R(u,v)$ represents the real part of the transform and $I(u,v)$ its imaginary part. We met functions which perform this separation in section 3.3.9.1. Now we can express the transform as

$$F(u,v) = |F(u,v)| e^{j\phi(u,v)} \tag{7.6}$$

where

$$|F(u,v)| = \sqrt{R^2(u,v) + I^2(u,v)} \tag{7.7}$$

and

$$\phi(u,v) = \tan^{-1}\left[\frac{I(u,v)}{R(u,v)} \right] \tag{7.8}$$

$|F(u,v)|$ is the magnitude of the transform. Equation (7.7) shows how we can compute the magnitude of any particular Fourier component from the real and imaginary parts of the corresponding pixel in the transform. An image, composed of these values, is known as the **Fourier spectrum** of the image $I(x,y)$. It is a real quantity and it is the image which we view when we display a Fourier transform. The magnitude of the transform shows the amplitudes of all of the sine and cosine waves which can be used to represent the original image. This image is the two dimensional equivalent of the frequency response graphs often used to illustrate the performance of audio equipment, such as microphones, amplifiers and loudspeakers. The quantity $\phi(u,v)$ is the phase of the transform. It contains the information about the phases of the individual sine and cosine wave components. Equation (7.8) shows us how to compute the phase for a given pixel in the transform.

At this point, we should perhaps summarise the representation of the two dimensional, discrete, Fourier transform as an image. The Fourier transform is an image composed of pixels which represent spatial frequency components. The position of each pixel encodes the spatial frequencies which it represents, one in the x direction and one in the y direction of the original image. The further a pixel is from the origin, the higher the spatial frequency which it represents. The amplitude and phase of the sine and cosine waves with particular frequencies are coded as a complex value stored in the appropriate pixel of the image. The actual amplitude and phase can be recovered from the stored value using equations (7.7) and (7.8).

7.1.1.2 Displaying Fourier spectra

There are some practical difficulties to be overcome when displaying the Fourier spectrum of an image. The first of these arises because of the wide dynamic range of the data in the frequency domain. The spectrum is a real image with a floating point value at each pixel location. The values must be re-mapped to an integer range compatible with the chosen display device. Given the limited range of contrast available on typical displays, it is common for a few spatial frequency components to dominate the spectrum, making it impossible to discriminate many, low amplitude components. The zero frequency term is commonly the largest single component. It is also frequently the least interesting when inspecting a spectrum. One solution to the problem is simply to ignore this component completely for purposes of display. Sometimes it may be necessary to ignore other low frequency components as well if they also have significant amplitude. This can be done, provided that these components are not of any interest.

Another possible solution to the problem is to display the logarithm of the spectrum rather than the spectrum itself. We saw, in section 3.3.8, how the logarithmic functions can be used to reduce the dynamic range of an image, and they are just as effective for the Fourier spectrum. In this case, the scaled logarithm function is exactly what is required as it reduces the dynamic range of the spectrum and re-maps it to the desired grey level range in a single operation. The problem of zeros in the spectrum, which are invalid as input to logarithm functions, is usually overcome by adding 1 to the spectrum before taking the scaled logarithm. This has the added advantage that zero values in the spectrum map to zero values after the logarithm has been taken.

Figure 7.3(a) shows the Fourier spectrum of the train image without modification. Hardly anything can be seen. Figure 7.3(b) shows the same Fourier spectrum without its zero frequency component and without the one and two cycle compo-

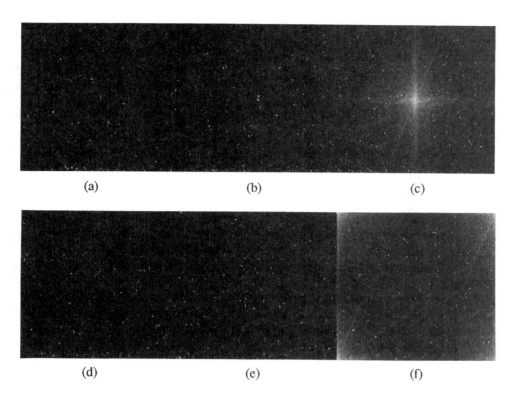

Figure   7.3. Displaying Fourier transforms as images. (a) Optical form of the Fourier transform of the train image, (b) (a) after removal of the zero, one and two cycle
components, (c) logarithm of (a) after adding 1 to avoid the zero problem, (d)
standard form of (a), (e) standard form of (b), (f) standard form of (c).

nents. There is more detail visible then when these low frequency components are
present, but there is still much of the spectrum which cannot be seen. With the low
frequency components removed, the other components, which have lower amplitude,
can be re-mapped to use the full grey scale range of the display. This is the origin of
the modest improvement in the visibility of other components. Finally, Figure 7.3(c)
shows the scaled logarithm of the spectrum after adding 1 to avoid the problem of
zeros. This image shows the most detail. Low amplitude components can be seen
right out to the limiting frequency of 1 cycle per pixel.

    A further issue arises when displaying spectra. It is the question of the position of
the origin of the spectrum. Because images are indexed from their top left hand
corner, the resulting spectrum is as well. This is in contrast with the normal method
of displaying Fourier spectra in which the zero frequency component is placed at its

centre. Because of the particular properties of the Fourier transform, this shift of origin can be carried out by the simple expedient of rearranging the data within the spectrum image array. The shift function, which we met in section 5.6.1, will perform the required operation. We need to shift the spectrum image by half its width and half its height to move the origin appropriately. Fourier spectra with the origin in the centre of the image are often called **optical transforms** since they are equivalent to Fourier transforms carried out optically, using diffraction gratings. Strictly speaking, they should be called optical spectra but this terminology seems not to be used.

Figure 7.3(a)-(c) show the optical form of the Fourier spectrum of the train image displayed in various ways. Figure 7.3(d)-(f) show the standard form of the same spectrum. The optical form is normally preferred when inspecting a spectrum.

7.1.1.3 The Fast Fourier Transform

We have already seen that the domain transforms are, in general, expensive to calculate. Direct computation of equation (7.3) requires of the order of N^4 operations. In this estimate, we ignore the computation of the individual values of the exponential term. These can be computed once and stored in a suitable table. For an image 512 pixels square, we need of order 6.9×10^{10} operations to form the Fourier transform. By exploiting the separability of the transform kernel and employing an algorithm known as the **Fast Fourier Transform (FFT)** the number of operations can be reduced to being of order $(N^2 \log_2 N)$. This reduces the number of operations to about 2.4×10^6 an improvement of nearly 30000 times.

Because of its computational efficiency, the Fast Fourier Transform is the preferred method of computing the Fourier transform. A practical restriction of most implementations of the technique is a requirement for images of a predetermined size. The image must have an x size and y size which is an integer power of 2, for example 128, 256, 512 and so on. In practice, this is not much of a restriction and the technique is very widely used.

7.1.2 Applications of the Fourier Transform

Now that we understand something of the computation of the Fourier transform, we are in a position to discuss some ways in which it can be applied in image processing. These applications include image filtering and correlation, which can often be carried out more efficiently in the frequency domain than in the spatial domain. The Fourier transform can also be used for image compression, and for feature detection.

7.1.2.1 Filtering in the Frequency Domain

Some useful filtering operations can be carried out on the Fourier transform of an image rather than on the image itself. When we discussed filters in section 6.2 we talked about them in terms of spatial frequency. Low pass filters, which attenuate the high frequency components, have a smoothing effect on the image whereas high pass filters which attenuate low frequencies have sharpening or even edge detecting properties. In the Fourier transform of an image, we have a direct representation of these very spatial frequency components. Consequently, we can perform high and low pass filtering, and others besides, by direct manipulation of the spatial frequency components in relation to one another. We will look at three such manipulations and discuss some difficulties which can arise.

7.1.2.1.1 The Ideal Filter

An ideal filter is one in which a certain set of frequencies is passed through unaffected whilst all others are completely blocked. The term 'ideal' arose because such filters cannot be directly realised using analogue electronic components and all practical filters are in some sense approximations to the ideal. Again, this terminology shows a historical origin in electronics and signal processing.

Actually, from the point of view of filtering an image, this filter is far from ideal. It shows some unpleasant characteristics as we shall see. We will consider a low pass filter. This filter has a value of 1 from the origin out to a certain frequency, ω_c, beyond which it is zero. Figure 7.4(a) shows a filter of size 512 by 512 pixels of which only pixels out to a radius of 60 are non-zero. In this image, white represents no attenuation by the filter and black represents 100% attenuation. If we make an optical transform from the image to be filtered and multiply this transform by the filter, we will set to zero all the transform components with frequencies greater than ω_c. The transform, and hence the image after transforming back to the spatial domain, have been low pass filtered. Figure 7.4(b) shows the Fourier transform of the train image. The bright circle shows the area of the transform which will be retained after filtering. The logarithmic form of the transform has been used for this figure so that the high frequency components can be seen. However, it should be emphasised that the filtering takes place on the transform itself, not on its logarithm. Figure 7.4(c) shows the transform after filtering. Clearly, all components beyond the radius of the filter have been set to zero. Finally, Figure 7.4(d) shows the result of transformation back into the spatial domain. This image has clearly been smoothed, but artifacts are also present. They are known as ringing, yet another piece of terminology from signal processing and electronics. Ringing is a characteristic artifact of this kind of filter, which effectively truncates the series of terms defined by equation (7.3). In general it is best to avoid the ideal filter and choose one of the smoother filters which overcome this problem.

(a)   (b)   (c)

(d)

Figure   7.4. The ideal filter. (a) Ideal filter of radius 60 pixels, (b) scaled logarithm of the
Fourier spectrum of the train image. Bright circle shows area of transform
retained after filtering. (c) Filtered version of (b), (d) filtered train image after
inverse transformation

7.1.2.1.2 The Root Filter

The ideal filter uses a simple but dramatic method of reducing the amplitude of
high frequency components of the frequency domain image. It just discards them.
Rather more subtle approaches reduce the amplitude of the high frequency components in relation to the low frequency ones. The most general case is that of convolution in the Fourier domain and we will look at that in section 7.1.2.2. There are
other approaches. For example, the roots of a series of values show lower dynamic
range than the values themselves. This is trivially shown by a simple example.
Figure 7.5 shows a series of values and their square roots. Clearly, the values have a
dynamic range of 64 to 1 whereas the square roots have a dynamic range of only 8
to 1. The implication of this reduction in dynamic range is that low amplitude values
have been increased in relation to those of higher amplitude. We have already noted

x	1	4	9	16	25	36	49	64
$\sqrt{x}$	1	2	3	4	5	6	7	8

Figure   7.5. Tabulated values of simple square roots

that high frequency components of Fourier transforms tend to have low amplitudes. Indeed, we needed to reduce the dynamic range of the spectra themselves in order to be able to see them on a display (section 7.1.1.2.) Consequently, by taking some root of the magnitude of the Fourier transform we will tend to increase the low amplitude, high frequency components in relation to the high amplitude, low frequency ones. This is the basis of the root filter, which is consequently a sharpening or high pass filter. We can express the filter in the Fourier domain as

$$V(u,v) = |F(u,v)|^{\alpha} e^{j\phi(u,v)} \tag{7.9}$$

This equation says that the root filtered Fourier transform $V(u,v)$ is the original Fourier transform but with the magnitude raised to the power α. Figure 7.6(a) shows the effect of root filtering the train image with α set to 0.5 . This is a square root filter.

In practice, the root filter is performed via a number of steps. First, we compute the normal Fourier transform $F(u,v)$. Most image systems will deliver this as a standard transform and not in magnitude and phase form. Consequently, we must convert to magnitude and phase form using equations (7.7) and (7.8) before the root operation can be applied to the magnitude term. Then we need to convert back to standard form before finally applying the inverse Fourier transform and recovering the result image in the spatial domain.

Though we have discussed this filter as the root filter, values of α greater than 1 make it a power filter. It is not referred to as such in the literature. The converse of our argument for roots leads us to expect that this will be a low pass filter, since it increases the high amplitude, low frequency components in relation to the low amplitude, high frequency ones. Figure 7.6(b) shows the effect of an α of 1.5. The filter is indeed smoothing the image, though the effect it produces, of viewing the Festiniog[†] railway locomotive through a thick Welsh mist, is rather hard to explain convincingly.

[†] In Welsh, the place name Ffestiniog is spelled with two F's. The name of the railway, on the other hand, is spelled with just one. Apparently, the railway's Act of Incorporation was drawn up in London by Englishmen unable to spell the name correctly!

(a)   (b)   (c)

Figure   7.6. Root filtering. (a) The result of root filtering the train image with α of 0.5, (b) with α of 1.5, (c) and with α of 0

As a final example of the root filter, consider the case when α is 0. This has the effect of making the amplitude of every component the same, namely 1.   Any resulting variation in the spatial domain result must be entirely due to the effect of phase. Figure 7.6(c) shows the effect of root filtering the train image this way. The outline of the locomotive is discernible despite the fact that this image was reconstructed with essentially no amplitude information whatsoever.

7.1.2.1.3 The Generalised Cepstrum

We have already used logarithms to reduce the dynamic range of a Fourier spectrum so that we can see detail in it when displayed (section 7.1.1.2.) We have also seen that high pass filtering can be performed by reducing the dynamic range of the magnitude of the transform using the root filter. The **generalised cepstrum** of an image is performed in the same way as root filtering, but instead of taking the root of the magnitude, its logarithm is used instead. We can express the operation in the Fourier domain as:

$$S(u,v) = (\log |F(u,v)|) \, e^{j\phi(u,v)} \qquad (7.10)$$

As with the root filter, this operation is defined on the magnitude of the Fourier transform. Consequently it is necessary to convert between the standard and magnitude and phase representations of the transform during the operation. Once again, this operation is a high pass filter. Figure 7.7(b) shows the generalised cepstrum of the train image.

(a)   (b)

Figure   7.7. Generalised Cepstrum. (a) Train image, (b) generalised cepstrum of (a)

7.1.2.2 Convolution in the Fourier Domain

In chapter 6 we mentioned that convolution could be carried out in the frequency domain. Performing convolution in the frequency domain does not change the nature of the operation nor does affect the results. The filters which we discussed in section 6.2 work in exactly the same way in the frequency domain as in the spatial domain. The difference is one of implementation. As we saw in section 6.1.1, the computational load for convolutions in the spatial domain increases rapidly with filter size. In the frequency domain there is no such correlation. The cost of the forward and reverse Fourier transforms required to allow the the convolution to be performed in the frequency domain can be more than recovered by the simplicity of the convolution calculation itself, provided the filter mask is large enough. We have already remarked that the precise break even point, when convolution in either domain carries the same computational cost, depends on the particular processor on which the calculations are being run. However, it can be worth going into the frequency domain for filter masks as small as 9 pixels square.

What, then, is the origin of the reduction of the computational burden of the convolution calculation in the Fourier domain? It arises because of what is sometimes termed the **convolution theorem**. This can be written:

$$f(x,y) \otimes g(x,y) \Leftrightarrow F(u,v)\,G(u,v) \qquad (7.11)$$

The left hand side of this expression represents the convolution of image $f(x,y)$ with a filter $g(x,y)$. The symbol $\otimes$ denotes convolution. The right hand side represents the product of the Fourier transform $F(u,v)$ of the image and the Fourier transform $G(u,v)$ of the filter. The symbol $\Leftrightarrow$, which links the two sides, indicates that they form a **Fourier transform pair**. This means that the left hand side can be converted into the right hand side by a normal Fourier transform. Likewise the right hand side can be converted into the left hand side by an inverse Fourier transform.

(a)   (b)

Figure   7.8. Image and convolution mask for the Fourier domain. (a) Image, (b) convolution mask. The active area of the mask is shown by the white circle. Values beyond this region are zero.

The practical significance of equation (7.11) is that in the Fourier domain, the convolution requires only a single multiplication for each image pixel, rather than the expensive sum of products operation required in the spatial domain, as defined by equation (6.10). The steps needed to perform a frequency domain convolution are as follows

- Perform a Fourier transform on the image

- Perform a Fourier transform on the filter

- Multiply the two transforms together

- Form the spatial domain result by an inverse Fourier transform on the product.

This still leaves a couple of questions unanswered. For example, what do we mean when we talk about the product of the Fourier transform of the image and mask? After all, the masks we looked at in section 6 were very much smaller than the images involved. What size must the transform of the mask be and how do we create it? In fact, the answer is quite simple. We make the mask the same size as the image by padding it out with zero pixels. The active part of the mask, that is to say the part other than the padding, must be centred on the zero frequency component of the transform of the image. If we are using the optical form of the Fourier transform, we create the convolution mask by placing the active part of the filter in the centre of an image the same size as the image to be filtered. Then we transform this image to form the convolution mask in the Fourier domain. Figure 7.8 shows the image, the active part of the mask and the padding in the spatial domain.

Now that we have a mask of the appropriate size, the formation of the product in the Fourier domain is trivial. It is the normal multiplication operation described in section 3.2, albeit for the complex data type.

One further issue which we have not covered is that of normalisation. When we transform the image back to the spatial domain we have essentially the un-normalised version of the filtered image. If the mask components in the spatial domain sum to a value other than 0 or 1, it may not be possible to hold the result image in the same data type as the original. One solution is to normalise the spatial domain result image by dividing by the sum of the mask elements before conversion to the data type of the original. An alternative approach, which we did not consider in chapter 6, because we were dealing with integer images and masks, is to convert the mask to floating point form in the spatial domain and to normalise it before taking its Fourier transform. Normalisation of the mask involves dividing each mask element by the sum of the mask elements. The resulting sum of the mask elements is then 1, leading to a normalised convolution.

7.1.2.3 Correlation in the Fourier Domain

As with convolution, correlation can also be performed in the Fourier domain. The considerations of computational efficiency are almost identical, due to the similarity of the operations performed. As with convolution, we can express a Fourier transform pair for correlation.

$$f(x,y) \circ g(x,y) \Leftrightarrow F(u,v) \, G^*(u,v) \tag{7.12}$$

The left hand side of this expression represents the correlation of image $f(x,y)$ with window $g(x,y)$. The symbol $\circ$ denotes correlation. The right hand side represents the product of the Fourier transform $F(u,v)$ of the image and the complex conjugate of the Fourier transform $G(u,v)$ of the window. The symbol * in this case denotes the complex conjugate. The steps needed to perform the correlation are very similar to those required for convolution.

· Perform a Fourier transform on the first image

· Perform a Fourier transform on the window

· Form the complex conjugate of the transform of the window

· Form the product of the transform of the image and the complex conjugate of the transform of the window

· Form the spatial domain result by an inverse Fourier transform on the product.

As with spatial domain correlation, normalisation may be needed.

Once again, the window needs to be padded with zeroes to bring it to the same size as the image. As with the convolution mask, if the optical form of the transform is being used, the window is placed in the centre and padded around the edges in the same way as shown in Figure 7.8 for convolution masks.

As with convolution, the use of the Fourier transform for correlation is to enable an efficient implementation when large windows are in use. The results obtained in the spatial domain are identical with those obtained in the Fourier domain.

7.1.2.4 Other Applications of the Fourier Transform

There are many other applications of the Fourier transform in image processing. Several of the more important of these applications are discussed in other sections of the book. For completeness they are listed here.

inverse filtering

> A restoration technique which attempts to correct for deficiencies in the image acquisition system (section 8.3)

Weiner filtering

> Another restoration technique which attempts to correct for deficiencies in the image acquisition system (section 8.4)

transform mapping

> An image compression technique based on the Fourier domain representation of the image (section 7.3.1.1.4)

detection of periodic features

> Use of characteristic features in the Fourier domain image to indicate the presence of some feature in the spatial domain (section 9.2)

7.1.3 Other Domain Transforms

We saw the general form of a domain transform in equation (7.1). There are a number of well known examples of these transforms which differ in the kernel which they use. Though we will not cover the other domain transforms in detail, they are described briefly here for completeness. Once again, though the equations of the transforms are given, it is not necessary to understand them fully to appreciate the applications of these domain transforms. We will encounter these transforms again in section 7.3.1.1.4 when we look at transform mapping, an image compression technique.

7.1.3.1 The Walsh Transform

The Walsh transform is a domain transform with some particularly attractive properties, from the point of view of its computation. Like the Fourier transform, its kernel is separable. It can be implemented via an algorithm similar to the FFT, with similar saving in computational overhead when compared with direct calculation. It is a real transform and as such requires less storage per pixel than the Fourier transform, which is complex. It does not require any trigonometric or exponential functions in its computation. The forward and inverse transforms are identical. Any algorithm capable of implementing one can implement both.

Since domain transforms represent all the data in the spatial domain image, but in different form, the Walsh transform is just as valid a representation of the data as is the Fourier transform. It does not have the properties of the Fourier transform which allow us to compute convolutions and correlations effectively. However, it does provide an efficiently computed, domain transform which can be used for image compression.

The forward and inverse Walsh transforms are defined, in two dimensions, by

$$W(u,v) = \frac{1}{N} \sum_{x=0}^{N-1} \sum_{y=0}^{N-1} I(x,y) \prod_{i=0}^{n-1} (-1)^{[b_i(x)b_{n-1-i}(u) + b_i(y)b_{n-1-i}(v)]} \tag{7.13}$$

and

$$I(x,y) = \frac{1}{N} \sum_{x=0}^{N-1} \sum_{y=0}^{N-1} W(u,v) \prod_{i=0}^{n-1} (-1)^{[b_i(x)b_{n-1-i}(u) + b_i(y)b_{n-1-i}(v)]} \tag{7.14}$$

In these equations, terms of the form $b_i(x)$ mean the ith bit of the value x. For example, if $x = 128$, $b_7 = 1$ and all other values are 0. Also, in these equations, $N = 2^n$ and the transform is defined only for images whose sizes are integer powers of 2. Though the equations may initially appear complex, the kernel of the transform involves only the product of terms which are 1 or -1. The lack of exponential or trigonometric terms makes the transform simple to compute.

7.1.3.2 The Hadamard Transform

The Hadamard transform is closely related to the Walsh transform. The forward and inverse Hadamard transforms are defined in two dimensions by

$$H(u,v) = \frac{1}{N} \sum_{x=0}^{N-1} \sum_{y=0}^{N-1} I(x,y) (-1)^{\sum_{i=0}^{n-1} [b_i(x)b_i(u) + b_i(y)b_i(v)]} \tag{7.15}$$

and

$$I(x,y) = \frac{1}{N} \sum_{x=0}^{N-1} \sum_{y=0}^{N-1} H(u,v) \, (-1)^{\sum_{i=0}^{n-1} [b_i(x)b_i(u) + b_i(y)b_i(v)]} \qquad (7.16)$$

Once again, in these equations, terms of the form $b_i(x)$ mean the ith bit of the value x. As with the Walsh transform, $N = 2^n$ and the transform is defined only for images whose sizes are integer powers of 2.

Like the Walsh kernel, the Hadamard kernel is separable. However, it cannot be implemented directly via an algorithm similar to the FFT without some additional work being performed. Like the Walsh transform, it is a real and as such requires less storage per pixel than the Fourier transform, which is complex. Again, it does not require any trigonometric or exponential functions in its computation. Finally, the forward and inverse transforms are identical, and any algorithm capable of implementing one can implement both.

The Hadamard transform provides another method of representing the data from a spatial domain image be used for image compression.

7.2 PRINCIPAL COMPONENTS ANALYSIS

So far in this book we have really only considered single images. We have mentioned that colour images are often digitised as groups of three images, one containing the red, one the green and one the blue component, but we have not considered how such groups of images might be used together for any purpose. Groups of images of the same scene but differing in spectral properties are known as **bands**. The ensemble of bands is known as a **multi-band** or **multi-spectral** image.

The archetypal source of multi-spectral images is the earth observation satellite. Satellites, such as Landsat, are designed to send back detailed information about the surface of the earth. This information is used in a wide range of endeavours from the monitoring of agricultural activity to prospecting for new mineral deposits. Multiple bands are acquired to aid in solving the segmentation problems associated with this sort of data. Certain kinds of ground cover have characteristic spectral signatures which can be detected by having data for each ground point at a variety of wavelengths. Indeed, later Landsat spacecraft have a detector, known as the thematic mapper, in which the detectors have been chosen specifically to aid differentiation between soil, vegetation and water. Using the many bands available from this kind of satellite it is possible to make quite subtle distinctions in ground cover, even to the extent of identifying different crops.

Later versions of the Landsat series of spacecraft carry a 5 band instrument, known as the multi-spectral scanner (MSS), as well as one known as the thematic mapper, which has 7 bands. The MSS records data in the green and red part of the visible spectrum and has two near infrared bands and one in the far infrared. The thematic mapper has a band in the green, one in the yellow and two in the red part of the visible spectrum. It has two near infrared bands, at longer wavelength than those of the MSS, and a far infrared band.

The information gathered by each of the bands in the two instruments aboard a Landsat satellite is not unique. Each detector responds to a range of wavelengths of visible or infrared radiation. These ranges overlap and consequently different detectors 'see' each other's data. This phenomenon is called **spectral overlap**. The result of this overlap is that the the 4 bands of the MSS, for example, are quite highly correlated. This means that, in principle, we could hold an amount of information, equivalent to that in the 4 MSS bands, in less storage. Each image for each MSS band contains some 7.6 million pixels. It covers a ground area approximately 185 kilometres square with 3240 pixels on each of 2340 rows. Consequently, the 4 shortest wavelength bands of the MSS require a little over 30 megabytes of storage for each multi-spectral image. If we can reduce that figure, by removing the effects of the correlation, we should be able to store the same information in substantially less space. The process by which this can be achieved is known as **principal components analysis**.

In addition to the purely practical benefits of storage reduction, principal components analysis is also often a first step in the automatic classification of ground cover. We will look at classifications in section 9.1.4.

7.2.1 The Hotelling Transform

Principal components analysis is based on the Hotelling transform. Rather in the way that the Fourier transform is an equivalent way of representing a single band image, the Hotelling transform provides a new but equivalent way of representing a multi-band image. If the original image has m bands, the Hotelling transform of the image will also have m bands. However, the bands in the transformed multi-spectral image are ordered in terms of their information content. The first band has the largest information content, the second the next largest and so on. The later bands may contain so little information that visually they resemble noise. The storage saving comes from discarding these low information content bands.

The Hotelling transform can be written as a vector equation

$$\mathbf{p} = \mathbf{H}(\mathbf{b} - \mathbf{m}) \qquad (7.17)$$

In this equation, $\mathbf{p}$ is a transformed vector, $\mathbf{H}$ is the transformation matrix, $\mathbf{b}$ is the original vector and $\mathbf{m}$ is vector representing the expectation value of $\mathbf{b}$. We will look at the specific meaning of each of these values shortly. For the moment, the point to note is that equation (7.17) shows us how to transform from our original data in $\mathbf{b}$ to the result in $\mathbf{p}$.

The vector $\mathbf{b}$ represents the set of pixel values in each band at a given position. For the Landsat MSS data, excluding the far infrared wavelengths, this vector is of

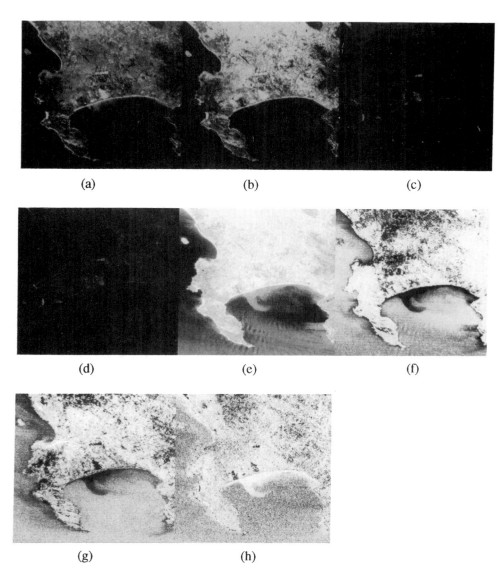

Figure 7.9. Principal components of a multi-spectral image. (a) the green MSS band (band
4), (b) the red MSS band (band 5), (c) the first near infrared MSS band (band 6),
(d) the second near infrared MSS band (band 7), (e) the first principal component, (f) the second principal component, (g) the third principal component, (h)
the fourth principal component

length 4. The choice of ordering of the elements within **b** is arbitrary so long as we use the same ordering at each pixel position. An ordering based on wavelength would make the first element of **b** the pixel from the green MSS band, the second element the pixel from the red MSS band, the third element the pixel from the shorter wavelength near infrared band and the last element the pixel from remaining near infrared band. In a sense, we are reorganising the data as a large number of short vectors rather than as a small number of large images. Applying the Hotelling transform to this large collection of vectors gives us a new collection of vectors which we can subsequently view as images. If we apply the transform to a set of full size Landsat images, we will be processing 7.6 million such vectors.

Before we can apply equation (7.17) we need to evaluate **H** and **m**. We'll look at **m** first. It was referred to earlier as the expectation value of **b**. This simply means that it is a vector in which each term is the mean of the value of the terms in the same position in each of the **b** vectors. So, in our example, the first element of **m** is the mean pixel value of the green MSS band, the second is the mean of the red MSS band and so on. To be strictly accurate, the mean pixel value (section 4.1) is an approximation to the expectation value under the assumption that each possible value of a pixel is equally likely. We assume that the approximation is valid.

All that remains, then, is to compute the transformation matrix **H**. This is defined as being the matrix whose rows are the normalised **eigenvectors** of the **covariance matrix** of the original images. That sounds a little complex, so we'll take it a step at a time. First we need to understand what the covariance matrix of the images is and how it is computed. Covariance is a measure of how two variables move together. If two bands of the MSS data are highly correlated, we would expect that their brightness values would move together. Bright pixel values in one band would correspond with bright pixels in the other. The covariance of the pair of bands would be high. The measure of how well the bands move together is very simple. For each band we compute the difference between the pixel value and the mean. The entry in the covariance matrix for a given pair of bands is just the product of these differences. If a given pair of bands is well correlated, when one of them is above its mean value the other will be as well and the product of differences is positive. Likewise, when one of the bands is below its mean, so is the other and again the product is positive. Summation over the whole image will tend to give a positive value. If the bands are not correlated, the situation where one is above its mean whilst the other is below it is as likely as that when both are above or both are below. Summation over the whole image will give values close to zero.

In our example, where we have 4 bands, we can compute 16 covariance values. However, there are only 8 independent values because the covariance of A with B is just the same as the covariance of B with A. We can produce a 4 by 4 covariance matrix for our 4 band image with each element representing the covariance of one particular combination of bands. We can compute a covariance matrix for every one of the **b** vectors, as described above. We can write this calculation for the ith **b** vector as follows

$$\mathbf{B}_i = (\mathbf{b}_i - \mathbf{m})(\mathbf{b}_i - \mathbf{m})^T \tag{7.18}$$

In our example, using Landsat MSS data, there will be 7.6 million such covariance matrices. To compute the overall covariance matrix for all the **b** vectors we need to form the expectation value of all these $\mathbf{B}_i$ matrices. As before we approximate this as an average:

$$\mathbf{C} = \frac{1}{N} \sum_{j=0}^{N-1} \mathbf{B}_i \tag{7.19}$$

In this equation the summation of the matrices simply involves summing the terms in equivalent positions. For our example of the 4 band MSS image the result of the summation is a 4 by 4 matrix. The division by N, the total number of pixels in each band, also simply divides each term in the matrix which results from the sum. **C** in our example is a 4 by 4 matrix. **C** is the covariance matrix of the original images, which we need in order to compute the transformation.

The final part of the computation of the **H** matrix is to determine the eigenvalues and eigenvectors of **C**. These quantities are characteristics of any given matrix. They can be computed directly from the values within the matrix. Eigenvalues and eigenvectors are defined in terms of the solutions to particular kinds of matrix equation. They occur commonly in the solution to problems in applied mathematics, physics and engineering, for example. In our example of the 4 bands of MSS data, our matrix **C** is a 4 by 4 matrix. It is a property of the eigenvalues of a matrix of size m by m that it will have at least 1 and at most m eigenvalues. We can expect there to be 4 in our example. Associated with each eigenvalue will be an m element eigenvector. Again, in our example these vectors will have 4 elements and we can expect 4 of them. Consequently, we can build a 4 by 4 matrix by making each of its rows one of the eigenvectors. This matrix is the desired transformation matrix **H**. It is normal, when constructing **H** to use the eigenvectors in the order of decreasing eigenvalue. Then, after application of equation (7.17), the resulting image bands will be in order of decreasing information content.

In this discussion of the computation of the transformation matrix, two important elements have been ignored. First, we have not discussed why this particular form of transformation has the desired property of removing the correlation between the bands from the lower numbered principal components. A proof of this property is well beyond the scope of this book. However, Figure 7.9 demonstrates the effect. Figure 7.9(a)-(d) show show the 4 MSS bands we have been discussing. These images are corrected forms of the raw satellite data and have been reduced to 512 pixels square. Figure 7.9(e)-(h) show the resulting principal components. It is clear that the majority of the information from the 4 bands is in the first two principal components. Indeed the last principal component contains almost nothing but noise, the third one being little better. The eigenvalues of the C matrix indicate the information content of each band. Typically, with this type of data, 95% of the information is in the first two principal components.

The second element in the computation of H which we have not discussed, is the derivation of the eigenvalues and eigenvectors from the covariance matrix C. Fortunately, eigenvalues and eigenvectors are so widely used that, like the Fourier transform, extensive studies have been made to find general purpose ways of computing them. The available methods are efficient and maintain accuracy. Consequently, given the matrix C there are standard, computational techniques available which allow us to compute its eigenvalues and eigenvectors without our needing to be concerned about the details. Most mathematical subroutine libraries contain implementations of these techniques.

Principal components analysis allows us to remove correlation between the bands of multi-spectral images. The technique can be used to reduce the amount of data needed to represent a particular set of images. The removal of redundant information has the obvious practical effect of reducing the amount of storage required to hold the data. It is also a useful precursor to image classification, a process which we will discuss in section 9.1.4.

7.3 IMAGE COMPRESSION

Image compression is a thoroughly pragmatic operation. Images require large amounts of data. Storing and transmitting this data places a significant load on the computer systems and data transmission facilities used. Compression of the data can reduce the cost of image storage and increase the effective speed of transmission.

There are two broad categories of image compression techniques. Before using a particular compression technique, it is important to know to which category it belongs. The first category consists of methods which completely preserve the original data. When the compressed image is converted back into its uncompressed form, it is identical with the original image. For this kind of compression to be effective, there must be some redundancy in the original data. There usually is, but the scope for compression is somewhat limited. For a grey-scale image consisting of 8-bit, unsigned integer pixels, information preserving compression techniques typically achieve compression ratios of 2:1 at best. The compressed image requires half the storage of its uncompressed form. Images from satellite are normally compressed by techniques which preserve information. It is important not to loose data which may be important in the future. Medical images also normally fall into this category.

Indeed, some countries are already investigating legal requirements for the kinds of compression which can be used for archiving medical images in digital form. An ironic consequence of this desire for absolute fidelity is that future medical archives, as well as accurately recording the images of their patients, will also faithfully reproduce the original noise, from the medical imaging instruments, for years to come.

The second category of compression techniques consists of methods which only approximate the original data. In general, the less accurate the resulting image needs to be, the greater the compression which can be achieved. In this class of techniques, we can exploit not only any redundancy in the data, but also the ability to make approximations.

With this second category of techniques it is obviously important to know, for any given application, how much degradation in image quality can be tolerated. It is possible to apply objective measures of quality. For example, the original image can be compared with the result of compression followed by decompression. The differences can be expressed as a kind of signal to noise ratio which characterises the compression technique. This might be the ratio of the average difference to the average pixel value in the original image, for example. If the purpose of the image data is for use in some automated segmentation and analysis process, the real criterion for fidelity is that enough information is preserved to allow the necessary subsequent operations to be carried out. In this case an objective quality measure may be appropriate. If, on the other hand, the purpose of the images is to be viewed and analysed by a human operator, a more subjective measure of fidelity may be required in which people are asked to judge the resulting images by looking at them and giving their opinions.

Binary images represent a special case as far as image compression is concerned. Partly, this is because of the tremendous commercial possibilities of replacing paper documents with scanned, binary images. It is also because relatively poor reproductions of the original images, in terms of objective fidelity, are still eminently legible. There is plenty of scope for compression ratios well beyond 10:1 when binary image data is involved.

There are two major components in any compression scheme. The **encoder** takes the original image and compresses it. The **decoder** takes the compressed image and reproduces the original image, or an approximation to it. In the next section we will look at encoders in detail and discuss a number of the approaches which can be used. In a subsequent section we will look at decoders. Finally, we will discuss some common compression schemes as combinations of these basic building blocks.

7.3.1 Components of the Encoder

There are three basic components in an encoder. The first stage is called the **mapper**. It converts pixel data into another form which can be more effectively used by the subsequent stages. The second stage is called the **quantizer**. This stage applies the approximation in compression techniques which do not preserve information. The quantizer assigns the mapper output to one of a smaller number of different values. In compression techniques which preserve information, the quantizer is normally absent. The final stage is the **coder**. It converts the output from the mapper or quantizer into some bit pattern and it is this which is the final compressed form of the image.

7.3.1.1 The Mapper

The job of the mapper is to convert the pixel data of the original image into a form which is more amenable to quantization or coding. We will examine four techniques for mapping input values in this section. They become progressively more expensive to compute.

7.3.1.1.1 Run-Length Mapping

One of the simplest forms of mapping which is commonly used is **run-length mapping**. Compression techniques based around this mapping, and using an appropriate coder, are known as **run-length encoding** techniques. In run-length mapping, each row of the image is treated as a separate sequence of pixels. The mapping involves locating sequences of l_j identical pixels, each with pixel value p_j and using the value pair (p_j, l_j) to represent the whole set of pixels. The group of l_j pixels has been mapped to the value pair (p_j, l_j). The effectiveness of this mapping relies on there being many groups of consecutive pixels of identical value within the image. Clearly, it is going to require more data to represent a large number of individual pixels as value pairs than as the pixel values themselves. Only when we can replace large numbers of pixels by a single value pair can we see any compression. Actually, it is not always wise to judge the overall performance of a compression technique on the basis of the mapper alone. Its job is not so much to compress as to provide the opportunity for compression. However, in the case of run-length encoding, much of the compression actually does come from the mapper.

For general grey-scale and colour images, run-length mapping is normally quite unsuitable. Runs of identical pixels almost never occur. However, one kind of image does offer significant opportunity for this technique. A thresholded image, such as that shown in Figure 3.5(a), has large areas of contiguous pixels of a given value. Such images compress well using a run-length mapper. Other binary images also offer the scope for compression using run-length mapping.

7.3.1.1.2 Differential Mapping

Differential mapping is commonly employed in the compression of grey scale images. It exploits the observation that, whilst typical images do not contain runs of identical pixels, neighbouring pixels are often of a similar value to one another. We can verify this observation by looking at figure Figure 3.6. This figure shows the gradients in the train image. Much of the gradient image is dark, indicating that in most places, the gradient is small. Consequently, except at edges, neighbouring pixels are similar in value. The difference between one pixel and the next is normally small. The number of occurrences of pixel to pixel differences of a given size falls rapidly as that size increases. This turns out to be very favourable from the point of view of coding, as we will see in section 7.3.1.3. Briefly, if we can induce statistics in which a small number of values occur with high frequency, we can assign very short codes to them and so achieve a large amount of compression. We reserve longer codes for less frequent values. Differences between one pixel and the next normally show these favourable statistics.

In differential mapping, we start with the first pixel value on a row and compute the difference between it and the second pixel. Then we move to the second pixel and compute the difference between it and the third pixel. The process continues along the row. We store the first pixel value and all the differences. It is worth pointing out that the differences can require more storage than the original pixels. For our normal 8-bit unsigned integer image, pixel to pixel differences vary from +255 to −256, a total range of 512 values which requires 9 bits of storage per pixel. Clearly, unlike the case of run-length mapping, there is no compression which results from the mapper alone. Differential mapping relies on providing input which the coder or quantizer can compress well.

7.3.1.1.3 Differential Predictive Mapping

A small modification of differential mapping can modify the statistics further in the direction which aids coding. Instead of storing the differences between successive pixel values, the next pixel value is estimated or **predicted** from some simple model of the image. The values stored are the differences between the predicted pixel values and the actual pixel values. If the model accurately predicts the pixel values, the differences will be small.

In this technique, we are effectively replacing some of the image data by a model of the way the image varies. If the image is predictable, we are saying that some of the data is redundant and can be replaced by a simple computation which can regenerate it. The data that we need to send represents the deviations of the actual image from the model. We can use a very simple model to predict the image. It is called a **linear estimator**. It predicts the next pixel on a given row from the previous pixel value and some image statistics. The form of the estimator is

$$\hat{x}_i = \rho x_{i-1} + (1 - \rho)\bar{x} \tag{7.20}$$

In this equation, $\hat{x}_i$ is the estimate of the pixel value at position i, x_{i-1} is the actual pixel value at position $i - 1$ and $\bar{x}$ is the average pixel value for the entire image.

The value ρ is the coefficient of correlation between successive pixels. It is normalised and is given by

$$\rho = \frac{E(x_i\, x_{i-1})}{E(x_i^2)} \qquad (7.21)$$

Here, E indicates expectation value, as before, and we approximate this by a mean value. When adjacent pixel values are highly correlated, ρ tends towards 1 and equation (7.20) leads to estimates which are close to the value of the preceding pixel. If ρ is 1, the technique reduces to differential mapping. When the pixels are not highly correlated, ρ tends towards 0 and equation (7.20) leads to estimates which are close to the mean pixel value of the image. In fact, ρ is typically in the region of 0.9 and equation (7.20) estimates pixels primarily on the basis of their predecessors.

The result of applying this technique is a set of values given by

$$d_i = x_i - \hat{x_i} \qquad (7.22)$$

The differences passed to the quantizer or coder are those between the actual pixel value and the estimate, rather than between successive pixels. For values of ρ approaching 1, the variance of the d_i values is much lower than that of the pixel values themselves. As with the differential mapper, this confinement of the range of values which occur commonly is the source of the compression available in the coder.

7.3.1.1.4 Transform Mapping

A further method of reducing the correlation in an image, and thereby enabling its compression, is by transforming it into a different domain. We have already seen what a prodigious amount of computation is required for these transforms. Also, the resulting, transformed image is floating point or complex and requires a significant amount of storage. One way to mitigate these difficulties is to divide up the transform process into a series of smaller transforms. We can, for example, divide a 512 by 512 image into 1024 subimages, each 16 pixels square. These subimages can be transformed and coded separately.

The Fourier and Hadamard transforms are commonly used in transform mapping. We have already noted that the result of these transforms is a floating point or complex image. Consequently, since the transform is the same size as the original image, there is an increase in the amount of data during the mapping process. Compression using these techniques comes from the relatively greater importance of the low order terms in the transform. This means that higher order coefficients in the transform can be ignored. Further savings can be made by quantizing the values which result from the mapping and coding them appropriately, as we shall see in section 7.3.1.2

Image compression is concerned with removing redundancy from image data. We saw, in section 7.2, that the Hotelling Transform could be used to remove redundancy from sets of images. It is equally applicable to removing it from a single image composed of subimages. For this application, the vectors **b** are composed by concatenating together the rows of one of the subimages. For the 16 by 16 pixel subimage of our example, the vector has 256 elements. The first 16 are the first row of the subimage, the second 16 are its second row and so on. Equations (7.17-7.19) hold for this situation and allow the relevant transformation matrix to be computed. The resulting transform, like the Fourier and Hadamard transforms, has the majority of the image information in its low order coefficients, allowing high order terms to be ignored. Indeed, the Hotelling transform is theoretically the best transform from this point of view, though in practice all three transforms perform similarly well.

7.3.1.2 The Quantizer

Compression techniques which are not information conserving employ a **quantizer**. This component maps its input into a smaller number of possible output values. A range of input values is converted to the same output value by the quantizer. Consequently, the quantizer is not reversible and information cannot be conserved. As an example, consider the problem of coding the result of a transform mapping. The transforms produce floating point or complex valued images. The pixels have huge dynamic range, as we saw in section 7.1.1.2 when we were trying to find suitable techniques for displaying them. To make the task of compression manageable, we need to reduce the total number of different values which need to be transmitted and allow a compact code to be used. In our example, we might try to find a set of integer values which could adequately represent the transform. This is the job of the quantizer.

A typical quantizer works as follows. The set of possible input values is divided up into a number of ranges. Each range is associated with one of the possible values which can be output by the quantizer. Each input value is examined to determine the range to which it belongs and the associated quantizer value is output.

Most quantizers work on this simple principle. What distinguishes them from one another is the manner in which the total input range is divided up. There are two basic categories of quantizer. In uniform quantizers, each input range is of identical size. This approach is suitable for images in which each pixel value is approximately equally likely. In non-uniform quantizers, the individual ranges differ and are chosen to allow the best approximations for the particular form of the input data. The basic idea is to provide smaller input ranges in the vicinity of the most common pixel values. This allows a better approximation to common values, at the expense of poorer approximations to rarer ones. The overall effect is to reduce the total error, introduced by the quantizer.

7.3.1.3 *The Coder*

The final mapping, during image compression, takes place in the **coder**. The coder input is an integer, constrained to be one of a fixed set of possible values. Coder input may come directly from the mapper, in information conserving compression techniques, or it may be the output of a quantization stage. For each possible input value, the coder outputs the associated **code word**. Unlike the quantizer, the coder is reversible. Each input value is associated with exactly one code word. A coder which can accept 256 input values, will produce 256 different code words. No additional error is introduced into the compression process by the coder.

Codes comprised of code words which are all the same length are known as **equal length codes**. Whilst simple to generate and decode, equal length codes fail to exploit a property of most image data which can allow additional compression. For most images, whether in the spatial domain or after transformation, the probability of a pixel having a particular value varies significantly with that value. Only for spatial domain images which have been histogram equalised (section 4.5.2) is this untrue. Also, most mappers try to modify the statistics of the data to obtain this property. Consequently, if we use short codes for high probability pixel values, we can reduce the overall amount of data which needs to be used to code the image. Once again, the cost of needing to use longer codes, for low probability pixels, is more than recovered by the frequent use of short codes. Codes which use this approach are called **unequal length codes**.

As you might expect, there is a theoretical lower limit to the amount of data required to code a given image without loss of information. This lower limit, expressed in bits per pixel, is given by the entropy of the image (section 4.6.) Indeed, schemes based on unequal length codes are sometimes referred to as **entropy coding**. The entropy represents a limit on the performance of any coding scheme we might choose. As a simple example, in the case of the perfectly histogram equalised image which we used in section 4.6, there is no point in looking for a code which can reduce the number of bits needed to represent the image. All pixel values are equally likely and the image's entropy is 8 bits per pixel. Direct coding of the image, without some prior mapping step, cannot result in compression without loss of information. However, in the case of the thresholded image, the entropy is only 1 bit per pixel and we can look for codes which provide compression. In this case, one particularly obvious equal length coding can be used. We can represent the pixels with values below the threshold as 0 and those with values above it as 1. Clearly this satisfies the 1 bit per pixel requirement. It is also satisfies the criterion of being as compact as theoretically possible, without loss of information.

The statement, that the best possible compression for our thresholded image is 1 bit per pixel, may have caused some consternation. Does this mean, for example, that the theoretical limit on run-length mapping of binary images is a compression to 1 bit per pixel? Actually, no. To see this we have to remember one of the premises of the entropy calculation. The calculation assumes that the input values are independent of one another. In terms of images, this amounts to discarding information about the spatial relationships between pixels. This is information which we exploit in run-length mapping. Consequently, we may expect to find some situations in which we can compress more than we might expect, from the entropy considerations, by exploiting spatial information.

In this section we are interested in how entropy relates to the coder. We have already noted that the job of the mapper is to reduce correlation between the values used in subsequent stages of the compression scheme. Consequently, we can expect that, if a suitable mapper has been employed, the entropy of the data presented to the coder will fairly accurately represent its information content. An interesting case to consider here is that of a perfectly histogram equalised image being presented, first without mapping, and then after differential mapping. We have already seen that entropy considerations lead us to the conclusion that the image itself cannot be compressed since all of the possible pixel values occur an equal number of times. However, if we perform differential mapping, there is no reason to suppose that the histogram of the differences will be equalised, simply because that of the image is. The differences depend on the spatial arrangement of the pixels as well as on their values. The unequal histogram of the difference image gives a lower entropy, and the possibility of compression in the coder. Since the mapper and coder are reversible, we can re-create the original image without loss of information.

We have not reduced the entropy of the original image by taking differences. All we have done is allowed ourselves to get a better estimate of it. It is important to bear in mind, that the entropy calculation is based on the assumption of un-correlated data. We can apply it to the coding stage of the compression because the data coming from the mapper or quantizer is normally not highly correlated.

7.3.1.3.1 Huffman Codes

Huffman codes can be shown to be the most compact coding for any given set of data to be compressed. In fact, it can be shown that Huffman codes will achieve bit per pixel rates equal to the entropy of the data if the associated probabilities are all negative powers of 2. Even when they are not, Huffman codes usually achieve rates close to this theoretical limit. Huffman codes are relatively easy to construct, but do rely on explicit knowledge of the probabilities of each possible value in the data. Figure 7.10 shows a table of values which we can use to demonstrate formation of a Huffman code. The data to be coded can take 4 different values. The probability associated with each value is shown in the column headed *Pr*. This column is in decreasing probability order. From the probability data we create the column 1, with one less term than the probability column, combining the two lowest probability terms. In this case the terms are 0.2 and 0.1 and their sum, 0.3, is used in column 1. Once again, column 1 is ordered by decreasing probability. Since we have two identical terms, it is arbitrary which we place higher in the column. Column 2 is created

Code	Pr	Col 1	Col 2
1	0.4(1)	0.4(1)	0.6(0)
00	0.3 (00)	0.3 (00)	0.4 (1)
010	0.2 (010)	0.3 (01)	
011	0.1 (011)		

Figure   7.10. Huffman coding

from column 1 in just the same way. This time the two 0.3 terms are combined to produce 0.6. Again, column 2 is written down in decreasing probability sequence.

The formation of columns stops at column 2 as it contains only two terms. We can now begin assigning bits for the codes. The bit patterns used at each stage are shown in parentheses in Figure 7.10. In each case, when assigning bits to adjacent pairs of values, we assign 0 to the upper one and 1 to the lower. Hence the 0.6 term in column 2 receives the value 0 whilst the 0.4 term is assigned 1. If we follow the 0.4 term back through column 1 to the probability column, we discover that it was never the result of a combination. Its code, for the data given, is 1. Following the 0.6 term back, we discover that it was the result of combining the two 0.3 terms in column 1. Both of these terms retain the prefix 0, gained from column 2. We add a second 0 to the upper term and a 1 to the lower term as before. Once again, if we follow the upper 0.3 term back to the probability column, it takes part in no further amalgamations and its code is 00. The lower 0.3 term in column 1, however, resulted from the combination of the 0.2 and 0.1 terms in the probability column. These both inherit the 01 code from column 1 and again we append a 0 to the upper term and a 1 to the lower, resulting in codes 010 and 011 respectively.

The resulting set of codes illustrates a crucially important attribute. No individual code is ever a prefix of another code. This means that there is never any ambiguity in the decoding step. Once a string of bits which corresponds to a code has been detected, the value corresponding to that code can be emitted by the decoder. Codes with this attribute are sometimes called **instantaneous** codes, because they can be decoded unambiguously as soon as a given code is recognised. Other kinds of code may require that the decoder look at the subsequent one or more bits before it can decide how to decode the bit string.

Because of their efficiency, it might appear that Huffman codes are universally the best for use in compression. However, this is not necessarily true. There are two factors worth considering. Most important, because Huffman codes are so compact, there is no redundancy and errors due to the transmission or storage medium cannot be corrected. This may not be a problem for images stored on highly reliable media, such as magnetic disk. However, for transmission over noisy channels, such as telephone lines, error recovery, or at least the minimisation of difficulties caused by errors is very important. Consequently, other codings are frequently used. The second factor which must be considered is that each image to be transmitted has its own Huffman code. The coder must first determine the codes to be used and construct a table which represents the mapping. This table is sometimes known as the **code book**. The code book must be stored or transmitted with the compressed image, adding to the amount of data. Usually, the code book is much smaller than the image to which it relates, but its size must be taken into account. If the mapper or quantizer for a given compression technique also have characteristic parameters or tables, these too will form part of the code book.

7.3.1.3.2 Shift Codes

Shift codes can be implemented by a simple technique, which requires less work than a Huffman code. The resulting codes are still reasonably efficient. Again, the use of these codes assumes that the mapper has arranged the data values in order of decreasing probability. As an example, consider using a shift code based on 2-bit code words to code 8 different values. A 2-bit code word allows us to implement 4 code words. We use 3 words to represent the first 3 data values to be coded. The final code word represents a shift. The second set of 3 data values is represented by the 3 normal code words, but prefixed by the shift code word. The final 2 data values are coded by the first 2 code words prefixed by 2 shift code words. Figure 7.11 shows the table of code words produced.

The code is much simpler than a Huffman code and does not need a separate code book, though as we already mentioned, mapper data might need to be passed to the decoder. The number of bits used in the code, will affect the overall size of the compressed image. Too few bits for a given class of image will result in an excessive number of shift words being necessary. Too many, will result in unused bits being present in the compressed image. Either situation is suboptimal.

7.3.2 Components of the Decoder

The decoder in any compression scheme is very similar to the encoder. Naturally it works in reverse. First, the coded data must be decoded using the inverse code mapping. If this is a Huffman code, the code book must be available to the decoder.

Input	Code
0	00
1	01
2	10
3	1100
4	1101
5	1110
6	111100
7	111101

Figure   7.11. Shift coding. Use of a 2-bit shift code to represent 8 possible data values. The code words 00, 01 and 10 are used for data. Code word 11 represents a shift.

The result of applying the code mapping must now be mapped back to the original pixel values. Next, the inverse of the quantization stage must be performed, if quantization was used. We have already noted that this step is not full reversible. Finally, the inverse of the initial mapping needs to be applied.

7.3.3 Some Complete Compression Schemes

We have seen that a compression scheme consists of a mapper, optional quantizer and coder. Though we have looked at these components individually, we have not yet seen how they can be used together to implement a complete compression scheme. Consequently, we now look briefly at two complete encoders, one of which is information conserving, the other of which is not.

Gonzalez and Wintz (1977)   describe an information preserving encoder for remote sensed data from Landsat. The basic data is 7-bit unsigned integers and this is mapped to 8-bit signed integer differences. No quantization is performed, as this is an information preserving compression. Histograms of the differences show that the vast majority lie between +8 and -8. Consequently, they use a 4-bit shift code to represent the difference data. The 14 values between -7 and +6 are directly coded. The remaining code words are used to indicate shifts of more than +6 and less than -7. Gonzalez and Wintz (1977) report compressions of about 2:1 on typical Landsat data. Their technique compares favourably with Huffman coding of the same data.

As an example of a compression technique which does not preserve information, we will look at a form of transform coding. First, we map the image with a Hadamard transform. Using subimages of about 16 by 16 pixels has been found satisfactory and indeed smaller subimages do not appear to degrade the images much visually. Next, we have to quantize the pixels of the subimage transform. There is considerable dynamic range in the coefficients which makes it difficult to quantize them. Consequently it is usual to compute the mean and variance of the transform and then to normalise the pixels by dividing by the variance. Compression is achieved by discarding the higher order transform components and usually, about half of the pixels will be retained. This approach once again yields compression ratios of about 2:1 for grey scale images. It can be improved a little by employing a Huffman code on the quantized transform components.

In encoders like this one, it is possible to increase the amount of compression beyond 2:1, at the expense of the quality of the resulting image. The number of transform coefficients retained during encoding can be reduced. Also, the quantization step can be made less precise. Most compression techniques which are not information preserving allow this kind of trade off, of compression against quality, to be made.

7.4 TRANSFORMING PIXEL REPRESENTATIONS

In this section we look at transformations suitable for converting grey scale and colour images to be compatible with particular forms of output device. We will see that all of these transformations are based on properties of the human visual system. First, we look at grey scale transformations. Subsequently we will look at colour transformations.

7.4.1 Transforming grey levels

It is often necessary to modify the range of grey level values which an image uses. We saw one kind of transformation in section 3.6, when we looked at grey scale re-mapping. However, there are other techniques which are more suitable to solving the particular problem of displaying a grey scale image on a device with a smaller number of distinct grey levels than the image itself.

One way of reducing the number of grey levels in an image to some arbitrary value, to satisfy display requirements, is known as **error diffusion**. As with all techniques for representing grey level images with a smaller number of shades, it exploits known properties of the human visual system. In particular, it makes use of the human visual system's tendency to average brightness values over small areas. Patterns of light and dark pixels tend to merge together and are perceived as an area of intermediate brightness. In effect, we are trading off a small amount of spatial resolution in order to improve the perceived grey scale.

Input range	Threshold	Output Value	Equiv- alent Input
0—63	64	0	0
64—127	128	1	64
128—191	192	2	128
192—255	256	3	192

(a)

	*	7/16
3/16	5/16	1/16

(b)

Figure   7.12. Error diffusion.   (a) Input ranges for thresholding for 4 level error diffusion, (b)
       fraction of error diffused to neighbouring pixels. The pixel marked * is the
       current pixel.

The general principle of error diffusion was reported by Floyd and Steinberg
(1976) and it has been used, subsequently, in a variety of ways. The technique consists of two steps. First, we evaluate the error caused by the new representation of
the pixel. For example, we can set up a number of threshold values for the input
image, as shown in Figure 7.12. Input image pixels are assigned to the output value
associated with the value range into which they fall. In our example, an input pixel

(a)   (b)   (c)

Figure 7.13. Error diffusion and Thresholding. (a) Original image, (b) image thresholded
         according to Figure 7.12, (c) image fully error diffused according to
         Figure 7.12

of 73 will be given an output value 1. On its own, this process yields images
showing a significant amount of contouring. It is, after all, a 4 level version of the
normal threshold operation. Figure 7.13(b) shows the train image processed this
way.

    Having assigned the output pixel value, we can now also assign an error. We
give each input range a notional value. For example, we could consider that the
output value 0 really does mean 0 displayed intensity. An input value of 42, say,
which gets assigned an output of 0 has been darkened by 42 units. The pixel is too
dark and we can correct the error by lightening surrounding pixels before thresholding them. In a similar way, each output level is associated with a nominal input
level to allow the error to be calculated. These values are shown in Figure 7.12 in
the column labelled 'Equivalent Input'. In this particular case, all the errors will be
positive.

    The final part of the technique involves spreading, or 'diffusing', the error around
neighbouring pixels. This is done before the pixels are themselves thresholded and
converted. It is normal to process the image from top left to bottom right, the natural
image sequence. As a consequence, error can only be passed to pixels to the right,
on the same row, and to rows below the current one.   The second table in
Figure 7.12 shows a simple error diffusion matrix. The fractions shown normalise
the error. The pixel whose error is being diffused is shown as *. The pixel to its
right gets 7/16 of the error. The nearest neighbours in the next row get 3/16, 5/16
and 1/16 respectively. Figure 7.13(c) shows the effect of the full error diffusion to 4
levels. This is clearly a much better approximation to the original image, judged
visually.

There are a number of ways in which the process can be tuned for different devices. One is to alter the effective input values associated with each input range. These can be moved to account for non-linearity of the display brightness as it varies with pixel value. The modified error values which result, will help to compensate for the non-linearity. Naturally, the effective input value should remain within the input value range with which it is associated. A second way in which the technique can be tuned is by using different error diffusion matrices. In particular, on devices with pixels which are physically smaller, it can be beneficial to use larger matrices.

The major advantage of the error diffusion technique is that it is very simple to implement and does not require much computation. Indeed the technique can be implemented in hardware. The major drawback is that the regularity of the diffusion matrix means that patterns do tend to appear in the resulting image. This happens in regions devoid of texture and where the grey level is changing smoothly. They are not particularly unpleasant, but might be mistaken for real image features if the user is unaware of their real cause. The patterns become more noticeable as the number of available output levels decreases. On a 16 level display, for example, they are almost invisible at normal viewing distances.

7.4.2 Binary Approximations to Grey Scale Images

One of the commonest requirements, in pixel transformation, is to generate a binary representation of a grey scale image. The obvious application is in image printing. Also, many computer screens, particularly those on personal computers or older workstations, are limited to showing 1 bit per pixel. Conversion is necessary before images can be displayed. Whilst it is possible to view images on such displays, they are not normally suitable for serious, grey scale image work.

Since image printing is by far the commonest requirement for conversion of grey scale to binary, we will concentrate on it here. However, the techniques described are in general suitable what ever the output device. There is one difference, however, between printers and displays which is worth noting here. The dots which make up an image on a display are bright. Those on a printer are dark. The device dependent tuning, which we will mention later, operates differently in the two cases.

7.4.2.1 Damped Error Diffusion

A very simple modification of the error diffusion technique (section 7.4.1) works reasonably well for binary images. A single threshold is established, typically at grey level 128. Pixels are assigned to a white output value if above the threshold and to a black output value otherwise. Normally, for a printer, the black output value is 1 and the white output value is 0. The output value represents the presence of ink. Error is diffused in the same pattern as shown in Figure 7.12. The difference is that the denominator of the fractions used for spreading the error is changed to 19 from 16. The numerators remain unchanged. Consequently, not all of the error in a given

(a)   (b)   (c)

Figure   7.14. Damped error diffusion and ordered dither. (a) Original image, (b) expanded
             view of part of (a) rendered using damped error diffusion, (c) expanded view of
             part of (a) rendered using ordered dither

pixel is spread to the neighbours. This is the origin of the term 'damped' used to
describe the technique.

The patterning effect, already described in relation to error diffusion, afflicts
damped error diffusion in much the same way. Patterns in smooth areas tend to be
quite noticeable in binary images produces this way. However, the technique is
simple and relatively fast and capable of generating reasonable quality printed
images. Figure 7.14(b) shows an expanded view of part of the train image rendered
by damped error diffusion. In this case, the image was processed for output on a
display, so the dots used are white.

7.4.2.2 Ordered Dither

The **ordered dither** technique is another relatively simple approach to the task of
generating a binary approximation to a grey scale image. In this case, the approach
is to lay a small mask over each portion of the image in turn. The movement of the
mask **tiles** the image. Once computation is complete at one point, the mask is moved
on by an amount equal to its width. This is in contrast with mask movement in, for
example, spatial convolution (section 6.1), where the mask moves by only one pixel
each time.

The mask contains a set of threshold values. If the pixel underlying the mask is
greater than the threshold, a white value is placed in the output image. If it is less, a
black value is placed there. As before, black is usually represented by 1 for printer
output. One possible mask, or ordered dither matrix, for use with 8-bit unsigned
integer images is

136	192	160	128	116	60	92	124
168	232	224	212	84	20	28	40
200	248	244	180	52	4	8	72
152	184	216	148	100	68	36	104
112	56	88	120	140	196	164	132
80	16	24	44	172	236	228	208
48	0	12	76	204	252	240	176
96	64	32	108	156	188	222	144

Larger sized masks can be used. However, above about 8 pixels square there is normally little, visual improvement. Figure 7.14(c) shows an expanded view of part of the train image rendered by ordered dither.

The design of the mask is based on approximating the local grey level of the image by a black dot which is larger for dark regions and smaller for light regions. In this respect, the technique is very similar to **halftoning**.

7.4.2.3 Halftoning

Halftoning originated in the publishing industry as a way of converting photographs into a form in which they could be printed. Much of the terminology has been retained in the digital form. Basically, halftoning is another mask based approach. This time the mask is known as a screen. The screen is laid onto the image to be halftoned, and the area under each tile is examined. Its average brightness is calculated. From this, the number of output pixels, which need to be turned on is determined. If the tile corresponds to, say, 32 pixels and the average grey level of the input image under the tile is 128, clearly 16 output pixels need to be white and 16 need to be black. Notice that, unlike ordered dither, no account is taken of the number or value of the individual pixels, of the input image, which are under under the tile. Only the average value is used.

The second stage of the process involves determining which of the output pixels should be turned on. There are two common approaches, which correspond to spot and line screens in traditional printing. The spot approach turns on pixels in such a way that, for printing, a white spot appears in the centre of the tile and grows towards the edge of the tile as the pixel value increases. In the line approach a thin white line appears across the tile and gradually increases in width, as the pixel value increases.

The screens used are not normally parallel with the image rows and columns. The tiles may be angled at 45°, for example. One advantage of this technique is that the averaging which occurs makes the resulting image independent of the original image resolution. The size and resolution of the resulting image is determined by the screen parameters and scaling factors. The input image is automatically re-sampled.

Halftoning with very high resolution screens, for example more than 500 lines per inch, can yield printed results of the highest quality. These techniques are routinely used by publishers of high quality volumes. The same technique is also used by printers which support the PostScript[†] language. Unfortunately, PostScript is often used with laser printers which typically have resolutions of the order of 300 to 400 pixels per inch. Using screens of about 5 pixels square, to obtain about 25 different brightness values, reduces the spatial resolution available to some 60 dots per inch. Each dot is a tile, rather than an image pixel. The quality of images reproduced this way at these medium printer resolutions is poor. Error diffusion and ordered dither are much better approaches since they avoid the wastage of the available device spatial resolution inherent in the halftoning approach. Whilst with high resolution screens, very high quality results can be obtained, halftoning is best avoided for use with laser printers in the medium resolution range.

7.4.3 Transforming Colour Resolution

Colour images are often digitised at 24 bits per pixel. For example, in section 1.3.1.6 we saw how colour images could be digitise one primary colour at a time. Each band was an 8-bit unsigned integer image. Though there is an ever increasing number of 24-bit colour displays available, the amount of storage they require to hold the image and the data bandwidth which they require to achieve reasonable display speed mean that they are expensive and tend to require high performance computer systems to drive them. In the short term, at least, they will continue to be used for rather specialised purposes and for applications which demand the highest display quality.

Displays capable of showing 8-bit colour images are much more common and much less costly. Even though these displays are limited to showing only 256 colours simultaneously, it is still possible to achieve good quality colour reproduction on them. We will look at two basic approaches. One creates a custom colour look-up table, or palette, by investigating the colours which actually occur in the image. The other builds a **universal palette** which contains sets of colours from which reasonable representations of all colours can be derived.

7.4.3.1 Custom Palettes

The basic philosophy of custom palette techniques is to try and find a palette which will allow the image to be displayed as nearly perfectly as possible. First, a histogram is constructed of the colours which actually occur in the image. When it is complete we can, for example, look-up how many pixels have a red value of 42, a green value of 97 and a blue value of 3. Usually, most possible pixel values will be unused. There are after all over 16 million possible different pixel values for a 24-bit image. The worst possible case is that every pixel is different. Consequently, for a

---

[†] PostScript is a trademark of Adobe Systems Incorporated.

512 by 512 pixel image, about 256 000 different values will occur. Usually, however, it is much less than this. Even so, there will usually be many more than the 256 colours actually available.

The histogram of pixel values can be arranged in order of decreasing pixel count. The assumption is made that the more pixels there are of a particular colour, the more important that colour must be. The crudest method of selecting a palette consists of simply taking the 256 most populated colour entries from the histogram. A pixel value is assigned arbitrarily for each palette entry and the 24-bit image is transformed accordingly. Those colours not represented in the palette are approximated by using the nearest available palette entry. To measure the distance between one colour and another, the red, green and blue component values are used as if they are a three dimensional coordinate. The distance between two colours (r_1, g_1, b_1) and (r_2, g_2, b_2) is just

$$d = \sqrt{(r_2 - r_1)^2 + (g_2 - g_1)^2 + (b_2 - b_1)^2}$$ (7.23)

as we expect from normal coordinate geometry.

The problem with this approach is that there is no guarantee that there will be a suitable palette entry close to all of the unrepresented pixels. Poor approximations can have dramatic effects, especially when there are only a few palette entries available. Once, when trying to use this sort of approach for a 16 colour display, a small, but very prominent butterfly, which was bright orange in the original image, was purple in the processed image. The purple shade was the nearest available colour to the required orange and was used despite the fact that it was wholly unsuitable. The technique clearly does not fail gracefully. Though the likelihood of such a problem occurring with a 256 entry palette is less, it is a real possibility.

One approach, which can reduce the likelihood of this problem, is based on trying to avoid the palette being used up by colours which are very similar. Having established the histogram, the approach is to try and combine colours which are within some specified distance of one another. Again, equation (7.23) can be used to compute the distance. If a cluster of colours is found, it is replaced by a single palette entry which represents a reasonable approximation to all the colours. This clustering frees up palette entries for use by other, less common colours.

Whilst custom palette techniques are capable of good results, their susceptibility to sudden failure, and blatantly incorrect colour rendition, coupled with the high cost of analysing the image statistics mean that the trend is towards the use of universal palettes. A final drawback of custom palettes is due to the increasing use of window systems in image processing workstations. Normally, only one colour palette can be used at a time in a given display. Some more advanced displays can support multiple palettes simultaneously, but the number available is small and fixed. A custom palette means that only one, or at best a small number of images can be correctly rendered simultaneously. With a universal palette, all images will appear correct, regardless of how many are displayed.

7.4.3.2 Universal Palettes

A universal palette provides a single colour mapping which will render any colour image with reasonable fidelity. Rather than look at the image statistics, the 24-bit image is transformed to a representation defined by the universal palette. Several techniques are available, but all are equivalent to finding the nearest palette entry to each of the pixels in the image. However, because, in this case, the palette has been constructed to cover a good range of colours, rather than being tailored to the specific image, a reasonable approximation to every possible colour is guaranteed and no gross errors occur. The error is distributed amongst all colours rather than being confined to a few.

Universal palettes can be very simple. For example, Cowlishaw (1985) suggests that, since the human visual system is most sensitive to the yellow-green part of the spectrum, more resolution needs to be given to the green component than to the red or blue. He proposes a palette consisting of 16 shades of green, 4 shades of blue and 4 shades of red. Since these shades can occur in any combination, the total number of colours is the product of the three numbers, namely 256. This is just what is needed for an 8-bit colour display. This palette has another very desirable property. Since it is separable, in terms of the primary components, the palette entries can be ordered in a way which makes transformation of the 24-bit image to 8- bit very simple. The palette entries are arranged so that each pixel has the following struc-ture.

$$G \ G \ G \ G \ R \ R \ B \ B$$

The 4 most significant bits code the green component, the next 2 the red component and the low order 2 the blue component. The image transformation just requires error diffusion of the green component of the input image to 16 levels and the red and blue components to 4 levels each. The composite image can then be assembled by bit shifting and adding. This particular ordering of the bits in each pixel has the added advantage that the composite image is rendered quite well on grey scale displays too, though obviously not in colour.

The particular values chosen to be placed in the palette for each colour depend on the linearity of the display. For example, if the display is assumed to be perfectly linear and each colour table entry can range from 0 to 255, the 4 levels for the red component should be 0, 85, 170 and 255. These values will need to be modified to take account of display non-linearity. Actually, colour palettes should also be modi-fied in accordance with the colour response of the human visual system. After all, what we desire is that a pixel value representing twice as much red, for example, is perceived as being twice as bright when viewed. This kind of correction is known as

psychometric. High quality colour image display is possible using only 256 colours with a universal palette incorporating psychometric and display linearity corrections.

7.5 SUMMARY

In this chapter we have looked at a wide variety of ways of transforming image representations. We looked at the domain transforms and saw how useful the Fourier domain can be. We looked at the transformation involved in principal components analysis. We discussed techniques for representing images in compressed form, some of which preserve information and others of which do not. Finally we looked at ways of transforming individual pixels to make them suitable for display or printing on devices with restricted capability.

8

Restoration

In image restoration, we are interested in correcting for the known deficiencies of an image. These deficiencies may be very simple, such as a non-linearity in the brightness response of the detector used. Alternatively, they may be very complex, being caused by effects such as atmospheric turbulence or motion of the object being imaged relative to the detector. Whatever the source of the degradation, it must be possible to model it in some way, before restoration can be carried out. We will start our discussion of restoration by looking at this modelling process. Then we will look at basic brightness, contrast and geometric corrections. Finally, we will discuss the inverse filter and the Weiner filter, two powerful techniques.

8.1 MODELLING THE DEGRADATION

The fundamental problem in image restoration is to recover a corrected image from a degraded image and some information about the degradation. This information is usually called the **degradation model**. The model is normally either **analytical** or **empirical**. Analytical models arise from a mathematical description of the degradation process. Many degradations can be modelled as point spread functions. for example, atmospheric turbulence, which affects astronomical observation made from earth, can be modelled as the point spread function

$$m(x,y) = e^{-\pi\alpha^2(x^2 + y^2)} \qquad (8.1)$$

Here, α is a parameter indicating how much turbulence there is. It could be said that this equation is the reason that NASA, in collaboration with the European Space Agency, launched the Hubble space telescope in 1990. Being above the atmosphere, it should not suffer from this rather severe limitation on telescope resolution. Unfortunately, a rather embarrassing error in the manufacture of the telescope's mirror has meant that its optical performance is many times worse than it should be. The degradation has been modelled and it is ironic that it is spatially dependent and therefore more complex than the atmospheric turbulence. It is, however, not time dependent and can be corrected by a suitable restoration.

The model for a degradation which can be represented as a point spread function indicates that the degraded image can be thought of as a perfect image which has been filtered. The filter can be specified in terms of an equation like equation (8.1). Analytical models exist for a wide variety of degradations, including focus errors, blurring caused by diffraction and various forms of motion.

Empirical models result from direct measurement of the degradation. It might be possible, for example, to measure the point spread function of a given optical system. This would give us $m(x,y)$ but directly in numerical form rather than as an equation. Geometric degradations can be modelled empirically by imaging an object of known geometry and then measuring the distorted image. We will see an example in section 8.2.2. Similarly, brightness and contrast errors can be measured by imaging special targets.

As well as the brightness and geometric distortions and blurring, images usually suffer from one other degradation, namely noise. The details of noise models need not concern us here, except to say that such models do exist for photodetectors, film and a variety of other optical and electronic systems used in image capture.

8.2 BASIC CORRECTIONS

In this section we look at the most basic corrections of all. The techniques are based on forming an image of an object with known properties. This image can then be compared with a perfect image, deduced directly from the properties of the object. First we will discuss simple techniques for correcting non-linearity in the brightness response of the detector. Then we will look at making geometric corrections.

8.2.1 Brightness and Contrast Corrections
Most photodetectors show some non-linearity in their brightness response. When the intensity of the light striking the detector is doubled, the detector output voltage does not double. Typically some kind of power law is involved, though the analyt-

ical form of the relationship need not worry us. An empirical means of determining the relationship is readily available.

We can make use of a standard target, often called a **grey scale wedge**. This can be a transparency or a print. It is divided into a number of areas each of which has a known relative brightness. Grey scale wedges appear on typical test charts available for setting up and calibrating video equipment. By imaging an evenly illuminated, grey scale wedge, the photodetector response can be calibrated. The average grey level in each of the wedge areas appearing in the image can be measured and related to its actual brightness. It is not absolute brightness which is important here. Instead, it is the relationship between the brightness of each wedge area and its neighbours. A table can be constructed between photodetector output and wedge area brightness. For example, if the wedge has 9 equal steps between full black and full white, each should correspond to a change of pixel value of 32 (the range includes 0 remember). We can build a 9 entry table showing the photodetector output for each of these steps. By linear interpolation, we can complete an entire 256 entry table which corrects our camera output and makes it linear. After capturing an image, we transform it by looking up each pixel value in the input image in this table and writing out the table entry to the result image.

8.2.2 Geometric Corrections

Geometric distortions arise from a wide variety of sources. These include, aberrations of the lens or other optical components, distortions which can arise in tube based cameras and undesirable viewing angles, which are most commonly encountered in remote sensing, as we saw in section 5.5.3. However, in terrestrial applications, geometric errors can often be ignored, especially with modern, high performance optics and solid state cameras. Applications involving X-rays, on the other hand, suffer from considerable distortion. This is a consequence of the great penetrating power of this kind of radiation which makes it all but impossible to build high quality optical systems. Many image processing applications involving X-rays do not require geometrically corrected images. The diagnosis of pneumothorax from an enhanced image, which we saw in section 6.2.4, is a case in point. The objective is to make the diagnostic feature more visible, not to measure its size.

However, in one particular X-ray based medical application (Mol (1984)) geometric correctness is vital. In this application the aim is to form quantitatively correct, three dimensional models of structures within the body. To do this, pairs of X-ray images of the patient are taken simultaneously and later are used to infer the three dimensional structure. The technique is basically stereoscopy, but the angle between the two views is typically 90°. In order for the stereoscopy to work and for the resulting models to be quantitatively precise, it is vital that the images be geometrically corrected before use.

Once again, we need not be concerned with the details. However, use is made of a standard test object which can be placed in the X-ray apparatus at the same position as the patient. The test object is a perspex cube into which steel ball bearings have been fixed at known positions. The ball bearings show up clearly in the images. Given a sufficiently large number of known points visible in the images, the warping necessary to perform correction can be deduced. Due to the tendency for the X-ray apparatus to drift, the test object must be imaged, and the corrections computed before each session with a patient.

8.3 THE INVERSE FILTER

The **inverse filter** is a technique for restoring images degraded by processes which can be modelled as linear, shift invariant systems. These are the processes, discussed in section 8.1, which can be described by a point spread function. Inverse filtering is based on the idea that applying the inverse of the degradation point spread function, as a filter, to the degraded image will reconstitute the original. We can see what is meant by the inverse filter if we consider the original degradation as a filtering process in the Fourier domain. If $F(u,v)$ is the transform of the original image and $M(u,v)$ is the transform of the degradation, we can express each term in the transform of the degraded image as

$$D(u,v) = F(u,v)\,M(u,v) \tag{8.2}$$

Equation (8.2) follows from the fact that convolution in the spatial domain corresponds with multiplication in the Fourier domain (section 7.1.2.2.) Simple rearrangement of equation (8.2) yields $F(u,v)$ in terms of quantities which we know, namely the degraded image and the degradation.

$$F(u,v) = D(u,v)\left[\ \frac{1}{M(u,v)}\ \right] \tag{8.3}$$

We simply divide the transform of the degraded image by the transform of the degradation, term by term. Equation (8.3) is deliberately formulated to make the point that the restored image is formed by filtering the degraded image with the inverse of the degradation. If we have enough information about the nature of the degradation, we can actually evaluate $1/M(u,v)$. Consequently we can implement this filter. Though equation (8.3) is formulated in the Fourier domain, we can of course perform the filtering in the spatial domain if desired. The spatial domain form of the inverse filter is just the inverse Fourier transform of $1/M(u,v)$.

Though in principle this technique is very simple, there are serious, practical difficulties with this filter. In particular, if $M(u,v)$ has any zeroes, the inverse filter is undefined. A simple modification to the filter is to locate any values of 0 and to replace them by 1. This effectively ignores these values in the calculation. The

| (a) | (b) | (c) |

Figure 8.1. Inverse filtering. (a) Image degraded with Gaussian blur, (b) image restored
          with a perfect inverse filter, (c) failure of restoration due to a small number of
          errors in the inverse filter.

resulting filter is known as the **pseudoinverse filter**. Unfortunately, even this does
not overcome all of the difficulties inherent in the technique. We saw, in section
7.1.1.2, that the dynamic range of Fourier transforms tends to be large and that the
coefficients drop off rapidly the further we get from the origin. Because we are
dividing by the Fourier transform of the filter, these very small values of coefficients
can have disproportionately large effects on the result. These small values, which
can arise as a result of the necessary approximate definition of the filter, can cause
large, spurious terms to appear in the transform of the restored image, and lead to
artifacts in the final result.

   Figure 8.1 illustrates the use of a perfect inverse filter and shows what can
happen if a few spurious terms occur. Figure 8.1(a) shows an image which has been
blurred with a fairly broad Gaussian mask. Figure 8.1(b) shows the result of inverse
filtering the blurred image. The restoration is essentially perfect. We know precisely
the form of the degradation and hence we can compute precisely the right inverse
filter. The quality of the restoration should come as no surprise. After all, the degradation was performed as a Fourier domain multiplication. The restoration is simply a
Fourier domain division, using exactly the same values. Apart from rounding errors
in the calculation, the Fourier transform after the restoration is identical with the
transform of the original image, and hence, so is the spatial domain image.
However, Figure 8.1(c) shows how badly just a few erroneous terms, in the inverse
filter, can affect the restoration. A small number of terms, with amplitudes about 10^5
times smaller than the largest term in the filter, were made significantly smaller.
This dramatic effect was achieved by modifying about 10 terms from a transform
which was 512 pixels square. In the presence of noise or when the degradation is
being approximated, erroneous terms are likely and it is important to restrict their

effect. One means of doing this is to restrict restoration by ignoring those terms in $1/M(u,v)$ which have absolute values closer to zero than some some predefined value. For example, we could choose to ignore all terms smaller than 1% of the largest term in $1/M(u,v)$. To ignore the terms, we simply set them to 1 in the inverse filter. The precise value to use for the threshold needs to be determined manually by trial and error.

Image degradations frequently consist of some blurring component, often due to the optical system being used, and a noise component, due to the recording medium or electronics. If the form of the noise component is known, and its Fourier transform can be established, the inverse filter can be extended to deal with it as well. Equation (8.3) becomes

$$F(u,v) = D(u,v) \left[\frac{1}{M(u,v)} \right] + N(u,v) \left[\frac{1}{M(u,v)} \right] \qquad (8.4)$$

Here, $N(u,v)$ is the Fourier transform of the noise and the other terms are as before. The difficulty with this formulation is that it is very rarely the case that the form of the noise component is known in sufficient detail to allow its Fourier transform to be derived. Consequently, a technique has been devised which can cope with noise, without needing to know its form in such detail. This technique is known as the **Weiner filter**.

8.4 THE WEINER FILTER

The full form of the Weiner filter can be derived after a significant amount of complex mathematics. Its objective is to provide a restoration which can cope with a linear, shift invariant degradation and a noise component. In its full form, as with the inverse filter, complete descriptions of both the degradation and the noise are required. The full formulation is

$$F(u,v) = \left[\frac{1}{M(u,v)} \quad \frac{|M(u,v)|^2}{|M(u,v)|^2 + S_n(u,v)/S_f(u,v)} \right] D(u,v) \qquad (8.5)$$

As before, this equation is in the Fourier domain. $F(u,v)$ is the restored, image and $M(u,v)$ is the model of the degradation. $D(u,v)$ is the degraded image. The term $|M(u,v)|^2$ is defined as

$$|M(u,v)|^2 = M^*(u,v)\, M(u,v) \qquad (8.6)$$

It is the product of the complex conjugate of the degradation model with itself. $|M(u,v)|^2$ is known as the **spectral density function** or the **power spectrum** of the degradation model.

In equation (8.5) the new terms $S_n(u,v)$ and $S_f(u,v)$ are also spectral density functions. $S_n(u,v)$ is the spectral density function of the noise component, and $S_f(u,v)$ is the spectral density function of the original image. It is worth pointing out, that when there is no noise component, with the consequence that $S_n(u,v)$ is 0 for all u and v, the second term in equation (8.5) becomes 1, and the filter reduces to the normal inverse filter.

As has already been mentioned, it is unusual for the necessary amount of information to be available about the noise component to allow its Fourier transform, and hence its spectral density function, to be computed. However, an approximation is possible, on the assumption that these functions vary in a similar way to one another, as u and v vary. If this is true, we can approximate the ratio of the two functions by a constant value. Equation (8.5) then reduces to

$$F(u,v) = \left[\frac{1}{M(u,v)} \frac{|M(u,v)|^2}{|M(u,v)|^2 + K} \right] D(u,v) \qquad (8.7)$$

This approximation will tend to work best in those cases where the noise varies with the signal. The noise power spectrum will then tend to resemble the image power spectrum and their ratio will tend to be reasonably constant. Of course, if there is a significant amount of, for example, **white noise**, so-called because the amplitude of its coefficients in the Fourier domain is constant, this will not be a good approximation. Real noise tends to contain both sorts of component. Weiner filtering using the approximation will work well if the signal dependent noise dominates.

One advantage of the simplicity of the form of equation (8.7) is that it possible to try a range of values of K to see which has the best effect in noise removal. This can be done even when nothing is known about the actual form of the noise component.

8.5 SUMMARY

In this short chapter, we have covered briefly some techniques which can be used to make quantitative corrections to degraded images. We have looked at simple corrections for brightness and geometric errors. We also discussed powerful techniques which can correct for a variety of image degradations and noise.

9

Analysis

The vast majority of this book, indeed all of the material in the preceding chapters, is concerned with the manipulation of images to form other images. This is true whether we are considering the enhancement of a medical X-ray, to allow a doctor more easily to diagnose an illness, or whether we are doing something more frivolous, such as warping an image to make it appear as if it is painted onto a cube. We have examined a whole host of techniques for making images bigger or smaller, for changing their shape, for re-mapping their brightness range, for changing their number of bits per pixel, for compressing them and even for converting them into entirely new representations. But throughout our discussion of this vast array of manipulations, never once have we properly considered how to extract information from images. This is the subject for the present chapter.

For most image processing applications, the corrections and modifications, which we have discussed in previous chapters, are nothing more than preliminaries. It is in the analysis of the resulting images where the real value of the techniques is finally exploited. The first stage of the analysis of an image is segmentation, its division into physically meaningful sections. A discussion of segmentation makes up the first part of this chapter. After segmentation, we will look at the identification and location of characteristic features within images and finally we will discuss how structural information can be extracted.

9.1 SEGMENTATION

Segmentation is the process of dividing an image up into areas which have some physical significance in terms of the original scene. For example in the train image, which we have used throughout the text, segmenting the locomotive would involve marking every pixel in the image to show whether it belonged to the locomotive or not. We could make an intrinsic image in which all locomotive pixels white and the rest black. The result would be a white locomotive shaped patch on a black background. We could then use the intrinsic image and the original image together to answer questions about the locomotive itself. We could determine its average brightness, or the length of its perimeter. We could look at the statistics of locomotive pixels and contrast them with background pixels. We might even try to deduce some descriptors for the locomotive's shape.

Given the vast array of analysis techniques which we might wish to apply, it is unfortunate that no current, computer based, segmentation technique can provide the discrimination required to distinguish the locomotive from its background. Automatic segmentation of real scenes represents the single most difficult step in modern image processing practice. In many applications, no attempt is made to segment the images automatically. Instead, use is made of the extraordinary segmentation capability of the human visual system. An operator provides the necessary input. Another technique, frequently used in practical systems, is to arrange the image capture system so that only the object of interest is in the field of view and that the background is grossly different in brightness. Under these special conditions, thresholding can be used to segment the object from its background. It is worth taking another look at Figure 3.5, to see how poorly thresholding performs on normal scenes.

Segmentation is a spatial analysis of the image. Unlike almost all the other techniques we have discussed, it is intimately concerned with the spatial relationships between pixels. It is based on being able to group pixels into discrete regions, either because they have some attributes in common or because they are bounded by a discontinuity, such as an edge. These regions must be strongly related to areas in the original scene, since we will want to use them to infer information about the objects which were imaged. For example, we might want to detect the presence of an object by finding a suitably shaped region in the image. The real difficulty is one of inference. From a spatial distribution of brightness or colour values we are trying to infer the properties of the three dimensional objects which were originally present when the image was formed. We can confidently expect that any solution to the problem, which can rival the human visual system, will require not only the brightness or colour patterns themselves, but also a great deal of additional knowledge about the world in general and about the method by which the image was acquired, in particular. After all, we saw in section 2.4 how sophisticated is the knowledge brought to bear on the segmentation problem by our own visual systems. None of the machine based techniques available today comes close to matching that level of performance.

However, despite the lack of powerful, general purpose methods, there are many interesting segmentation techniques. Some of these can be used quite successfully to provide full or partial solutions to the segmentation problem. These techniques form the topics for this section.

9.1.1 Segmentation by Thresholding

We have already seen that thresholding is not generally a useful form of segmentation technique. However, it can be used under controlled conditions, particularly if special illumination techniques are applied. The typical situation, in which thresholding might be used, is in a parts identification application as part of a manufacturing process. A number of special conditions must be satisfied. First, whenever an image is acquired, there must be only one part in the field of view. Actually, this constraint can often be relaxed so long as multiple parts do not touch or overlap. Even partially overlapping parts can be accommodated in some applications. Next, by the very fact of choosing thresholding, we have to arrange that the brightness of every visible part of the object is significantly different from that of the background. If we fail to achieve this, the shape of the object may be distorted by the thresholding technique making recognition harder. A simple way to arrange this distinction is to illuminate the background, rather than the object itself. The result is a silhouette of the object against a bright background. Under these conditions, we can use a simple threshold operation to discriminate between the object and background. A histogram of the silhouette image is bi-modal with a large separation between object and background pixel brightness. Consequently, it is a simple matter to determine the threshold value to use and this process can be automated. The thresholding step assigns different values to object and background pixels. This process is known as **labelling**. The result of thresholding the silhouette image is an intrinsic image in which the object and background have been labelled.

Though this silhouette based technique does allow simple segmentation, the images used are relatively poor in terms of information content. When compared with a normally lit, grey scale image of the same object, the silhouette is lacking in all the detail of texture and surface shading. This information is deliberately discarded to allow segmentation to be performed easily. This feature of the silhouette image makes it ideal for simple applications, but limits its usefulness.

9.1.2 Edge Detection

Edge detection is one of the commonest approaches to solving the segmentation problem. Unlike thresholding, which detects and labels regions in the image, edge detection is concerned with detecting the boundaries which separate distinct areas. The labelling of the areas themselves is a separate step. Edge detection relies on the observation that discontinuities in brightness or colour are often associated with physical boundaries between objects. They are also associated with boundaries between different parts of the same object. Consequently, dividing an image on the basis of these discontinuities should result in segments which correlate strongly with complete objects, or with important parts of objects. It is important that the resulting segments are related to regions and objects in the original scene so that we can extract information based on them.

There are many forms of edge detector. Much research has been carried out to improve the performance of the techniques used, in terms of accuracy of edge location and immunity to noise. We will look at some specific examples shortly. However, regardless of the particular detector used, they all suffer from the same difficulties to a greater or lesser extent. This stems from the fact that they all make the same fundamental assumption about the equivalence of colour or brightness discontinuities and physically important boundaries. Whilst this is often the case, there are many exceptions. For example, a shadow lying across an object causes brightness discontinuities which are not due to any boundaries of the object itself. Also, whilst real physical boundaries are always complete, their images are sometimes not. Factors such as illumination play an important role in the visibility of boundaries. Since neither of these factors is a property of any particular technique, but is instead a fundamental property of the world, no edge detection technique will be 100% reliable. The intrinsic image resulting from any edge detecting operation will contain indications of edges which do not exist. It will also contain incomplete representations of real object boundaries. The major challenge in using edge detection for segmentation is in interpreting the resulting edge maps. The interpretation step must suppress spurious edges and complete the discontinuous boundaries. This step often utilises inference. It is required, however good the performance of the basic edge detector used.

In the sections which follow, we will look at problems associated with the computation of edge maps and at how some common edge detectors behave. Then, we will look in more detail at one edge detector in particular. The Canny edge detector has been claimed as optimal in terms of its edge location accuracy and its ability to suppress noise. Finally, we will look at how edge maps can be used to provide geometric descriptions of segment boundaries.

9.1.2.1 Computing Edge Maps

Edge detectors produce edge maps. An edge map is an intrinsic image in which each pixel represents a measure of 'edgeness' or **edge strength**. This is a measure of how likely it is that the pixel belongs to an edge. Actually, there may be other attributes associated with an edge. Many edge detectors estimate the direction of the edge as well as its strength. We will return to this shortly. We did discuss the intrinsic images associated with edge detectors in section 6.2.3.1. However, it is worth repeating here that when we view an edge map, (for example Figure 6.8), the appearance of the edges as lines is a result of our own visual system processing the data. There is no explicit connectivity in the edge map. It is merely a collection of pixels which we interpret as connected structures as we view them.

We have already met a number of directional edge detectors commonly used in simple applications.   The Prewitt, Sobel and Isotropic filters were described in 6.2.3.2. We discussed difficulties with these filters including their poor noise performance and, at the small sizes usually used, their inability to detect broad or **slow** edges. Broad edges are edges which are wider than the filter mask used in the edge detector. Since these simple, directional edge detectors are often implemented as 3 by 3 convolutions, edges which take more than a few pixels to make the transition from one pixel value to another will not yield a response from the detector. In fact, this phenomenon is a general property of any edge detector implemented as a filter. Even relatively sophisticated edge detectors respond poorly to edges which are broad when compared with their mask size.   Marr (1982)   suggested using a range of Marr-Hildreth filters of different widths to try and overcome this problem. The idea is that the wide masks detect the broad edges and that narrower and narrower masks are used to detect the sharper discontinuities. In addition, any real edge detected at a particular filter size should be present in the output of all larger filters. If it is not, the filter response is probably not due to a simple edge, but to some more complex phenomenon. The observation of responses at the same location and with the same basic properties in the output of several filters of different size increases the level of confidence that a real edge exists.

Actually, the situation is by no means as simple as that just described. First of all, certain kinds of discontinuity may not be detectable by the larger filters, though they are clearly resolved by the smaller ones. A good example is a strip, ribbon or bar which has a pair of parallel edges which can be resolved as two nearby discontinuities in the small filters. In larger filters, the extra smoothing may average the responses and remove both of them. This particular situation can be detected in the output of the narrow filter given sufficient post processing. However, the post processing has then to be carried out without the benefit of the noise reduction which should arise from combination of the filter outputs. A second difficulty, which arises in attempting to combine the output from different sized filters, is that of identifying the common responses. Canny (1986) has shown that there is a kind of uncertainty principle relating the precision of the location of an edge and the signal to noise ratio of the filter. Narrow filters locate edges more accurately, but have worse noise performance than broad ones. The change of precision with filter size means that it is unlikely that a broad and narrow filter will report the same position for the same edge. We will return to this problem, and look at one possible solution in section 9.1.2.4. For the moment, it is worth noting that there is physiological evidence that animal vision systems do have the equivalent of edge detectors which operate at a variety of scales.

Edge maps tend to contain many weak responses as well as the stronger ones caused by major brightness discontinuities. These weak responses come from two main sources. The first is noise. Random fluctuations in the image, usually caused by noise in the acquisition system's sensor and associated electronics, cause spurious, low amplitude responses from the edge detector. A second cause of these low amplitude responses are discontinuities with widths significantly different from that of the filter. We have already discussed broad edges and thin ribbons or bars. Textures can have the same effect. The multitude of edges which are close to one another tend to be averaged by the filter unless the texture size is similar to the filter width. These low amplitude responses are usually considered to be unreliable and consequently are discarded. The simplest way to do this is to threshold the edge map at some predetermined value, leaving only the strongest responses. If only a single filter width is being used, we can expect to loose important edge responses by doing this. These responses could be reliably detected by wider or narrower filters, but are too different from the given filter's width to be located from its output alone. One way to think about using multiple scales is that it allows us to be more selective when thresholding each individual filter's output in the knowledge that edges with different widths will be detected by other filters. Of course, the reconciliation of edges detected at different scales is still a problem.

9.1.2.2 *Extracting Directional Information*

So far, the only property we have considered in the output from an edge detector is edge strength. However, as well as a measure of the likelihood that a given pixel forms part of an edge, edge detectors can determine the edge's orientation. Directional edge detectors, such as the Sobel, Prewitt and Canny operators, can yield edge orientation directly for each pixel in the edge map. This orientation information can be useful in subsequent steps in which a geometric description of the edges is constructed. Omnidirectional edge detectors, such as the Marr-Hildreth operator do not provide this additional information.

For the simple edge detectors, such as the Prewitt and Sobel operators, masks can be defined at a number of orientations. The horizontal and vertical forms of the masks are shown in 6.7. In fact, for these 3 by 3 masks, 8 possible orientations can be generated by a circular shift of the outer 8 elements. Each shift changes the orientation by 45°. By applying all 8 masks to the image, 8 separate edge maps can be formed. Comparing corresponding pixel positions in these 8 intrinsic images, we can select the maximum value. The particular intrinsic image from which this pixel originates defines the mask orientation which gives the best response. This indicates the orientation of the edge to the nearest 45° Because of the symmetry, or rather the anti-symmetry, of the masks, it is not necessary to perform all 8 convolutions in order to compute the 8 intrinsic images.

The Canny edge detector uses a slightly different approach to determining edge orientation. We will look at this detector in some detail, now, as it addresses most of the problems we have already discussed in relation to the detection and localisation of edges in images in the presence of noise.

(a)   (b)   (c)

Figure   9.1. Canny   Edge   Detector.   (a) Result   of   basic   non   maximum   suppression,   (b)
strongest edges extracted from (a), (c) strongest edges displayed on the original
image

9.1.2.3 The Canny Edge Detector

The Canny edge detector (Canny (1986)) is one of a number of operators which
have been proposed after a fundamental examination of desirable characteristics.
Canny proposed three criteria which should be satisfied by an edge detector.

Good detection   The detector should only occasionally incorrectly assign edge
                          pixels, either by failing to mark true edge points or by incor-
                          rectly marking non-edge points.

Good localisation   Points marked by the detector as edge points should be as
                          close as possible to the actual position of the edge.

Single response   The detector should produce only a single response to a
                          given edge.

It should be clear that these properties are desirable for any edge detector. In fact,
the third criterion is actually contained implicitly in the first. However, it needs to
be made explicit in the mathematics used to derive the form of the detector from the
criteria.

Canny found that a sort of uncertainty principle applies when considering location
and detection performance. A limit is reached beyond which improved detectability
can be achieved only at the expense of poorer localisation, and vice versa. A com-
promise between these conflicting requirements can be reached and this leads to the
particular edge detector which Canny proposed. In fact the derivation of the operator

is anything but simple, mathematically. Fortunately, we need only be concerned with the result.

Basically, the Canny detector works by first convolving the image with a Gaussian and then taking its derivative. Local maxima in the resulting intrinsic image are taken as being edge points. In fact, Canny uses zero values in the second derivative to locate the edges, rather as Marr and Hildreth do. The difference here is that whilst the Marr-Hildreth operator finds zeros in the total derivative, the Canny operator uses directional derivatives. We can express the condition for an edge point as

$$\frac{\partial^2}{\partial \mathbf{n}^2} \, G \otimes I = 0 \tag{9.1}$$

Here, I is the image being processed and G is the two dimensional Gaussian function

$$G_r = e^{-\left(\frac{x^2 + y^2}{2\sigma^2}\right)} \tag{9.2}$$

In equation (9.1), the derivative is directional. The term $\partial^2/\partial \mathbf{n}^2$ is the second derivative in a particular direction defined by vector $\mathbf{n}$. The idea is to determine the derivatives at right angles to the edge which we are trying to detect. Vector $\mathbf{n}$ is said to be **normal** to the edge. Taking an image cross section in the vicinity of the edge and in the direction defined by $\mathbf{n}$ would show us the edge's grey level profile. A profile at right angles to the edge direction should give the best estimate of edge location.

The main difficulty in applying equation (9.1) is that we do not know the direction $\mathbf{n}$. We need to calculate it for each pixel in the image. Fortunately, this is a simple matter. We can derive $\mathbf{n}$ from the simple two dimensional gradient which we met in section 3.7. The gradient operation yields two components, one along the x axis and one along the y axis.. Equation (3.7) shows one way to extract the gradient direction from the components as an angle. Canny uses an alternative formulation which yields the vector $\mathbf{n}$ directly. This can be expressed as

$$\mathbf{n} = \frac{\nabla(G \otimes I)}{|\nabla(G \otimes I)|} \tag{9.3}$$

Here, ∇ represents the standard gradient operation which leads to the x and y components of the first derivative. Represented as a two element vector, and normalised by the magnitude of the total gradient, these components form a representation of the gradient direction consistent with equation (3.7) but easier to apply in this case. The magnitude of the total gradient can also be used as the measure of edge strength.

The steps in computing the basic Canny operator can be summarised as

1. Convolve the image with the chosen Gaussian. This convolution is separable, as we saw in section 6.2.5.2.
2. Compute the gradient components at each pixel in the resulting image
3. Compute the gradient direction **n** at each pixel
4. Compute the second derivative along the gradient direction at each pixel
5. Locate the zero values in these directional second derivatives
6. Mark the zeros as edge points.
7. Use the magnitude of the total gradient as a measure of edge strength.

The location of edge positions involves finding the local maxima in the first derivative. Consequently it is known as **non-maximum suppression**. It can be carried out by locating zeros in the second derivative, as we have seen. Particularly in the case of sharp edges, it is unusual for there to be zero values in the second derivative image. Instead, the zero values must be inferred from the behaviour of neighbouring pixels. Since the direction of the edge is known, so is the normal on which the zero lies. A simple nearest neighbour approach can be used to find the approximate location of the pixel. When the sign of the second derivative changes in moving from one pixel to the next along the normal, the zero is assigned to whichever of the neighbouring pixels has the smaller absolute value. However, a better estimate can be obtained, if desired, by linear interpolation or by fitting a simple curve through a small number of neighbouring pixels. Locating an edge point to sub-pixel accuracy in this way is known as **hyperacuity**.

Figure 9.1 shows the results of applying a Canny edge detector to the train image.

9.1.2.4 An Approach for Reconciling Multiple Scales

We have already noted that it is desirable to use a number of edge detectors of different widths when dealing with real scenes. Narrow edge detectors respond best to sharp edges whilst wider edge detectors respond to more blurred edges. A major difficulty in using a range of detector widths is in matching the responses from different filters to the same edge. Canny (1986) proposed a novel approach. It starts with the smallest filter and works upwards in size. Edges detected in the smaller filter are blurred by the Gaussian used in the larger filter. This effectively synthesises the output which would be detected in the larger filter if the only edges present are the ones detected by the smaller filter. Any discrepancy between the real output from the large filter and the synthesised output must be due to edges not found by the smaller filter. These new edges are added to the overall edge map. The process is then continued with the next largest filter and so on. The practical experiences with this technique are interesting. It turns out that the majority of edges are found by the smallest filter. Larger filters tend to locate shadow edges, shading, and boundaries between textures.

9.1.2.5 *The Search for the Ultimate Edge Detector*

The search for the ultimate edge detector has been under way for some time now. New detectors are proposed regularly.   Often, the improvement over previous approaches is marginal.   The edge maps produced by different filters are often similar, differences being due to noise performance or accuracy of location.   For example, because the Canny operator is computed only in one direction, namely at right angles to the edge, it has a noise performance superior to omnidirectional edge detectors, such as the Marr-Hildreth operator.   Contributions to the output of an omnidirectional operator from directions approximately parallel with the edge contribute no signal but do increase the noise.   Hence the worse performance of these operators.

The Canny operator does indeed seem to perform better than many other edge detectors, but it is by no means perfect, as we can see from Figure 9.1. Edge detectors, no matter how sophisticated, all suffer from similar problems, though some perform better than others. They all have a tendency to break edges which should really be continuous and to join edges which should be separate. None is perfect. This situation is unlikely to change. New operators may be proposed with better performance, but no matter how good they become they will never be able to overcome the limitation that brightness discontinuities are not always associated with object boundaries. In addition, these discontinuities are associated with other phenomena such as shadows. The consequence is that however good our edge detector, there will always be a need for some kind of post processing to turn an edge map into a believable set of geometrically described object boundaries. This post processing is likely to require the use of heuristic techniques or additional knowledge to resolve ambiguity about the edges.

9.1.2.6 *Boundary Representations*

Edge detectors produce intrinsic images in which the value of each edgel measures the likelihood that it lies on an edge. Some edgels will be genuine edge points, others will be artifacts due to noise. Edge detectors are frequently followed by some kind of thresholding of the edge map to try and reduce the effects of noise. Edgels with values less than the threshold are not considered to be edge points at all. The result is that some edges which should be continuous become broken. Even when more sophisticated thresholding schemes are used, the problem persists. Techniques which try to extract some geometric description of the edges from the edge map must try and repair these breaks without introducing spurious connections between distinct edges. This is difficult and requires some level of reasoning about the relationship between the various pieces of boundary.

The first step in extracting boundary descriptions is to find groups of connected edge points. Normally, groups are formed from sets of **8-connected** edgels. In this approach, an edgel is considered to be part of a group if it is an edge point and any of its immediate 8 neighbours is also part of the group. Groups formed this way

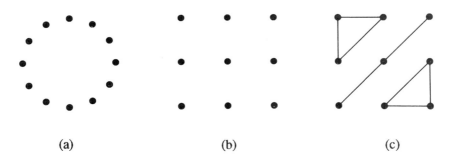

Figure   9.2. Visual grouping.. (a) Circle formed from dots (b) Square formed from dots (c)
A valid interpretation of (b) which is not spontaneously seen

typically represent pieces of an edge. The complete boundary can be found only
after the pieces are connected together. One way to do this is to utilise the information about the direction of the edge. This is available from directional edge detectors, such as the Canny operator. If another piece of edge begins not too far away
from the current one and its direction and position are consistent with it being part of
the same edge, the intervening edgels can be marked as belonging to the edge. The
pieces of edge can then be merged together to form a larger piece. The process can
be repeated in an attempt to close all the gaps in the edges.

The second step in extracting boundary descriptions is to replace the group of
edgels by some geometric description. This might be a straight line, an arc or some
other basic curve. The geometric description of the boundary is the set of parameters
which define the straight line or curve. For example, a straight boundary can be
described by its two end points and an arc can be described by its start and end
points and by a further point through which it passes. Simple geometric primitives
like these can often be described in a number of ways. The goal of the process is to
find a set of geometric primitives which describe the boundaries in the image.

This description makes the process sound deceptively simple. There are difficult
questions to answer before the technique can be applied.   For example, when
grouping edgels, how close must a pair of edge pieces be before we can consider
joining them, and how well must their direction match? If the constraints are too
restrictive, we may fail to close all the real gaps. If we are not restrictive enough,
we may join gaps between edges which are really distinct. The precise answers to
these questions are application dependent and usually have to be set by trial and
error. This is intellectually unsatisfying. Today's techniques are essentially incapable
of solving the edgel grouping problem without some help from a user.

Again, when trying to represent a group of edgels as a primitive, it might be possible to fit a straight line or an arc through the data. We need to know what the level of error must be before we abandon trying to represent the group as a straight line segment and try fitting the curve instead. The group of edgels might, in fact, represent a corner, in which case trying to fit a curve through it will also be difficult. What we probably need is a pair of straight line segments. Recognising these situations, knowing when to stop fitting with one primitive and when to start with another, spotting junctions, intersections and other larger scale arrangements is intrinsically difficult. Techniques applied tend to be based on heuristics, with the rules being deduced after observing the behaviour of algorithms on real data. Often the rules apply to one particular kind of structure and may need to be modified or extended for other applications. For example, Rake (1989) describes the steps needed to locate and describe extended, branching ribbon-like structures found in some medical and industrial images.

The boundary extraction problem is clearly soluble, however. The human visual system manages to locate and describe boundaries, apparently with consummate ease. It is also capable of performing grouping operations at long range. This may be the key to the problem of locating and representing boundaries in the presence of noise and gaps. Figure 9.2(a) is immediately recognisable as a circle. We place a simple interpretation on the dots. Even though they are quite widely separated, we recognise the figure. Similarly, we need very little information before recognising a square, as can be seen in Figure 9.2(b). Though the triangles and line shown in Figure 9.2(c) are an equally valid interpretation of the figure, it is not what we spontaneously see. Clearly, there are rules at work here. Some process is able to take disconnected elements of an image and propose an underlying arrangement which accounts for the phenomena. This is true whether it is the assumed boundaries in the Kanizsa figure of Figure 2.1(d) or the circle which we perceive in Figure 9.2(a). As yet, there are no known techniques which can allow image processing systems to achieve anything like the grouping performance of the human visual system. Nor are the rules by which this grouping takes place well understood.

Many mental processes can be described in terms of the generation of hypotheses. The brain's 'explanation' for some phenomenon appears to result from a hypothesis about its cause. The hypothesis is supported by the detected stimuli. Such 'explanations', or perceptions, often appear to be parsimonious. They are the simplest explanation possible which can account for the observations. The Kanizsa figure (Figure 2.1(d)) is a case in point. The assumed boundaries are straight, though they could have been any shape consistent with the breaks in the circles and triangle. Grouping might operate in a similar fashion. Each spot in Figure 9.2(a) adds weight to the hypothesis that the underlying shape is a circle. Competing hypotheses, such as one which postulates a set of straight lines as explaining the dots, are overruled.

There is one image processing technique which is capable of detecting long range phenomena which might be accounted for by simple geometric primitives. When compared with the abilities of the human visual system it is very restricted. However, it can be a useful tool and it does indicate that long range grouping can be detected in images. The technique is called the Hough Transform. It is interesting because, in a way, it emulates the scheme of competing hypothesis believed to be at work in human mental processes.

9.1.2.7 The Hough Transform

The Hough transform is very much simpler than the domain transforms we met in chapter 7. It does not attempt to produce an equivalent representation of the image. Instead, it collects statistics about the image which enable deductions to be made about its content. We will look at the simplest form of the Hough transform. In this form, the transform can be used to detect straight line segments in an edge map.

The equation of a straight line can be written

$$y = mx + c \tag{9.4}$$

m is the slope of the line and c is the intercept, the value of y when x is zero. If we consider x and y to be the coordinates of an edge point in our edge map, we can compute values of m and c for which equation (9.4) is true. Each pair of values represents one straight line on which our point lies. If we set up another intrinsic image in which each pixel is a count and which has m as its x coordinate and c as its y coordinate, we can accumulate counts of the number of edgels which lie on each possible straight line through the edge map. This intrinsic image is the Hough transform of the edge map. The accumulation is a little like that for a histogram. It proceeds as follows.

First we set all pixels in the Hough transform to zero. We then look at each edgel in the edge map in turn. From its x and y coordinate we find pairs of m and c values which satisfy equation (9.4). Each time we find such a pair, we increment the count in the pixel in the Hough transform which has those coordinates. When we have processed the entire edge map, we examine the Hough transform to look for local maxima. Pixels with large counts in the transform represent lines on which a significant number of edgels lie. Even if some of these edgels are rather weak, the other edgels which lie on the same line support the hypothesis that there is a boundary with those particular parameters.

The Hough transform can locate boundaries and give a geometric description of them. It works reasonably well for straight lines. However, it is computationally quite expensive. Deducing the straight lines on which a given pixel might lie involves the equivalent of a two dimensional search of the possible values of m and c. Also, this particular form searches only for straight lines. Other forms are possible which search for curves. However, curves require more parameters to specify them. For example, a circle requires the x and y coordinates of its centre and its radius. The Hough transform is no longer an intrinsic image it is a volume and its computation now involves a three dimensional search. More complex curves are consequently more expensive to identify.

As well as the increased burden of computation, the introduction of searches for edgels matching other geometric primitives brings the possibility that some groups of edgels might be accounted for by either a straight line or a curve. This is the competing hypothesis situation which we have already referred to. Some measure of goodness of fit is needed to decide how to assign the boundary.

The Hough transform has been extensively studied. Its ability to detect long range groupings of edgels makes it an interesting approach, despite the amount of computation which it requires.

9.1.3 Segmentation by Region Growing

In edge based segmentation, the aim is to locate the boundaries which separate the various regions in an image. From these boundaries, we can subsequently deduce the location and extent of each region. Often, it is the regions in which we are interested. Instead of trying to find the boundaries, we might instead attempt to deduce the extent of the regions directly. Edge detection is based on the discontinuities which occur at region boundaries. Region finding techniques are based on the absence of discontinuities within the regions themselves.

The region based approaches try to form clusters of similar pixels. Initially, clusters can be formed by grouping adjacent pixels with the same value. Naturally, for most images this tends to create a large number of clusters containing a single pixel each. The clusters are enlarged by merging neighbouring clusters. The incorporation stops when the neighbouring clusters fail to meet some measure of similarity. Various approaches are distinguished by the particular rules used to decide when to merge regions and when to keep them distinct. The rules are normally based on some measure of the strength of the boundary between the regions. The strength of the boundary at any particular position is based on examination of the values of the pixels which lie on either side. If the difference in value exceeds some threshold, the boundary location is said to be strong. If the difference is less than the threshold, the boundary location is said to be weak. If enough weak boundary locations exist, the regions can be merged.

As with edge detection, the description is temptingly simple. There are, however, difficulties in store. The variety of possible criteria for deciding whether or not to merge adjacent regions makes it necessary to try out a range of conditions before deciding what to use in any given application. Not only can the overall criteria for merging be changed, there is at least one threshold value involved as well and this may need to be tuned. Also, since the termination of the growth of a region relies on a strong boundary with the adjacent region, merging may take place incorrectly when a real region boundary is weak because of illumination effects. This is just the same sort of situation which will produce broken edges from an edge detector.

9.1.4 Classification

Classification is another approach to segmentation. Most classification techniques ignore the spatial relationships between pixels. Instead, they use statistical measures of the image to partition pixels into one of a small number of classes. Each class is associated with some particular kind of property of the scene which was imaged. The commonest application of classification techniques is in remote sensing. Typically, the goal is to classify each image pixel as one particular type of **ground cover**. It might, for example, be water, urban area, forest or some particular crop. The difficulties arise because within any one pixel, there may be multiple forms of ground cover. A simple example is a pixel centred on an area of foreshore. It will contain both land and sea. Individual forms of ground cover often have quite distinct **spectral signatures**, particular brightness ranges in each band of a remote sensed image. Despite this, when multiple forms of ground cover occur in the area covered by a single pixel, it is difficult to assign that pixel to any particular class. Classification techniques try to use statistical information to assign pixels to the most likely form of ground cover, given the particular brightness values in each band.

There are two basic approaches to classification. One requires a user to help by indicating examples of each type of ground cover to be used for the classification. The other attempts to divide the image into classes which have distinct properties. Once the classification is complete, a user must associate each class with a particular ground cover. We will look at each approach in more detail in the following sections. We will also look at a technique known as **relaxation** which can be used once a basic classification is available.

9.1.4.1 Supervised Classification

In supervised classification, areas are selected from an example image and used to train the algorithm to recognise particular types of ground cover. The data used is known as the **training set**. A user marks suitable training areas on the image and statistics are gathered from them. Normally, several examples of each class of ground cover are used and the statistics are combined. In a subsequent stage, the statistics are used to classify the rest of the image or even other images. Since the classification is based solely on the grey scale values of pixels in each band of the image, it is important that other images to be classified are acquired under similar conditions. The statistics can be modified by many different factors, including the time of day, which affects the illumination, and the time of year, which has a marked effect on the appearance of vegetation.

In the following sections we will look at two specific techniques for supervised classification.

9.1.4.1.1 Minimum Distance Classification

Minimum distance classification is simple, though not as accurate as other techniques. Consider the problem of classifying a single band image into k classes. From the training set, we can compute the mean value for pixels of each of the k classes. When we classify another image, we simply assign each pixel to the class whose mean is nearest to its value.

The technique is equally applicable to multi-band images. However, in this case the mean value is not a single value but is instead a set of values which we can think of as a geometric coordinate. For example, in a two band image we can think of the class mean values as a two dimensional coordinate. The x coordinate is the class mean in the first band and the y coordinate is the class mean in the second band. Similarly, each pixel value can be thought of as a coordinate and is assigned to the class whose mean is closest, in a geometric sense, to the pixel's value.

9.1.4.1.2 Bayesian Maximum Likelihood Classification

Another commonly used approach, particularly in remote sensing, is known as Bayesian maximum likelihood classification. The technique is more accurate than the minimum distance classifier, though its computation is more expensive and there are some practical difficulties. Once again, we can follow the basic principles of the technique by considering the classification of a single band image into k classes. In this approach, we first estimate how probable it is that a particular pixel belongs to each one of the k classes. Then we assign it to whichever class gives the highest probability. This is intuitively a sensible approach. The problem is in estimating how probable it is that the pixel belongs to particular class. This is where the image statistics play their part.

We can get some probability information from the training image. In particular, we can compute k histograms, one for each class identified in the training set. Each histogram shows how probable it is that a given pixel value belongs to that particular class. This is just the same as the histogram of an entire image, which shows how probable a particular pixel value is (section 4.4.), but it is applied to a chosen subset of the pixels. Unfortunately, this is not quite the probability we need. However, Bayes formula allows us to compute the probability we need from the histogram values as long as we can estimate the overall proportion of pixels belonging to each class. For example, we might have an image which is 20% water, 60% forest, 10% wheat, and 10% urban. These values represent overall probabilities of pixels belonging to each class. If we picked a pixel at random, without even looking at its value we know that there is a 60% chance that it represents forest. Bayes formula can be written

$$Pr(i|v) = \frac{Pr(v|i)\,Pr(i)}{Pr(v)} \tag{9.5}$$

$Pr(i|v)$ is the value we are looking for. It is the probability that a pixel with value v belongs to class i. For a given pixel value, we compute $Pr(i|v)$ for each of the k classes and find the class which gives the maximum value. Then we assign all pixels with the given value to that class. In equation (9.5), $Pr(v|i)$ is the probability that a pixel from class i has value v. We get this value from the histogram of each particular class. $Pr(i)$ is the probability that a pixel chosen from the image at random belongs to class i. $Pr(v)$ is the probability that a pixel of value v belongs to any of the classes. It is a normalisation term to take account of the fact that we may choose not to assign all the pixels in the image. For example, some of them may represent ground cover other than that in which we are interested. Alternatively, they may have such a low probability of belonging to any of the classes on which training was carried out, that it is safer not to classify them. $Pr(v)$ is simply the sum of the $Pr(v|i)$ values for class i. Consequently, for the purposes of finding the maximum value of $Pr(i|v)$ we can ignore it, since it is a constant.

Finding the class which maximises the value of $Pr(i|v)$ for every value of v gives us a mapping which allows us to classify the entire image. Every pixel with a particular value is assigned to the same class, regardless of the classification of its spatial neighbours. The mapping can easily be implemented in the form of a look-up table, with different colours being used to indicate the various classes.

There are practical difficulties associated with implementing the technique this way. For a single band image, computing the histogram for each class is straightforward and does not require much storage. However, as the number of bands grows, the size of the histograms increases rapidly. For a single band, 8-bit unsigned integer image, we need k 256 element histograms. For a two band image, we need k 256 by 256 element histograms. In this case the histogram is two dimensional. The element at location (p,q) represents the probability that when a pixel in the first band has value p that in the second band has value q. As we increase the number of bands, the amount of data which must be used to store the $Pr(v|i)$ values rapidly exceeds that which is available in typical computing systems. For an n band image, we need an n dimensional histogram.

To overcome this difficulty, an approximation to $Pr(v|i)$ can be used. The approximation models $Pr(v|i)$ as a Gaussian distribution and stores only the mean and standard deviation, rather than all the values. For a single band image, this is equivalent to the assumption that the histogram of the class is a Gaussian curve. Individual values of $Pr(v|i)$ can be computed from v and the parameters of the Gaussian. If the pixel values in each class do follow a Gaussian distribution, the approximation works well. Unfortunately, it is often the case that they do not and the approximation is poor. It is important to check that the Gaussian assumption is valid before using this classification scheme. If it is not valid, one solution is to split the chosen classes into a larger number of subclasses in the hope that their distributions will be more nearly Gaussian. Often, this will be found to work reasonably well and a satisfactory classification can be achieved.

9.1.4.2 Unsupervised Classification

Unsupervised classification can be thought of as an extension of the minimum distance classifier. Instead of a training set be used to allow the computation of the class mean pixel values, techniques are used which try to locate clusters in the n dimensional histogram of the n band image. Each cluster forms the basis for a class.

As an example, consider classifying a two band image. As with the minimum distance classifier, we consider each pixel as a two dimensional coordinate. The x coordinate is the pixel value in the first band and the y coordinate is the value in the second band. This coordinate system defines a two dimensional **pixel space** in which we can plot the position of any pixel value. The position plotted is independent of the pixel's spatial location, depending solely on the values in the image bands. The only difference between this pixel space and the two dimensional histogram we met earlier is that in the histogram we plot the counts of pixels with particular pixel space coordinates.

We might expect to find pixels for a particular kind of ground cover clustering together when plotted in pixel space. After all, pixels in a particular class should resemble one another reasonably closely. The goal of unsupervised classification is to identify clusters in pixel space and to assign each image pixel to one of them. The basic approach to cluster detection is very simple. First, we manually seed the algorithm with k cluster centres, one for each cluster which we are seeking. As with supervised classification, this requires prior knowledge of the number of different classes into which the image is to be divided. From the seed values, each pixel is assigned to the cluster centre nearest to it in pixel space. From these initial assignments, a new cluster centre is computed for each class by taking the mean values of the coordinates of the pixels assigned to it. Now the algorithm iterates. A new set of class assignments can be computed from the new cluster centres and then the cluster centres can be recomputed. The process can be halted after a few iterations.

This basic method is known as the **K-means algorithm**. Some additional rules can be added to remove the necessity of knowing precisely how many classes there are. These rules allow nearby clusters to merge and clusters which have large standard deviations in coordinate to spilt. Naturally, when these kinds of rules are added, more controls are required to prevent undesirable occurrences. For example, a tendency to produce large numbers of very small classes needs to be countered. Small clusters can be removed, forcing their pixels to become part of other clusters. Even when rules like these, and others, are applied to make the K-means algorithm more sophisticated (Duda and Hart (1973)), the best classifications require at least some human intervention during the iterations. Consequently, these classifications are not truly unsupervised.

9.1.4.3 Relaxation

Relaxation (Rosenfeld and Kak (1982)) is an approach to classification which attempts assign pixels to classes so as to maximise a measure of compatibility between the pixel and its immediate neighbours. Unlike the techniques we have looked at so far, it makes explicit use of spatial information. The compatibility measure, used in relaxation, could be based on grey level but it might be derived from other image properties. Suppose we want to try and divide the image into k classes. We need to establish measures which define how compatible adjacent pixels are when assigned to different classes. We might make positive values indicate compatibility and negative values indicate incompatibility, for example. Given these measures, and the current class for each pixel in the image we can compute an average value of compatibility for each pixel based on its class and that of its 8 immediate neighbours. This is just the average of the 8 individual compatibility measures.

On its own this value does not get us very far. However, instead of considering that each pixel has a current class, we can, once again, think in terms of the probability of the pixel belonging to any class. This gives us a set of k values associated with each pixel, just as we had with the Bayesian maximum likelihood classifier. Each of the values is the probability of the pixel belonging to one of the classes. However, in this case, rather than trying to compute these probabilities directly to allow us to choose the classes, we include this probability value when calculating the compatibility measures. This ensures that improbable class assignments have lower weight than more probable ones. Now, we can compute the compatibility measures for assigning a given pixel to any class, based on the current classes assigned to all its neighbours. Again, this is a set of k values saying how compatible each class assignment for the pixel would be, given the current assignments for its neighbours. Clearly, class assignments which are incompatible with the neighbouring pixels should be associated with lower probabilities than those which are compatible. Indeed, we can compute new probabilities for each of the possible class assignments, for the current pixel, from the compatibility measures. We now have enough information to iterate. From the probabilities we can generate the average compatibility measures. From these measures we can generate a new set of probabilities. We can continue processing, iterating over the whole image. As we do, the probabilities tend to converge to reasonable certainty of a particular class assignment for each pixel and this constitutes the classification of the image.

We will not explore the precise expressions used to compute the compatibility measures and the probabilities. In fact, these can be formulated in a number of different ways. This makes it necessary to experiment before applying the technique for any particular application. Relaxation offers benefits over other classifications because it takes into account the local neighbourhood of each pixel during the classification. It is, however, rather expensive, computationally. It also needs some initial estimates of the class probabilities for each pixel. Consequently, relaxation is usually run after some initial classification has been undertaken.

9.2 FEATURE EXTRACTION

Features are identifiable components of images. Features can be detected in normal grey scale or colour images, in intrinsic images, in transformed images or even in derived data, such as histograms. Features are manifestations of objects in the original scene. They are used to deduce the presence of objects and often to infer position, orientation and size information. For example, in Figure 1.6 the diagnosis of an astrocytoma was based on the presence of a particular object within the patient's skull. The presence, location and size of the object was itself deduced from identifiable features in the MRI images. The overall goal of the process was diagnosis of the medical condition. Steps on the way to that goal included segmentation and feature extraction. In the example, all of the necessary steps were carried out by the doctors involved with the case. Current machine based techniques cannot yet adequately segment and analyse medical images of that level of complexity. However, there are techniques available for carrying out some forms of feature extraction automatically.

Feature extraction is the identification of segments which have particular relevance to the task in hand. If, for example, we had an application for examining industrial parts and which used thresholding for segmentation, the feature extraction stage might involve looking at the dark areas of the segmented image in order to find one of the appropriate size and shape. Having located a recognisable feature we could then identify the particular part and might go on to infer its location and orientation. This is the kind of information which is the goal of the system. Location and orientation information might be used, for example, to allow the part to be grasped and manipulated by a robot arm.

There are a variety of feature extraction techniques. We will look at some of the more commonly used ones in the following sections.

9.2.1 Spatial Feature Extraction

Some of the most important feature extraction techniques are based on shape. Shape offers the most direct correspondence between an image and the objects of interest. It is much more direct than brightness, for example. This is the reason why thresholding rarely segments images in a useful fashion unless conditions are carefully established. In this section we will look at two techniques for shape based feature extraction. In both cases, the major task is to locate the feature within the image. Once located, processing to extract more information about the feature, for example its orientation, can be performed. Finally, we will mention approaches based on the deduction of three dimensional information from images which are much more sophisticated in their approach to feature extraction.

9.2.1.1 Template Matching

Template matching can be applied under controlled conditions to locate features. It is a brute force technique whose simplicity belies its difficulties and which may require large amounts of computation. Template matching is based on correlation. As we saw in section 6.3, a particular feature can be located within a grey scale image with great precision. However, for the technique to work, certain conditions must be met. The mask or **template** must contain an image of the feature being searched for. It must be exactly the same size as the feature and in exactly the same orientation. The grey level values in the template must be similar to those in the image. Indeed, the technique is often used after the image has been thresholded so that only black and white pixels occur.

If the size of the feature or its orientation is unknown, the correlation must be repeated with the template at a variety of orientations and sizes. Frequently this causes a **combinatorial explosion**. The amount of work required to perform all the necessary correlations increases to such an extent that the method becomes unworkable. Consequently, in practical applications, such as those employed in simple manufacturing systems, scale is made constant by the simple expedient of placing the camera at a fixed distance from the objects being inspected. Then only the orientation is potentially uncertain and the process may become practical.

Naturally, if the objects are always in a particular orientation, the problem is much simpler. A good example of this situation is in the recognition of printed characters. In simple text, the orientation is fixed, and only a small number of different character sizes occurs. Spaces between characters are reasonably regular, as are those between adjacent lines. All these factors help to reduce the search space. Recognition can normally be performed rather easily, though it is hardly ever 100% reliable. Poor quality reproductions, for example photocopies, tend to introduce noise and breaks in the characters which can lead to them being incorrectly matched. Nevertheless, correct recognition rates of 90% or more are by no means uncommon.

Except in these very special sorts of circumstances, where the features being detected and extracted are closely controlled, template matching is of little practical value. Much more powerful techniques are available based on derived properties of the regions in the image.

9.2.1.2 Parametric Shape Features

Instead of trying to match image features with templates on a pixel for pixel basis, it is possible to match them based on parameters derived from the segments themselves. Even the simplest derived parameters, such as perimeter length or area, can be used to discriminate between known objects, if the values are significantly different. These simple measures are clearly dependent on the distance of the object from the camera. However, they are not dependent on the orientation of the object within the field of view. They are called **rotation invariant** parameters. Actually, calling these parameters rotation invariant requires some qualification. First, the rotation involved is around an axis at right angles to the surface on which the object is lying. If rotated about any other axis, any general, three dimensional, object may present completely different views to a camera. In the situation, discussed earlier, of recognition of objects from their silhouettes (section 9.1.1), there will normally be a small number of classes of view from any given objects. Most three dimensional objects have only a small number of stable orientations which they can assume when placed on a horizontal surface, for example a conveyor belt. Given one of these stable orientations, we need only consider rotations about an axis at right angles to the surface. Under these conditions, area and perimeter are essentially rotation invariant.

There will be some variation in the measured values of the parameters due to the pixelation introduced by digitising the image. Change of orientation of an object will alter the number of pixels partially occupied by its edges. This will affect the average value of boundary pixels and consequently whether they are considered as object or background by the thresholding process. The consequence is that there will always be some level of uncertainty associated with a measure such as area or perimeter, and indeed with any parameter derived from the region. These variations can often be measured directly by observing the objects in a variety of orientations. As long as the parameter value range of one object does not overlap that for a different object, they can be discriminated. As more objects are added to the set of those which must be recognised, it becomes harder and harder to find simple parameters which can unambiguously identify them.

There are, of course, many parameters which can be derived for an image region. These parameters can be used both for recognition and for measurement. We will look at a variety of simple measures in the sections which follow. We will assume that segmentation has been carried out. In practice in typical systems being used today, this almost invariably means that some kind of simple thresholding operation has been performed and that the image is binary.

9.2.1.2.1 Area

The area of an object is simply the total number of pixels it contains. In typical situations, where only one object is in the field of view, the number of pixels in the image which are identified as part of the object is a measure of its area. The actual area can easily be computed if the size represented by a pixel is known in real space units, such as metres.

9.2.1.2.2 Perimeter

The perimeter of an object can be estimated by counting the total number of pixels on its boundary. Once again, in typical situations where only one object is in the field of view, the perimeter is simply the number of object pixels in the image which have at least one neighbouring background pixel.

9.2.1.2.3 Centre of Mass
For a binary image, the centre of mass of an object is the coordinate given by the mean of the x values of all object pixels and the mean of their y values.

9.2.1.2.4 Central Moments
Moments in image processing are distantly related to moments in mechanics. In mechanics, a moment indicates the turning effect which a force has about a particular point. In image processing, moments are not particularly interesting in themselves. However, parameters can be derived from them which can be very useful indicators of the overall shape of an object.

A central moment of order p is computed as

$$\mu_{jk} = \sum_{x=0}^{N-1} \sum_{y=0}^{M-1} (x - \bar{x})_j \, (y - \bar{y})^k \, I(x,y) \tag{9.6}$$

In this equation, $\bar{x}$ is the x coordinate of the object's centre of mass and $\bar{y}$ is its y coordinate. For our simple case of a binary image, the image function $I(x,y)$ is 1 for each object pixel and 0 elsewhere. The order p of the moment is just $j + k$. The point of making equation (9.6) explicit here is to show that moments of arbitrary order can be computed very easily, directly from the segmented image.

Combinations of moments are particularly interesting. For example, from the second order moments we can compute the directions of the object's **principal axes**. These axes define an orientation for the object which often coincides with that which a human observer would assign. The particular expression which gives this direction is

$$\tan 2\theta = \frac{2\mu_{11}}{\mu_{20} - \mu_{02}} \tag{9.7}$$

Rotating the object through angle θ brings its principal axes coincident with the image axes. This can solve the rotation dependence problem when recognising objects. The object can always be rotated to align its principal axes before template matching, for example. Also, the dimensions of the object along its principal axes can be used to adjust scaling parameters before attempting template matching. These can remove problems due to size differences.

Other combinations of moments are particularly useful as features. They have the property of being invariant under rotation, translation and scaling and so can be used in object recognition (Gonzalez and Wintz (1977).) These combinations are known as **moment invariants**.

9.2.1.2.5 Bounding Rectangle

The bounding rectangle is the rectangle which just encloses the object and which is aligned with its principal axes. It can easily be determined once the object's principal axes have been rotated to align with the image axes. The maximum and minimum x and y coordinates of the object's pixels define the corners of the rectangle.

9.2.1.2.6 Length and Width

The length and width of the object are just the length and width of its bounding rectangle.

9.2.1.2.7 Rectangularity

Rectangularity is a measure of how nearly an object approximates to being a rectangle. It is the ratio of the area of the object to that of its bounding rectangle. The nearer the ratio is to 1, the more nearly rectangular is the region.

9.2.1.2.8 Compactness or Circularity

The compactness of the object is a measure of how nearly circular it is. Compactness is computed as

$$\gamma = \frac{P^2}{4\pi A} \tag{9.8}$$

where P is the perimeter of the object and A is its area. For a circular object, equation (9.8) attains its minimum value of 1.

9.2.1.3 Extracting Higher Order Features

So far, we have only considered feature location and extraction in situations where the shape of the region in the image is known. In more general situations, where we are trying to identify a three dimensional object from a two dimensional image, things are less simple. The appearance of the object in the image depends on the viewing conditions. For all practical purposes, the object could appear at any orientation. Simple, two dimensional parameters extracted from particular views of these objects are of little use when so many different views are possible.

We should expect simple approaches to feature extraction, such as the use of silhouettes and simple shape parameters, to run into difficulty as the complexity of the feature extraction task increases. One important reason is that by simplifying the problem to that of a two dimensional silhouette, we are discarding a great deal of information about the object. Brightness, colour, texture and shading have all been ignored in an attempt to make the problem tractable. Whilst, as we have seen, there are applications for which this kind of approach is appropriate, it is not generally applicable. For more complex situations we should expect to have to exploit as much of the information in the image as possible.

The recognition of three dimensional objects from two dimensional images is known as **computer vision**. The subject has been widely studied. Since in computer vision the goals are very similar to those of human vision, the location and identification of objects in three dimensions, it is not surprising that the techniques involved tend to be rather complex. For example, some approaches use stereoscopy to derive distance information. This allows additional shape information to be recovered from the image. There are also techniques which allow shape to be inferred from the shading of the objects in the image. Shape information can also sometimes be inferred from the change in appearance of textures on the surface of objects. Recognition of three dimensional objects is complicated by the fact that in an image, only part of the object is seen. Even if a great deal of shape information can be derived from the image, using shading, texture, stereoscopy and so on, only part of the object's shape can be described. To recognise this particular object we need to match the partial shape information derived from the image with complete shape descriptions in a database of object models. This kind of matching is difficult. It is also true that the model description and the derived shape description must have the same representation to allow comparison to be made. The choice of representation is important. In particular, today it is common to use a geometric description based on primitives such as straight lines and mathematically defined curves. Whilst this approach works well for manufactured objects, it is not appropriate for the more general curvatures found in biological systems.

There are many problems still to be solved before general purpose computer vision becomes a reality. However progress is being made and certain tasks are already being being achieved using these techniques, particularly when the objects to be recognised are man made and relatively simple.

9.2.2 Transform Features

Sometimes it can be easier to recognise features in an image transform then in the image itself. For example, an extended structure which has a characteristic periodicity in the image may show up as a single, well defined peak in a Fourier transform. This may make it easy to deduce that the object is present in the image. This kind of approach can be used in industrial inspection tasks (Gregory and Taylor (1984).) An assembled part is presented in a defined orientation to the camera. Since the geometry of a correctly assembled part is known, it is possible to predefine specific areas of the image in which to look for the presence of the anticipated features. If an item, such as a spring, should be at a particular place in the image, a simple one dimensional Fourier transform along its length can be used to indicate its presence. The frequency of the peak in the transform can also be used to estimate whether the spring has the correct tension. Too high a frequency indicates that the spring is shorter than it should be. Perhaps it has not been attached properly at one end.

In addition to these simple, transform domain features, it is possible to define two dimensional shapes in terms of Fourier components. These representations of shape are known as **Fourier descriptors**. Their importance lies in the fact that scaling and rotation tends to affect them in very simple ways, making it easier to compare a standard shape with one from an image than if the comparison is attempted in the spatial domain. As with moments, it is possible to derive Fourier descriptors which are scale and rotation invariant. A full discussion of Fourier descriptors is beyond the scope of this book.

9.3 EXTRACTING STRUCTURAL INFORMATION

In many image processing applications, a simple representation of the objects in the image is needed. A description in terms of the line segments and curves which comprise the object's boundary is too complex for the task at hand. In this section we look at techniques normally applied to binary images of objects, for example the silhouettes which we have already discussed. The objective of the techniques is to allow the object to be described in sufficiently simple terms to allow its recognition. These techniques are usually of use in basic recognition or inspection tasks. Possible applications include inspection of manufactured parts, chromosome counting and in the initial analysis of the lines composing a fingerprint.

9.3.1 The Medial Axis Transform
Particularly where the object in question tends to be rather extended in one direction, a representation called the **medial axis** may be appropriate. A point in the object is on the medial axis if it is equidistant from at least two points on the object boundary. The value of the medial axis transform at a point on the axis is simply the distance to the boundary. However, frequently all that is needed for shape description is the set of points on the axis. Figure 9.3 shows some shapes and their medial axes transforms. An operation which converts the image of an object into its medial axis is known as a **medial axis transform**.

The transform may be useful for thinning broad lines. These might be produced by a simple edge detector or as a result of thresholding a line drawing or handwritten text. The simplified description of the object, in terms of its medial axis, may make it more easily recognisable. It may also give other information such as its approximate orientation and size.

Two common methods exist for computing the transform, or at least, the set of points on the medial axis. We will look at these in the following sections.

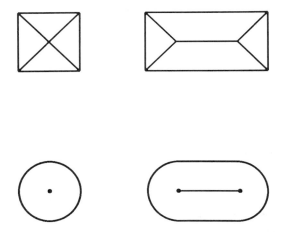

Figure   9.3. Medial axes of various shapes

9.3.1.1 Thinning

In **thinning** we gradually remove boundary pixels from the object whilst retaining connectivity. Thinning stops when no further pixels can be removed without causing loss of continuity. Points whose removal would cause loss of continuity will be visited more than once as the boundary is traversed. Consequently, the thinning algorithm needs to traverse the entire object boundary, marking pixels which are candidates for removal and remembering how many times each has been visited. Those candidates which have been visited only once are then removed. The process continues until no more pixels can be removed.

9.3.1.2 Distance Transform

The **distance transform** is a computation which measures the distance of points within the object from the boundary. Local maxima within the result are points on the medial axis. The technique is iterative. Consider the question mark shaped object in Figure 9.4(a). All object points are given a value of 1. Background pixels are given a value of 0. This leads to the rectangular block of pixels surrounding the

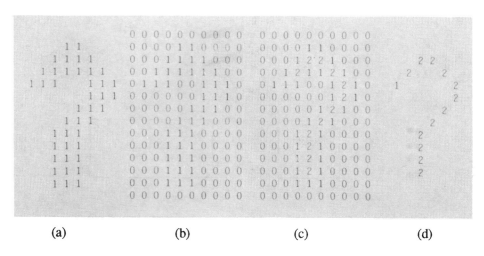

Figure   9.4. Distance transform.   (a) Object, (b) object and local background, (c) distances of
object pixels from background, (d) medial axis of object.

object shown in Figure 9.4(b).   The ability to distinguish object and background pre-
supposes a satisfactory segmentation, of course.   In each 3 by 3 neighbourhood we
examine the central pixel value from Figure 9.4(b) and add to it the minimum value
of its immediate neighbours which are **4-connected**.   These are the pixels immediately above, below, to the left and to the right.   Doing this yields Figure 9.4(c).
We can repeat the process, starting with Figure 9.4(b) again but looking at neighbour
values from Figure 9.4(c).   In fact, for this shape, no further changes happen when
we iterate.   The values in the array Figure 9.4(c) are the minimum distances from the
given pixel to a background pixel travelling horizontally or vertically, hence the name
of the transform.   The final step is to extract just the local maxima from the array
Figure 9.4(c).   Again, each pixel is examined and retained if it is the maximum of
itself and its 4-connected neighbours.   This leads to Figure 9.4(d), which is the
medial axis of the object.

9.3.2 Morphology
Morphology is the study of form and shape.   It has a rather specific meaning in
image processing applications.   A set of techniques have been developed based on
two primitive operations.   Usually applied to binary image data, morphological operations can be used to smooth object boundaries or to identify particular pixel config-
urations, such as corners.   In some ways, morphology is similar to template matching
but the template seeks out features rather than entire objects.   Also, the image is
normally modified based on whether the template matches or not.   In morphology,
the template is called a **structuring element**.

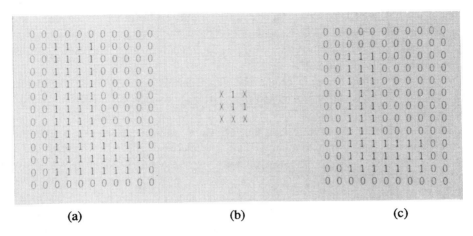

Figure 9.5. Erosion. (a) Object, (b) structuring element for eroding top and rightmost edges, (c) result of erosion.

The structuring element is a small image, typically 3 by 3 pixels. It has a defined origin. Each pixel in the structuring element can be set to values indicating

- object
- background
- don't care

The structuring element is placed in turn on each pixel in the image. If the image pixels underlying the structuring element are consistent with its values, the pixel in the output image corresponding to the position of the structuring element's origin is set on. Otherwise it is set off. The result is another binary image. The particular operation performed depends on the values of the pixels in the structuring element and on the position of its origin. Usually, the origin is the centre of the array.

Figure 9.5 shows an example of the use of a structuring element to **erode** part of the boundary of an object. The object is the simple L shaped area shown in Figure 9.5(a). Object pixels have value 1 whilst background pixels have value 0. The structuring element is shown in Figure 9.5(b). A value of 1 means that there must be an object pixel under that position for there to be non-zero output. An X means that any value can be present. The origin of the structuring element is its central pixel. Placing the structuring element over each pixel of Figure 9.5(a) in turn yields Figure 9.5(c). The upper row of pixels has been removed from the object, as has the rightmost column.

This erosion could be repeated. Eventually, all pixels in the image would be removed. This particular erosion is specific to top and right hand edges. Rotation of the template by 180° produces a structuring element which erodes bottom and left hand edges. A general erosion rule can be obtained with a 3 by 3 structuring element with all pixels set to 1. Only pixels surrounded by other object pixels in the original image are retained. This operation is almost equivalent to the thinning operation we saw in 9.3.1.1. However, we need to add more rules if we want to ensure that connectivity is retained.

As another simple example of morphology, Figure 9.6 shows a corner detector. It is specific for lower left corners. Consequently it is successful only once on the L shaped object.

We have seen an example of erosion. **Dilation** is an operation which adds pixels to the boundary, rather than removing them. It increases the size of the object. In general, erosion and dilation are not inverses of one another. This fact can sometimes be used to smooth away small imperfections in object boundaries. An erosion followed by a dilation can be arranged to achieve this.

Morphological operations suffer from exactly the same kinds of problems as does template matching. For example, the corner detector we looked at earlier will work only if the corner is aligned precisely on the grid of pixels. Different orientations of corner need different structuring elements. Also, the detection operations need perfect object boundaries. Often, boundaries defined by thresholding are a little imprecise. Rather than being straight, they wander by a pixel or two due to the imperfection of the thresholding technique mentioned earlier (9.2.1.2.) Nevertheless, they can be used under appropriately controlled conditions to detect simple features and to clean up the results of thresholding. In addition they are often used for thinning. A wide variety of operations can be performed by varying the structuring element and by altering what happens when the structuring element matches the underlying image.

9.4 SUMMARY

Analysis is the goal of almost all image processing applications. The division of the image into regions and the consequent recognition and measurement of objects allows image processing to be used in a wide variety of tasks. Though there are now many well known techniques for dealing with simple, two dimensional recognition and measurement applications, the more general problems associated with analysing arbitrary, three dimensional scenes have not yet been completely solved.

Whereas there are many techniques which are applicable to the location and identification of features within segmented images, the only commonly used segmentation technique in practical recognition systems is thresholding. We have seen several times how unsatisfactory this can be unless conditions are tightly controlled. The general segmentation problem is very difficult and it must be emphasised that when considering any new application of image processing, it is this step which should

0	0	0	0	0	0	0	0	0	0	0
0	0	1	1	1	1	0	0	0	0	0
0	0	1	1	1	1	0	0	0	0	0
0	0	1	1	1	1	0	0	0	0	0
0	0	1	1	1	1	0	0	0	0	0
0	0	1	1	1	1	0	0	0	0	0
0	0	1	1	1	1	0	0	0	0	0
0	0	1	1	1	1	0	0	0	0	0
0	0	1	1	1	1	1	1	1	1	0
0	0	1	1	1	1	1	1	1	1	0
0	0	1	1	1	1	1	1	1	1	0
0	0	1	1	1	1	1	1	1	1	0
0	0	0	0	0	0	0	0	0	0	0

(a)

0	1	X
0	1	1
0	0	0

(b)

0	0	0	0	0	0	0	0	0	0	0
0	0	0	0	0	0	0	0	0	0	0
0	0	0	0	0	0	0	0	0	0	0
0	0	0	0	0	0	0	0	0	0	0
0	0	0	0	0	0	0	0	0	0	0
0	0	0	0	0	0	0	0	0	0	0
0	0	0	0	0	0	0	0	0	0	0
0	0	0	0	0	0	0	0	0	0	0
0	0	0	0	0	0	0	0	0	0	0
0	0	0	0	0	0	0	0	0	0	0
0	0	0	0	0	0	0	0	0	0	0
0	0	1	0	0	0	0	0	0	0	0
0	0	0	0	0	0	0	0	0	0	0

(c)

Figure 9.6. Detecting a corner. (a) Object, (b) structuring element for corner detection, (c) result of corner detection. Only one appropriate corner exists. It is at the lower left of the object.

receive the most careful consideration. It may dictate the whole approach to the application.

In this chapter we looked at segmentation techniques, we saw how features within an image might be detected and measured and looked at morphological techniques for shape analysis.

Appendix 1: References

Angell, I.O. (1988) *A Practical Introduction to Computer Graphics*, Macmillan.

Bevington, P.R. (1969) *Data Reduction and Error Analysis for the Physical Sciences*, McGraw—Hill.

Canny, J. (1986) A Computational Approach to Edge Detection *IEEE Transactions on Pattern Analysis and Machine Intelligence* **PAMI-8** No 6, 679—698.

Cocklin, M.L., Kaye, G, Kerr, I.H, Lams, P. (1982) Digital Enhancement of Pneumothoraces, *First IEEE Computer Society International Symposium on Medical Imaging and Image Interpretation*

Cocklin, M.L., Gourlay, A.R., Jackson, P.H., Kaye, G., Kerr, I.H, Lams, P. (1983) Digital Processing of Chest Radiographs, *Image and Vision Computing* **1** 67—78.

Duda, R.O., Hart, P.E. (1973) *Pattern Classification and Scene Analysis*, John Wiley & Sons.

Dugdale, J.S. (1970) *Entropy and Low Temperature Physics*, Hutchinson University Library.

Floyd, R.W., Steinberg, L. (1976) An Adaptive Algorithm for Spatial Greyscale, *Proceedings of the Society for Information Display* **17** No 2, 75—77

Gonzalez, R.C., Wintz, P. (1977) *Digital Image Processing*, Addison—Wesley.

Gregory, P.J., Taylor, C.J., (1984) Knowledge Based Models for Computer Vision. In: Pugh, A. (ed.) *Proceedings of the 4th International Conference on*

Robot Vision and Sensory Controls (ROVISEC 4) IFS Publications and North-Holland, pp 325-330.

Hummel, R., Lowe, D. (1989) Computational Considerations in Convolution and Feature-extraction in Images. In: Simon, J.C. (ed.) *From Pixels to Features* . Elsevier Science Publishers (North-Holland), pp 91—102.

Jackson P.H., (1984) *The IAX Image Processing System: Reference Manual*, IBM UK Scientific Centre Reports 113—116.

Jain, A.K. (1989) *Fundamentals of Digital Image Processing*, Prentice Hall.

Kreyszig, E.(1972) *Advanced Engineering Mathematics*, John Wiley & Sons.

Lewis, J.R.T., Ibbotson, J. (1989) *IMPART Image Processing System Technical Reference Manual* , IBM UK Scientific Centre Internal Report.

Marr, D. and Hildreth, E. (1980) Theory of Edge Detection *Proceedings of the Royal Society of London B* **207** 187—217.

Marr, D. (1982) *Vision*, W.H. Freeman & Co.

Cowlishaw, M.F. (1985) Bit Requirements for Monochrome and Colour Pictures, *Proceedings of the Society for Information Display* **26** No 2, 101—107

Mol, C.R. (1984) 3D Reconstruction from biplane X-ray angiography *IBM UK Scientific Centre Report UKSC124*

Netravali, A.N., Haskell, B.G. (1989) *Digital Pictures Representation and Compression*, Plenum.

Niblack, W. (1986) *An Introduction to Digital Image Processing*, Strandberg.

Rake, S.T. (1989) Finding Parallel Structures *Proceedings of the IEEE Third International Conference on Image Processing and its Applications*, pp 628—632

Rosenfeld, A and Kak, A.C. (1982) *Digital Picture Processing Volume 1* , Academic Press.

Appendix 2: Typesetting this Book

This book was prepared using the IBM BookMaster typesetting program. A special style sheet was prepared to match the Ellis Horwood house style. Output, in PostScript format, was printed on an IBM 4216 laser printer, with a resolution of 300 dots per inch, and was supplied as camera ready copy to the publisher.

Images were processed using the IBM IAX Image Processing system and the IBM UK Scientific Centre IMPART image processing package. The images were then photographed from the front of display screens using black and white negative film. The negatives were printed at the final size of the illustrations and supplied to Ellis Horwood ready for halftoning.

Glossary

A

adaptive filter. A filter whose properties adapt to conditions in different parts of the image.

additive colour system. A technique for reproducing colour based on the addition of various amounts of three primary colours. The primary colours are red, green and blue. The technique is used in television and in the display of colour images.

alignment. A technique used to ensure that rows of an image start on appropriate storage boundaries. For example, images of 1 bit per pixel are often aligned so that new rows begin on a byte boundary.

amplitude. One half of the difference between the smallest and largest values attained by a periodic function, such as a sine wave.

analogue to digital converter (ADC). An electronic device which converts a voltage into a numerical representation. These devices are used in image digitisation systems.

analytic function. A function which can be represented algebraically. As a consequence, values of the function can be computed to arbitrary precision.

aspect ratio. The ratio of the width of an image to its height.

B

band. An image from a detector which responds to a restricted range of wavelengths. In colour image work, 3 bands are often acquired. These bands are the primary colours of an additive colour system.

bandwidth. Range of frequencies over which some particular system responds. The higher the bandwidth, the more detail is preserved, but the more susceptible the system is to noise.

bass. A term for the low frequency part of an audio signal.

bias. One of the parameters available in grey scale re-mapping. A constant added to each pixel in the image.

bi-modal histogram. A characteristic histogram pattern showing that image pixels partition into two distinct classes.

bit. The smallest individual piece of computer storage. A bit can be either on or off. Combinations of bits can be used to store integer or floating point values.

body scanner. A medical instrument which uses X-rays to deduce the three dimensional shape and constitution of tissues and organs within the human body.

byte. A group of 8 bits. It can be used to store an 8-bit unsigned integer, for example.

C

charge coupled device. A solid state device for detecting light. It forms the basis for many light weight, robust, television cameras.

classification. A technique which tries to divide an image up into regions according to the values of pixels in one or more bands. It is commonly used when processing remote sensing images when the classes are chosen to distinguish various forms of ground cover.

code book. The set of translations necessary to convert between an uncompressed image and its compressed form. In many compression techniques, the code book is constructed during compression and is used during decompression. The code book consists of a set of code words.

code word. One particular coded output from a coder.

coder. A component of an encoding device. The coder converts each possible input value which it can be given into the appropriate code word. For image compression, input to the coder is typically either directly derived from pixel values or is the output of a quantizer.

combinatorial explosion. A situation in which the number of eventualities which must be investigated grows sufficiently rapidly to become intractable.

computer aided tomography (CAT). The technique used to reconstruct three dimensional representations of tissues and organs inside the human body from X-ray data collected by a body scanner.

computer vision. A field of research in which attempts are made to make computers reason about image data. The aim is to try and build machines which can interpret images in terms of objects in the real world, in the same sort of way that human beings do. Much work remains to be done.

concatenation. The juxtaposition of two or more images horizontally or vertically to create a new, larger image.

contrast. A measure of the variation in brightness between the lightest and darkest portions of a given image.

control point. One of a set of points used to define the warping which must be applied to an image to correct it so that it corresponds to some predefined coordinate system. Such warping is necessary to align remote sensing images with particular cartographic coordinate systems, for example.

convolution. A technique which can be used to provide a wide variety of different filtering functions using a single algorithm. Optimisation of this one algorithm provides high speed implementations of all filters implemented this way.

correlation. A technique which can be used to locate particular areas in an image.

covariance matrix. A matrix which shows how a set of variables move together. Used when processing multi-band images, especially in principal components analysis.

cumulative histogram. Histogram in which each entry is the number of pixels with value less then or equal to the current value.

curve fitting. A technique for data reduction. Experimental data points are approximated by a curve which is an analytic function. The parameters needed to calculate the curve are used in subsequent processing, rather than the data points themselves.

D

data reduction. Representation of a set of data points by a small number of parameters. The reduced data is easier to manipulate than the points themselves. In addition, the parameters may be interpreted in terms of a model of the behaviour which gives rise to the data points.

decoder. The component of a data compression scheme responsible for converting the compressed data back into its uncompressed form.

degradation model. A model describing the ways in which a particular image has been degraded. An empirical degradation model is based on actual observation. An analytical degradation model is based on a mathematical description.

derivative. The rate of change of a function. For an image, the derivative shows the rate of change of pixel values along a particular direction. Normally, an image's derivatives are calculated along its rows and down its columns. The term derivative is shorthand for the first derivative. Higher order derivatives can be calculated. For example, the second derivative of an image is the derivative of its derivative.

differential mapping. A technique applied within the mapper component of an image compression scheme. Pixel values are applied to the mapper which outputs successive differences. The statistics of these differences are often more favourable, for the subsequent coding step, than are those of the pixel values themselves.

digital terrain model. An empirical model of the geography of part of the earth's surface usually given in terms of three dimensional coordinates. Data for these models comes from terrestrial surveys.

digital to analogue converter (DAC). An electronic device which converts numerical data into some kind of analogue output, frequently a voltage. The voltage can be used to drive other equipment. These devices are used in graphics and image displays.

dilation. A morphological operation during which an object is increased in size by the addition of pixels around its boundary. An object, in this sense, is a two dimensional region of the image which has been identified by some previous segmentation step.

display controller. An electronic device which converts a digital image into a signal which can be displayed. Normally, the display itself is a cathode ray tube.

distance transform. A transform in which pixels are replaced by their distance to the nearest object boundary. An object, in this sense, is a two dimensional region of the image which has been identified by some previous segmentation step.

domain knowledge. Knowledge or information applied to the solution of a problem and which is of a specific nature.

domain transform. A transform producing a representation which, although completely different from the original data, is equivalent to it in terms of the information contained.

dynamic range. The range between the maximum and minimum value of pixels within an image.

E

edge detection. An approach to image segmentation based on the assumption that discontinuities in pixel value often correspond to the edges of objects. Many implementations of edge detection are based on first and second image derivatives.

edgel. An edge map pixel with a value which indicates the likely presence of an object edge.

edge map. An intrinsic image in which each pixel represents the likelihood of an object edge at that point.

edge preserving smoothing. A group of techniques which attempt to remove noise from an image without excessively blurring discontinuities which are likely to be object edges.

edge strength. The value of an edgel. The larger the value, the more likely it is that an object edge exists at that point.

eigenvalue. One characteristic value of a matrix related to the solution of particular kinds of matrix equations. Numerical techniques exist for determining these values.

eigenvector. The characteristic vector associated with a given eigenvalue. Numerical techniques exist for computing these vectors once the associated eigenvalue has been determined.

encoder. The overall component of an image compression scheme responsible for converting pixel data into compressed form.

enhancement. A range of techniques for modifying the appearance of an image to make it visually more attractive or to improve the visibility of certain features. The aim is to make the analysis of the image easier for a human observer or for subsequent machine based processes.

entropy. A measure of the amount of disorder in a system. Entropy can be used to estimate the information content of an image.

equal length code. A code in which every code word consists of the same number of bits.

erosion. A morphological operation during which an object is decreased in size by the removal of pixels from around its boundary. An object, in this sense, is a two dimensional region of the image which has been identified by some previous segmentation step.

error diffusion. A technique for approximating a grey scale or colour image with fewer bits per pixel. Errors introduced by the approximation are spread amongst pixels yet to be converted as compensation.

F

Fast Fourier Transform. An algorithm for computing the Fourier transform requiring many fewer operations than the direct method.

fiducial marks. Recognisable marks introduced into an image during its capture to allow the actual geometry of the acquisition system to be recovered. These marks can be used to calibrate pixels in terms of real space units, for example.

finite impulse response. An optical system is said to possess a finite impulse response if a point source of light produces an output which is of a finite size. Most systems conform to this definition as do the filters used in convolution operations.

fixed point. A kind of arithmetic in which a fixed number of bits in an integer is assumed to represent a fractional part. This kind of arithmetic can be used to allow fractional calculations to be carried out even when floating point calculations are not supported.

floating point. A kind of arithmetic in which a large range of values can be handled. Fractions are catered for automatically. Often, floating point computations are slower than equivalent integer calculations. If this is the case, fixed point computation may offer a way to improve performance.

flux. The amount of light falling on a given area in a given time.

Fourier descriptors. A representation of shape in terms of Fourier components.

Fourier domain. Another term for frequency domain.

Fourier spectrum. An image in which each pixel is the magnitude of the corresponding element of the Fourier transform.

Fourier transform. A domain transform as a result of which an image is represented as a set of spatial frequency components.

Fourier transform pair. A pair of operations, one in the spatial domain and the other in the frequency domain, which are equivalent. For example, convolution and multiplication form a Fourier transform pair, under appropriate conditions.

frequency domain. The domain in which an image is represented as a set of spatial frequency components.

frame. One complete picture transmitted in a television system. In the European standard, 25 frames are transmitted every second.

frame grabber. An electronic device which can digitise and store one frame of a television signal in real time.

G

gain. One of the parameters which can be varied in linear grey scale re-mapping. The gain affects the slope of the linear mapping.

geostationary. A satellite which orbits the earth in such a way as always to be above the same point on the surface. Normally, this kind of orbit is appropriate for communications satellites.

grey level slicing. A thresholding operation in which an image is divided into a small number of pixel groups each of which has a particular range of values.

grey level re-mapping. Modification of the contrast and brightness of an image by mapping particular pixel values to new values.

grey scale. A type of image in which each pixel represents the overall brightness of a given point.

grey scale wedge. A calibration device consisting of adjacent strips with particular brightness relationships. When illuminated evenly, test images can be acquired and the image acquisition system can be calibrated.

ground cover. The particular kind of surface at a given point on the earth. It might be water, forest, or a particular crop, for example.

H

halftoning. A technique for approximating a grey scale image by a binary image. Derived from techniques used in the printing industry, the image is divided into a number of small areas. Depending on the average brightness within each area, a number of pixels is made black. Pixels are chosen in a particular order from within the area. The effect is that as the area gets darker, a single dot centred in the area gets larger.

high pass filter. A filter which allows high spatial frequencies to pass through whilst tending to attenuate low spatial frequencies. Such filters tend to sharpen the appearance of an image. More extreme filters can be sued as edge detectors.

histogram. A graph showing how many pixels of each value occur in an image.

hyperacuity. The ability to estimate the location of an edge to less than the width of a pixel. Normally, some kind of interpo-

lation is applied to values either side of the edge in order to compute this.

I

instantaneous code. A code which consists of code words which can be decoded individually. Codes which are not instantaneous require one or more subsequent code words to be investigated before the current code word can be decoded.

integer. A whole number.

interpolation. Estimation of the value of an image at points between those which are actually known.

intrinsic image. An image in which the pixels do not represent the normal, observable quantities such as brightness or colour. Intrinsic images usually represent rather more abstract quantities, such as edge strength.

inverse filter. A Fourier domain filter designed to remove some particular, known image degradation. These filters are usually derived from a degradation model.

K

K-means algorithm. An algorithm for classifying pixels into a relatively small number of sets. Initial sets are established and each pixel is assigned to the set whose value it most nearly approximates. A new value for the set is calculated as the mean value of the pixels belonging to it and the procedure is repeated. After a few iterations, or when no further changes occur, the classification is said to be complete.

kilobyte. A unit of storage equal to 1024 bytes.

L

least squares. A set of techniques for fitting models to data. The parameters of the model are adjusted until the sum of the squares of the differences between the data and the model's prediction is minimised.

linear estimator. One type of estimator used in predictive mapping. The value of the next pixel to be coded is predicted by extrapolating along a straight line from previous pixel values.

linear systems theory. A theory governing the behaviour of a particular kind of system. The theory works well for a variety of optical systems and also for digital image filtering. The theory forms the basis for the convolution technique.

linear superposition. A property of linear systems. The result of applying an image to a linear system is equivalent to applying its pixels one at a time and summing the results.

look-up table. An electronic device for converting pixel values into values which are used to drive a display. The appearance of the displayed image can be modified extensively by changing the values in the table. A number of simple image operations, such as thresholding, can be implemented this way.

low pass filter. A filter which allows low spatial frequencies to pass through whilst tending to attenuate high spatial frequencies. Such filters tend to smooth or blur the appearance of an image.

low resolution. Term used for an image with rather few pixels. It is a relative term since the adequacy of a given image's resolution depends on the application for which it is to be used.

M

magnetic resonance imaging (MRI). A technique for recording medical images based on the behaviour of atomic nuclei in the presence of a strong magnetic field and radio frequency emissions. Many different kinds of image are possible. The commonest appear as slices through the body at particular positions and with particular orientation. The technique has the ability to distinguish a wide variety of tissues under appropriate conditions.

mapper. A component of an image compression scheme responsible for converting pixel values into a form which can be more efficiently coded.

mask. A binary image defining an area in which an operation is to be performed on another image of the same size.

matrix. A table of values arranged in rows and columns, rather like a small image. However, matrices are subject to special rules for certain kinds of arithmetic operation.

medial axis transform. A transformation which reveals the medial axis of an object. The medial axis is a connected set of lines joining locations which are local maxima in terms of their distance from the object's boundary. An object, in this sense, is a two dimensional region of the image which has been identified by some previous segmentation step.

megabyte. A storage unit consisting of 1024 kilobytes or 1 048 576 bytes.

mixed mode arithmetic. Arithmetic involving values of different type, For example, the addition of an integer and a floating point value.

moment. A value, derivable from an image and which can be useful in defining shape properties of an object. An object, in this sense, is a two dimensional region of the image which has been identified by some previous segmentation step.

moment invariant. A particular kind of moment which is insensitive to translation, rotation and scale, making it very characteristic of a particular object.

monochrome. Literally meaning single colour, this term is normally used to describe grey scale images.

multi-spectral image. An image consisting of a number of individual bands each of which records a different part of the spectrum. This kind of image is most commonly seen in remote sensing applications.

N

neighbourhood operation. An operation involving a pixel and a set of its neighbours.

noise. Random variation in the pixel values in an image caused by the acquisition process rather than by the scene itself. Noise originates in all electronic equipment.

non-maximum suppression. Removal of all but the maximum value within some neighbourhood. This operation is carried out during edge detection to select the position of the edge as the largest member of a group of edgels.

normalisation. An operation applied to the result of another computation to bring the value into some consistent range so that it can be compared with other values.

O

optical transform. The form of the Fourier transform in which the origin is in the centre of the image. This form is equivalent to transforms obtained using optical apparatus, hence the name.

ordered dither. A technique for approximating a grey scale image by a binary image. Related to halftoning, this technique also involves dividing the image into small regions. Within each region, a mask defines a set of threshold values which, when compared with the underlying pixels, determine whether the corresponding output pixels are set to black or white.

origin. Position with both x and y coordinate of zero. For an image, the origin is in the top left corner. For graphics, the origin is often in the bottom left corner.

P

palette. The definition of the set of colours which can be displayed and their relationship to the individual pixel values in an image. Palettes are commonly implemented as display look-up tables.

parametric. A description, usually of a line, in terms of a model and some characteristic values. The values are known as parameters. As an example, a circle can be described by three parameters, the coordinates of its centre and its radius.

pel. Contracted form of pixel element.

phase. Property of a sine or cosine wave indicating where it passes through zero.

photoconductor. Light sensitive coating used in video cameras based on electron tubes.

picture element. The smallest individual part of an image which can be assigned a single brightness or colour.

pixel. Contracted form of pixel element.

pixel deletion. A technique for reducing the size of an image based on the periodic removal of pixels. For example, removal of every second pixel and every second row reduces the image to half its previous size in both directions.

pixel replication. A technique for increasing the size of an image based on the periodic duplication of pixels. For example, duplication of every second pixel and every second row doubles the size of the image in both directions.

pixel space. A space defined by using the values of corresponding pixels in successive bands of a multi-spectral image as if they were geometric coordinates. For example, for a colour image, the red band value might be the x coordinate, the green band value the y coordinate and the blue band value the z band coordinate. Similarity between two colours can then be considered as the geometric distance between the points, in this space, defined by their pixel values.

point spread function. The continuous function which describes the result of applying a point source to a linear system. A digital filter can be defined in as a sampled version of this function. The result is a convolution mask.

power spectrum. A spectrum, derived from the Fourier transform of an image. It estimates the power in each component of the transform. It is computed by multiplying each term in the transform by its complex conjugate. It is a real quantity.

predictive mapping. A technique applied within the mapper component of an image compression scheme. Pixel values are predicted based on some history of pixel values which have already been processed. The prediction takes place using some kind of estimator (for example a linear estimator.) Instead of the pixel values themselves being passed to the coder, the difference between the predicted value and the actual value is passed instead. The statistics of the differences are often more favourable, for the subsequent coding step, than are those of the pixel values themselves.

primary colour. One of a small number of standard colours which can be combined in various proportions to reproduce essentially all of the known, visible colours. The success of the reproduction depends on the chosen primary colours. For all practical purposes, specific red, blue and green colours are used today for additive colour systems such as image display and television.

principal axes. Directions through an object which generally correspond to its perceived orientation and the direction at right angles. The second order moments of an computed relative to its principal axes are zero. An object, in this sense, is a two dimensional region of the image which has been identified by some previous segmentation step.

principal components. A transformed set of bands, derived from a multi-spectral image. Principal components have minimised between band correlations, unlike the original bands. Consequently, they are more independent. The lack of repeated information means that it takes fewer principal components to represent the data than bands in the original image. There is a consequent saving in storage. In addition, their greater independence makes principal components more suited to classification schemes than the original data.

psychometric correction. A correction applied to the palette of a colour or monochrome display to take account of the non-linear brightness response of the human eye.

Q

quantizer. A component of an image compression scheme responsible for converting its input into a smaller set of values. Quantizers are components of compression schemes which do not conserve all of the information but which reconstruct approximations during decoding. The smaller set of values to be coded allow these schemes to achieve higher rates of compression than those which conserve information exactly.

R

re-sampling. A set of techniques which, given an image, approximate pixel values at points other than those at which the image was originally sampled. These techniques are required to compute pixel values when images are re-sized or rotated, for example.

relaxation. A technique which, given an initial classification of an image, uses the properties of neighbouring pixels to adjust the classification so as to minimise the occurrences of adjacent pixels being in different classes.

resolution. A measure of how accurately a sampled image represents the actual scene. Resolution can be used as a spatial measure or as an indicator of how faithfully brightness or colour is represented.

restoration. A set of techniques which attempt to correct images for specific defects caused during acquisition. The fundamental requirement for restoration is that a degradation model must be available. Models for the noise introduced are also frequently used.

rotation. Most commonly, this refers to rotation in the plane of the image. In image synthesis systems, when images are to be 'painted' onto a surface, a more general three dimensional rotation may be involved.

rotation invariant. A property of the image, or of some region within it, which remains almost constant as the image is rotated. These properties, such as the moment invariants, are very useful in recognition of objects from the two dimensional regions which can segmented out from simple silhouette images, for example.

run-length mapping. One particular kind of mapping technique used in image compression. A set of adjacent pixels of the same value is replaced by a single pixel of that value and a count of the number of pixels in the set. Though very high compressions can be achieved with this technique, it is not generally applicable to grey scale or colour images, in which such sets hardly ever occur. However, for synthetic images and especially for binary images, the technique is useful.

S

saturation. Condition when a photodetector has so much light falling on it that it has reached its highest possible output. Further increase in illumination produces no more detector output. Consequently, huge errors in pixel values can result from detectors operating in this region.

scalar. A single value. Not a vector or an image, for example.

scale invariant. A property of the image, or of some region within it, which remains almost constant as the image size is altered. These properties, such as the moment invariants, are very useful in recognition of objects from the two dimensional regions which can segmented out from simple silhouette images, for example.

scaling. The changing of the size of an image. The factors by which an image is scaled do not have to be the same in each of the two directions. If they are not the same, the aspect ratio of the image will change.

scene/sensor model. A transformation, derived from knowledge of the properties of the objects being viewed and of the image acquisition system. It defines how the image data must be warped geometrically to bring it to some standard coordinate system. Most commonly used in remote sensing applications.

scientific visualisation. A relatively new field of endeavour in which the properties of a system are represented graphically in some way. These properties are usually not directly observable, for example the probabilities associated with electron clouds around an atom.

segmentation. The division of an image into regions corresponding to objects or parts of objects.

separable filter. A filter, implemented as a convolution, which can be split into a horizontal and vertical component. The two, separate, one dimensional convolutions require significantly less computation than a full two dimensional version.

serialisation. The extraction of pixels in the correct order to form each row of the display.

serialiser. An electronic device for performing serialisation in a display controller.

sharpening filter. A filter which tends to increase the visual sharpness of an image. These filters are often also high pass filters.

signal to noise ratio. The ratio of the amount of real image data being collected to the amount of noise introduced by the process. Images of high quality also have high signal to noise ratios. Some kinds of image, for example those from hospital ultrasound scanners, suffer from inherently low signal to noise ratios.

smoothing filter. A filter which tends to smooth out the effect of noise in an image. These filters are often also low pass filters.

spatial domain. The domain of normal image data, that is of brightness or colour as a function of position.

spatial frequency. A measure of how quickly pixel values change on traversing an image. In the region of an object edge, or where there is texture, pixel values change rapidly. In this region, the image is said to exhibit high spatial frequencies. Conversely, in smooth regions of the image where the pixel values change slowly, the image is said to exhibit low spatial frequencies.

spectral density function. Another term for power spectrum.

spectral signature. A combination of responses at corresponding pixels in a multi-spectral image which is characteristic of some particular form of ground cover.

structuring element. A small neighbourhood of binary pixels used in morphological operations.

subimage. A set of adjacent pixels within an image. Most commonly, subimages are rectangular, but in principal can be any shape.

synchronisation pulses. Timing pulses added to the signal from a display controller to its display. These pulses ensure that the pixel data appears at the appropriate place on the screen by synchronising the sweep of the electron beam to the data signal. Similar techniques are used in broadcast television.

T

thinning. One technique for retrieving the medial axis of an object based on removing pixels from the object boundary. An object, in this sense, is a two dimensional region of the image which has been identified by some previous segmentation step.

threshold. A pixel value at which a decision is made about the value to assign to the output. Thresholds, under controlled conditions, can be used as a simple segmentation technique. Application of multiple thresholds leads to grey level slicing.

training set. A set of regions in an image used to train a classification algorithm to recognise particular properties. Normally, several examples of each kind of ground cover are used in the training set.

translation. Motion in the plane of the image which does not involve rotation.

translation invariant. A property of a region within an image which remains almost constant as its position is altered. These properties, such as the moment invariants, are very useful in recognition of objects from the two dimensional regions which can segmented out from simple silhouette images, for example.

treble. A term for the high frequency part of an audio signal.

U

unequal length code. A code in which code words consist of variable numbers of bits. Frequently used codes are assigned short code words to improve the degree of compression.

unsigned. A number which can hold only positive values.

V

vidicon. A type of video camera tube,

W

warping. Geometric stretching and shrinking of an image. Unlike pure scaling, the degree of size change varies from place to place over the image.

weight. One element of a convolution mask.

Weiner filter. A particular kind of restoration filter. The Weiner filter can be used to correct specific degradations and to help remove noise simultaneously.

white noise. Noise whose amplitude is constant across the range of frequencies of interest.

Numerics

8-bit unsigned integer. A number representation capable of holding positive, whole number values between 0 and 255. This is a very common representation for image data

16-bit signed integer. A number representation capable of holding whole number values between −32768 and 32767.

32-bit signed integer. A number representation capable of holding whole number values between about -2×10^9 and 2×10^9.

4 connected neighbours. The 4 nearest neighbours of a given pixel which are immediately above, below, to its left and to its right.

8 connected neighbours. The 8 nearest neighbours of a given pixel. These are the 4 connected neighbours together with the 4 pixels on the diagonals

Index

function   86

G

gain   245
Gaussian   212
    smoothing   127
generalised cepstrum   164
geometric correction   199
geostationary   245
gradients   68
grey level re-mapping   66, 245
grey level slicing   66, 245
grey scale   18, 246
grey scale wedge   199, 246
ground cover   170, 246

H

Hadamard transform   169, 179, 186
halftoning   191, 246
high pass filter   246
histogram   83, 246
    accumulating   83
    cumulative   84
    equalisation   87
    evaluating   85
    specification   89
    thresholding   85
Hotelling transform   171
Hough transform   217
Huffman code   182
human vision   44
hyperacuity   213, 246

I

ideal filter   161
illusion
    optical   44
image
    acquisition   28, 42
    analysis   42, 47
    applications   41
    arithmetic   53
    black and white   17
    colour   17
    compression   175

image *(continued)*
    coordinate system   18
    digital   17, 18
    display   27
    enhancement   42, 43
    monochrome   17
    re-ranging   67, 68
    restoration   42, 43, 197
    segmentation   42, 44
    warping   112
imaginary part   59
inference   206
instantaneous code   183, 246
integer   20, 246
integer image   20
interpolation   97, 246
    bi-linear   99
    curvilinear   100
    linear   99
intrinsic image   132, 145, 246
invalid values   52, 59
inverse
    filter   168, 200, 246
    function   86
    matrix   61
Isotropic filter   134

K

k nearest neighbour filter   80
K-means algorithm   246
K-means classification   222
kilobyte   21, 246
Kronecker delta   123

L

Landsat   170, 185
Laplacian   129
Laplacian of a Gaussian   136
least squares   247
line scan camera   34
linear
    estimator   178, 247
    re-mapping   66
    superposition   123, 247
    systems theory   123, 247